TRIBUTE FOR HARRIETTE

ANGELA
THIRKELL

*

Tribute
For Harriette

*THE SURPRISING CAREER OF
HARRIETTE WILSON*

*

A Common Reader Edition
The Akadine Press

Tribute For Harriette

A COMMON READER EDITION published 1999
by The Akadine Press, Inc., by arrangement with Hamish
Hamilton Ltd.

A COMMON READER EDITION and fountain colophon are trade-
marks of The Akadine Press, Inc.

ISBN 1-888173-95-5

10 9 8 7 6 5 4 3 2 1

Contents

FOREWORD

IF IN describing the early career of my heroine I have freely used her own words, it is for this reason: The *Memoirs* of her own life, first published in 1825, contain about a quarter of a million words, are inaccurate, and totally regardless of chronology. But the style is so dashing, the characterisation is so true, the conversations are so vividly reported, that re-telling gives but a poor idea of her brilliant, slip-shod impertinence. The best motto that could be found for her own account of her life would be in Charles Kingsley's *Water Babies:* "Remember, as I told you before, that this is all a fairy tale, and, therefore, you are not to believe a word of it, even if it is true."

I would like here to express my gratitude to the officials of the British Museum, the Victoria and Albert Museum, the Record Office, the Bodleian, the London Library, the Brighton Public Library, and the Westminster City Hall.

Sir John Murray has kindly allowed me to read the originals of Harriette Wilson's letters to Byron, and has given permission for the reproduction of part of a letter.

All the other illustrations are reproduced by the courtesy of the British Museum.

To Mr. Frederick Page my thanks are due for reading the proofs, and for many valuable suggestions, as well as for the Index.

I also have to thank Lord and Lady Berwick, Professor H. J. C. Grierson (who has allowed me to use published and unpublished material from Sir Walter Scott's correspondence), and Mr. G. T. Garratt for help and information.

A. T.

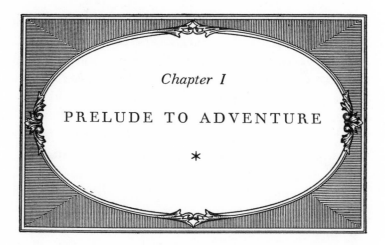

Chapter I

PRELUDE TO ADVENTURE

*

> But it seems a superfluous labour to weigh the propriety, unless we could ascertain the truth, of this singular event; which is attended with some circumstances of doubt and perplexity.
>
> GIBBON. Chapter XVIII.

IN THE first quarter of the eighteenth century there lived in Vevey, by the Lake of Geneva, a M. Dubochet, of good Swiss blood and of so intolerable a humour that he was proudly recognised by his compatriots as the worst-tempered man in the whole canton. This unenviable distinction was not confined to public life, and M. Dubochet made home so unpleasant to his three sons that they all ran away at an early age. Of the two younger nothing was ever heard again. The eldest, John, left his parents' roof at the age of thirteen in search of freedom and adventure, and joined a recruiting party journeying towards Holland. The officer in charge refused to take him on account of his youth, but allowed him to travel with the

soldiers and share their meals. The boy, who was tall
for his years, strong and good-looking, had the good
fortune after his arrival in Holland to be engaged as
secretary to a Colonel. After some years of this employment he had the further good fortune to please his
Colonel's mistress, but was unluckily surprised by his
employer in her arms. A duel followed. Young Dubochet fired on the guard who were sent to arrest him,
killed a soldier, and fled the country. His wanderings
took him to Italy, Spain, America, and finally to Portugal, where, having a turn for languages and mathe-
matics, he set up as professor of algebra, French, German, fencing and dancing, and saved enough money
to take him to England. He had during his travels acquired, though in no specified country or regiment,
the title of Captain, and so was qualified to stir female
hearts.

While looking, though not too eagerly, for employment in London, he made the acquaintance of a
worthy couple named Cook, who carried on the trade
of stocking-mending and grafting. At that time, about
1775, when the pantaloon was as yet undreamt of,
stocking-mending was a very profitable business. Silk
stockings, white, pink, pale green, pale blue, were
worn by every man of pretensions, and the Cooks
earned an income equivalent to about a thousand
pounds a year. This trade they had taught to their
adopted daughter, Amelia, natural child of a country
gentleman called Cheney and a country girl, who had
been packed off to America with a bank-note for a
hundred pounds, leaving the child with her neigh-

bours, the kindly Cooks. Amelia grew up a pretty, doc-
ile girl, patronised by Lady Frederick Campbell, who
later stood godmother to one of her elder daughters.

The nameless and portionless Amelia appeared to be
destined to a virtuous and hard-working life, suitable
for a child of shame, when John Dubochet came on the
scene with his handsome face, romantic air, and stories
of adventure. He was twenty years older than the four-
teen-year-old Amelia, but they fell in love and were
secretly married. When the Cooks discovered the connection they were in despair, for Dubochet had no
means, so Mr. Cook generously suggested to his wife
that, being childless, they should divide their business
and give part to Amelia and her husband. Mrs. Cook,
who had recognised Dubochet's capacity for living at
other people's expense, protested that he would never
settle down, but Mr. Dubochet was perfectly ready to
undertake a business which could be carried on by his
wife. Kind Mr. Cook also found him a position as a
coal merchant, but Dubochet had a soul above the
shop, and contented himself with attending at a coal
wharf in the city for an hour or two in the morning,
after which he would disappear from his family till
late at night, or lock himself into his room with his
mathematical instruments.

The Dubochets had fifteen children, the first being
born in 1777, the last in 1804. The first child died;
then came Jane; Amelia, shortened to Amy, who was
notorious as a liar from her earliest days; Frances or
Fanny, lively and delicate; Mary, very sharp, very
dark, very clever; then Harriette. The only other

daughter of whom much is known is Sophia, born in 1794, who made a good marriage. Of the boys, four in number, George is distinguished for having unfortunately carried the family trait of immorality into financial transactions. Henry, the youngest, was also given the name of Cook, a belated tribute to Mrs. Dubochet's kind foster parents.

Harriette Dubochet was born on February 22nd, 1786, when the family were living in Carrington Street, Mayfair, pulled down within the last few years. She was baptised at St. George's, Hanover Square, as Harriot, but seems to have adopted the more genteel name of Harriette early in her career. She was a child of fearless and independent temper, extremely trying to her father, whose natural selfishness and passion for mathematical problems made him a domestic tyrant of his own father's kind. None of his children was allowed to speak to him, or even speak to each other in his presence, for fear of disturbing his calculations. His sons he only valued according to their progress in his beloved science, while for his daughters he felt the contempt which they in their turn felt for x's and y's. His flashing white teeth, dark eyes, and ferocious eyebrows, used to frighten his children half out of their senses. When Harriette was about five years old she tore up one of his problems to make a fly-trap. Her father swore to use the birch till she promised never to offend again, but the spirited little creature submitted to a thrashing that left her almost senseless sooner than apologise or promise amendment. At last her father, exhausted by his efforts and her defiance, locked her, bruised and bleeding, into her room, but Harriette's stubbornness carried the day, and much against his will, annoyed at having to appear to give in to his wife's tears and entreaties, he was forced to let his daughter go. Harriette bore no rancour—it was one of her engaging qualities that she never remembered her wrongs with any malice—and in fact rather admired her father for this display of brutality.

Mrs. Dubochet, between a despotic husband who would not work and a very spirited young family, was not to be envied. She had married, so young, a husband so much older than herself that the habit of obedience and blind submission was ingrained. Nothing could be done in the home unless it suited Mr. Dubochet's convenience. He refused to discuss his affairs or plans, came in and out as suited him, bullied his children, and bragged to the neighbours. Mrs. Dubochet did what she could, tried to educate her children and make them happy, but she was too fully occupied in trying to earn enough by stocking-mending to keep her family clothed and fed, and could exercise no authority. Her girls looked upon her as an elder sister rather than a mother, and while they adored her, they took no other notice of her.

When Harriette was a growing girl the family moved to 23 Queen Street, Mayfair, where Mrs. Dubochet continued to carry on the trade of stocking-mending, and Mr. Dubochet to enjoy life in his own way, returning at intervals to make it intolerable for his wife and children. The stocking trade was beginning to feel the effects of a change in fashion. The days were passing when the Prince of Wales frowned at an officer who appeared one evening in pantaloons instead of breeches. What with the decline of the stocking-mending business and the high rent of 23 Queen Street, which was rated at £24, Mrs. Dubochet decided to take a first floor lodger. Fate sent to her a General Cheney of the Guards, her own half-brother. With proper feeling she concealed the discovery from her lodger, but her young daughters, with the artless precocity of childhood, adored the General, going so far as to collect clippings of his revered hair. Where all this might have led may well be wondered, but when this curious state of things had lasted for some years the General changed his lodging and the family lost sight of him.

There is still in Mayfair a large handsome house with a kind of obelisk outside the front door, No. 16 Charles Street, looking directly down Queen Street. Here lived the Earl of Craven and his brother Berkeley Craven, sons of the celebrated Lady Craven, daughter of the Earl of Berkeley, and later Margravine of Anspach. She had separated from Lord Craven and lived much abroad, where she was given the title of Princess Berkeley by the Imperial Court, though much to her annoyance the Court of St. James's would not recognise it. Her gifts, her charm, her ingenuous pleasure in her own beauty and talents, the plays that she wrote and acted in, are mentioned by many contemporaries. Horace Walpole wrote of her: She is very pretty, has parts, and is good-natured to the greatest degree; has not a grain of malice or mischief . . . and never has been an enemy but to herself.

Her second son, Berkeley, inherited all his mother's charm, and no one had a bad word to say for him, unless it were a few mothers of families who feared his reckless influence over their young sons. He was, like his mother, his own only enemy. With her gifts he inherited her extravagance, especially in gambling. In 1836 his losses at the Derby, won by Lord Jersey's 'Middleton', were greater than he could meet, and he shot himself. A Royal Duke, his attached friend, was so overcome by the news, that in getting out of his curricle he entangled the braiding of his pelisse in the hook of the dashing-board, and could only with difficulty be extricated.

Among Berkeley Craven's associates was Tom Sheridan, son of Richard Brinsley Sheridan and the lovely Miss Linley. Sheridan also inherited looks and charm from his parents, and from his mother the fatal tendency to consumption which had killed so many of her family. He was extremely popular in society and was associated with his father in his theatrical ventures. He married Henrietta Callander, a novelist of some repute and a beauty. One of his daughters was the celebrated Mrs. Norton, another became Lady Dufferin, and the third the Duchess of Somerset of Egliston Tournament fame. He was sent in 1813 to the Cape of Good Hope for his health, and there became Colonial Treasurer, dying in 1817, only a year after his father.

If Tom Sheridan called on Berkeley Craven and

Lord Craven, it was the easiest thing in life for the three young men, as they sauntered down Queen Street, to stare at Mr. Dubochet's good-looking girls; and the easiest thing in life for the girls to be at the door or the window when the young men passed. It was the fatal word 'propinquity' that was responsible for Harriette's first step from virtue; though if Craven House had not been in Charles Street, there would have been plenty of other temptations for such girls.

Harriette was now a lively girl of eleven or twelve, with a mother too busy to look after her, and four elder sisters, of whom two at least were ripe for any kind of mischief. Jane and Mary were steadier than Amy and Fanny, though this may have been less virtue than want of opportunity. Mary, at least, made a respectable marriage, as did Jane; and Harriette, with some consideration, never mentioned their names in her writings, disguising them as Paragon and Diana. If Harriette ever had any tendency to virtue, which seems improbable, her sisters' conversation and manners were enough to lead her astray.

Morning, noon and night, I heard of nothing but the softness of Tom Sheridan's hand, the brightness of Berkeley Craven's eyes, etc., and my elder sisters must still recollect how disgusted I used to be with their conversation, in return for which they called me 'Tell-tale and brown, ugly, straight-haired figure of fun.'

Fanny Dubochet, four years older than Harriette,

was already receiving love-letters from a young cousin, which she insisted on reading aloud to her sisters at night after undressing and cold-creaming her face for the freckles. As a love-letter one of them was an unsatisfactory composition if we are to take Harriette's verbatim report of it after hearing it for the hundred and fiftieth time.

> The love that but seldom requires the making of apologies is too frequently confounded in the attempt, whilst the gay and volatile, with hearts as light as their heads, pass over these matters with complete indifference, and escape with impunity. I should be happy to escape your censure, for daring to violate my engagement for our walk in the Green Park, but would fain convince you that the emergency of the case, etc.

Worn out by the nightly repetition of this passionate effusion, Harriette stole it and slipped it into a meat pie, just before it was carried to the baker.

The effect of this hotbed of love conversation was that Harriette began to curl her hair and look slyly under her bonnet at men in the street. Her parents thought it advisable to send her to a convent abroad to be out of the way. Accordingly her father, to whom she says she was much attached, in spite of the severe beatings he used to give her, went by coach to Brighton with her, to take ship for France. Sussex she found flat and ugly. During a tedious three days' passage to Dieppe, her father spent the first night on deck. Harriette felt very ill and remained in bed. A travelling companion, an aristocratic-looking young stripling, handsome, graceful, and particularly elegant in his attire, passed the whole night by her side, paying her every kind of civility, handing tea and various refreshing scents from his magnificent dressing case.

At last an old lady interfered and sent a message to warn Mr. Dubochet against the aristocratic stripling's intentions.

My father was annoyed, and a kind of talking at each other conversation took place, in which my father had much the best of it.

However, a reconciliation took place at Dieppe, and father and daughter went on to Rouen, where Harriette was left with 'the Abbess of the celebrated Convent of St. Ursulines.' The only boarder among a hundred girls whom she liked was 'la petite Comtesse de Richmond.' Harriette became a great favourite with the Abbess, Madame Cousin, who gave her pralines, jelly, Eau-de-Cologne and eau bénite, besides procuring for her the privilege of kissing the Archbishop of Rouen's shoes while she received his blessing, ' "*Bène, bène, Sancto Spiritu*", but I have forgotten my Latin.' She had several religious arguments with the Abbess's brother, confessor to the convent, a 'patient, willing, handsome priest' whom she persuaded to kiss her under the tolerant eye of the Abbess. Her entirely pagan point of view made the priest laugh so much that he had to beg her not to argue any more.

According to her own account, all she learned at the convent was the rule of three, in the hope of giving her father an agreeable surprise, the verbs *avoir* and *être*, for which she received a shilling, and a little daily prayer, for which she received nothing. Even if this convent only existed in Harriette's teeming imagination, it was worth inventing. As for her Latin, one cannot believe that she learnt enough to forget, but French she certainly did learn, and always spoke it fluently, if not with classical accuracy, so that she was quite at home in Paris when she went to live there in later years. Thus well prepared to face life she returned to a

> very uncomfortable home. My sisters Amy and Fanny had both run off; one with Mr. Trench, the other with Mr. Woodcock. Paragon and Diana still lived in all their purity, but they were both very cross.

To escape from this uncomfortable home life she took a situation as superintendent of the musical studies of young ladies, at a certain elegant boarding-school near Bayswater. She hated the life, and after a gross insult from a low-bred French woman teacher with whom she slept, she went back to her home, where her father told her that being nearly fourteen she must earn her own livelihood and not eat the bread of her younger brothers and sisters. Mr. Dubochet seems to have had no single redeeming quality.

Accordingly, a position was found for Harriette as

French teacher in the school of a Miss Ketridge at Newcastle-upon-Tyne. She travelled up in the coach with her old acquaintance Tom Sheridan, who was on his way to join his General, Lord Moira, at Edinburgh. Lord Moira was at that time Commander-in-Chief of the Forces in Scotland, where he was very popular, and Sheridan was one of his aides-de-camp. Sheridan begged to be allowed to correspond with her. Harriette, with much spirit, told him that if she had not wished to act rightly she would not have gone to Newcastle, as she found no lack of admirers in London who wished to get her under their protection.

But, I added, I do want a love-letter so very bad to send to Fanny and read to her over and over again, to pay her for tiring me so with her cousin's effusion, till I was forced to put it into the meat pye.

Touched by this artless confession, Tom Sheridan promised to write her such a letter as would not offend her pride, and with excellent feeling kept his word.

After two days and nights of uncomfortable journeying in the middle of winter, Harriette arrived at Ketridge House. It was a bitterly cold Saturday night and she was shown through a wet kitchen, which was being washed down for the following day, into a large dismal parlour with hardly a gleam of fire. Here she found Miss Ketridge and the English teacher, Miss Macdougal, a fat, smiling young lady in a Scotch plaid, at their supper. To a hungry girl of fourteen, fresh from a long journey, anything to eat would have been welcome, but even Harriette's appetite was hardly tempted by Miss Ketridge's very small beer and her very uninteresting little Dutch cheese, so she begged to be allowed to go to bed. Miss Ketridge showed her the room she was to share with another teacher, told her that she would be expected to have made her bed, dressed, and to be downstairs for prayers on the stroke of six, and left her.

So cold, so wretched a situation, was enough to daunt the courage of most girls. Jane Eyre had little worse to encounter at Lowood, but Harriette had two advantages over Jane Eyre. The religious element was wanting at Ketridge House, and Harriette brought with her the sense of humour in which Jane was so noticeably lacking. 'I naturally seize upon the ludicrous points of any subject,' she wrote of herself many years later, ' 'tis my forte or calling'; and seldom in her varied career was a sense of humour so much needed. After prayers came breakfast, in the dark cold parlour, consisting of one small roll for each person. Harriette, who had faced a father far more terrifying than any schoolmistress, asked for a slice of bread off the large loaf, which made Miss Ketridge and Miss Macdougal exchange significant looks. On the following morning, an eight-pound loaf was placed before her to shame her out of her appetite, but in spite of the tittering and laughing of the other teachers, Harriette helped herself to a thick slice, remarking as she did so ' 'Tis a brilliant invention, ladies, but you see it won't answer, as I shall never be the simpleton to quarrel with my bread and butter.' From this moment she and Miss Ketridge were at war, and though the headmistress had power and authority on her side, the girl of fourteen managed to hold her own with her sharp tongue.

The schoolroom was bitterly cold, the scholars a set of raw-boned, illiterate north-country girls. When Harriette was attempting to correct their barbarous pronunciation of French, Miss Ketridge gave her a heap of men's shirts, requiring her to sew them while she gave her lessons. These shirts, as Harriette afterwards found, were taken in by Miss Ketridge, who forced her teachers to make them and then pocketed the proceeds. With the cold weather, the long hours, the hard work and the lack of exercise, Harriette's health began to suffer severely and Miss Ketridge was unwillingly obliged to call in the apothecary. This person, who had some knowledge of the school, told the headmistress that her young teacher must have warm milk from the cow and early hours, or she would probably perish in a decline. On hearing this unwelcome advice, Miss Ketridge had a confidential conversation with Harriette, in which she advised her not to consult the apothecary again, and assured her that too much sleep was very injurious.

In spite of this friendly counsel Harriette grew worse and worse, till her father, at last alarmed by her letters, allowed her to return to London. Here it was necessary for her to find some work, so she consulted Tom Sheridan, who advised her to go on the stage. He said she was very like Siddons and asked her to read some Shakespeare to him, promising to use all his father's influence to get her brought out at Drury Lane if he thought well enough of her. Her mother consented to this proposal (which it was not thought necessary to mention to Mr. Dubochet) 'because Tom Sheridan's letters were so kind and brotherly, and we had known him with Lord Craven and his brother Berkeley all our lives, in consequence of their living in sight of our house and passing it constantly.' A day for the reading was arranged, and Harriette chose the part of Falstaff—hardly a Siddonian role—stuffing a pillow into a large waistcoat borrowed from a friendly coach-man. Harriette, saying that she knew that Falstaff, as far as manners went, was always a gentleman, and would not have laughed at his own wit and humour, managed to keep a steady face, while Tom Sheridan, who was reading the part of Prince Hal, laughed till he cried. The relations between Tom Sheridan, the Cravens, and the Dubochet girls seem to have been very agreeable. The young men found these girls, who were safely below their own station, very diverting companions, and if we are to take Harriette's account of Tom Sheridan, behaved quite sufficiently like gentlemen to them.

The inevitable family scene now took place. Mr. Dubochet was told of Sheridan's offer and chose to take violent offence. Mrs. Dubochet would like to have seen her daughter on the stage, but her father declared, in proper paternal fashion, that he would rather see her dead and in her grave. Here was Harriette at fifteen, with plenty of admirers, with two sisters already happily and illegally settled, doomed by her

father to drag on a forlorn existence and teach children
Clementi's lessons and the verbs *avoir* and *être* from
fifteen to sixty years of age, and then to retire, with-
ered and still more forlorn, to a workhouse. The prospect was not attractive.

At this point she made one last attempt to please her
father. Mr. Dubochet was extremely fond of a Swiss
dish which he used to prepare himself. Harriette
watched him attentively, and one night when he was
expected home to supper she took infinite pains to cook
this dish. The supper was ready at her usual bedtime,
ten o'clock, but she was so afraid it would get cold or
spoiled that she sat up till his return to watch it, and
got 'soundly boxed on the ears *pour commencer*.' Upon
this she resolved to leave her wretched uncomfortable
home on the following day. 'My dear mother would
forgive me and visit me. Of that I felt sure, for she
knew I should soon die if she forsook me.'

There was only one path open to a girl of spirit, and
she took it.

> I loved no one amongst those who sought to
> seduce me, but the Cravens were our near neigh-
> bours, and old acquaintances, and they were gentle-
> men. I was less afraid of them than of any other
> men, so I became the mistress of Lord Craven.

A more ingenuous apology has seldom been offered.

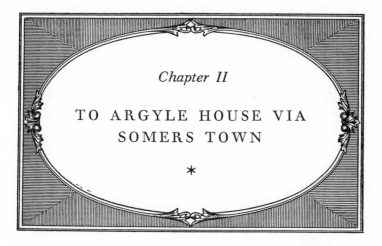

Chapter II

TO ARGYLE HOUSE VIA SOMERS TOWN

*

IT WAS at Brighton that Harriette, under Lord Craven's protection, made her first, and at the moment rather ill-assured, steps into the world of fashion. Her great friend in later years, Julia Johnstone, under whose name a very spiteful book about Harriette was published, protested that Lord Craven was not Harriette's first admirer, accusing her of having already had several lovers, including the washerwoman's son and a recruiting sergeant. But as she also stated that the Dubochet family were then living at Hammersmith, while they are known from the ratepayers' lists to have been living in Mayfair, her unkind words may be attributed to spleen rather than to a passion for accuracy. Harriette herself gave ugly hints in later life that her old friend Berkeley Craven had been her first seducer, then turning her over to his brother; but this was probably an unsuccessful attempt to blackmail a man who was known to have cut her, for good reasons, in after years.

27

Lord Craven, like many other young men of fashion, was a frequenter of Brighton, partly because the Prince of Wales lived there so much, partly because his regiment was stationed at Brighton or Lewes. He was also a patron of Rottingdean, already a kind of suburb of Brighton. 'The little watering place of Rottingdean,' says the *Sussex Weekly Advertiser and Lewes Gazette* in 1801, 'has been this year unusually full of company. The lovers of pure air, saline solution, and QUIET LIFE, will be sure of gratification.' Sailing was a popular amusement among the visitors, and Lord Craven's yacht, the *Griffin*, was a well-known sight off the Brighton cliffs, while Mr. Pitt, visiting Colonel Villars at Rottingdean, had performed a sailing expedition to Brighton and back, amid the enthusiastic cheers of the population.

It is in this year, 1801, that the *Memoirs*, which Harriette wrote many years later, begin, and about this time that she assumed—one name being as good as another—the name Harriette Wilson. Harriette shared with the minor Elizabethan poets the gift of unconsciously composing an opening phrase of great felicity, leaving the rest of the work to look after itself. Her *Memoirs* begin with these words:

I shall not say why and how I became, at the age of fifteen, the mistress of the Earl of Craven. Whether it was love, or the severity of my father, the depravity of my own heart, or the winning arts of the noble Lord, which induced me to leave my paternal roof and place myself under his protection, does not now much signify: or if it does, I am not in the humour to gratify curiosity in this matter. I resided on the Marine Parade at Brighton, and I remember that Lord Craven used to draw cocoa trees, and his fellows, as he called them, on the best vellum paper for my amusement. Here stood the enemy, he would say; and here, my love, are my fellows: there are the cocoa trees, etc. It was, in fact, a dead bore.

A more inviting beginning with its mixture of candour and nonchalance, its good-humoured self-depreciation, would be hard to find. Harriette, indeed, thought so well of her opening phrases that she used them again more than once when telling the story of her early life.

All these cocoa trees and fellows, at past eleven o'clock at night, could have no peculiar interest for a child like myself, so lately in the habit of retiring early to rest. One night, I recollect, I fell asleep; and, as I often dream, I said, yawning, and half awake, Oh, Lord! oh, Lord! Craven has got me into the West Indies again. In short, I soon found that I had made but a bad speculation by going from my father to Lord Craven. I was even more afraid of the latter than I had been of the former; not that there was any particular harm in the man, beyond his cocoa trees; but we never suited nor understood each other.

I was not depraved enough to determine immediately on a new choice, and yet I often thought about it. How, indeed, could I do otherwise, when the Honourable Frederick Lamb was my constant visitor, and talked to me of nothing else? However, in justice to myself, I must declare that the idea of the possibility of deceiving Lord Craven while I was under his roof never once entered into my head. Frederick was then very handsome, and certainly tried, with all his soul and with all his strength, to convince me that constancy to Lord Craven was the greatest nonsense in the world. I firmly believe that Frederick Lamb sincerely loved me, and deeply regretted that he had no fortune to invite me to share with him.

Lord Melbourne, his father, was a good man. Not one of your stiff-laced moralising fathers, who preach chastity and forbearance to their children. Quite the contrary; he congratulated his son on the lucky circumstance of his friend Craven having such a fine girl with him. 'No such thing,' answered Frederick Lamb; 'I am unsuccessful there. Harriette will have nothing to do with me.'—'Nonsense!' rejoined Melbourne, in great surprise; 'I never heard anything half so ridiculous in all my life. The girl must be mad! She looks mad: I thought so the other day when I met her galloping about with her feathers blowing and her thick dark hair about her ears.'

'I'll speak to Harriette for you,' added His Lordship, after a long pause; and then continued repeating to himself, in an undertone, 'Not have my son, indeed! six feet high! a fine, straight, handsome, noble young fellow! I wonder what she would have!'

In truth, I scarcely knew myself; but something I determined on : so miserably tired was I of Craven and his cocoa trees, and his sailing boats, and his ugly cotton nightcap. Surely, I would say, all men do not wear those shocking cotton nightcaps; else all women's illusions had been destroyed on the first night of their marriage!

I wonder, thought I, what sort of a nightcap the Prince of Wales wears? Then I went on to wonder whether the Prince of Wales would think me so beautiful as Frederick Lamb did? Next I reflected that Frederick Lamb was younger than the Prince; but then, again, a Prince of Wales!!!

I was undecided : my heart began to soften. I thought of my dear mother, and wished I had never left her. It was too late, however, now. My father would not suffer me to return; and as to passing my life, or any more of it, with Craven, cotton nightcap and all, it was death! He never once made me laugh, nor said nor did anything to please me.

Thus musing, I listlessly turned over my writing-book, half in the humour to address the Prince of Wales. A sheet of paper, covered with Lord Craven's cocoa trees, decided me; and I wrote the following letter, which I addressed to the Prince :——

BRIGHTON.

I am told that I am very beautiful, so perhaps you

would like to see me; and I wish that, since so many are disposed to love me, one, for in the humility of my heart I should be quite satisfied with one, would be at the pains to make me love him. In the meantime, this is all very dull work, Sir, and worse even than being at home with my father: so, if you pity me, and believe you could make me in love with you, write to me, and direct to the post-office here.

By return of post, I received an answer nearly to this effect: I believe, from Colonel Thomas.

Miss Wilson's letter has been received by the noble individual to whom it was addressed. If Miss Wilson will come to town, she may have an interview by directing her letter as before.

I answered this note directly, addressing my letter to the Prince of Wales.

SIR,

To travel fifty-two miles this bad weather merely to see a man, with only the given number of legs, arms, fingers, etc., would, you must admit, be madness in a girl like myself, surrounded by humble admirers, who are ever ready to travel any distance for the honour of kissing the tip of her little finger; but if you can prove to me that you are one bit better than any man who may be ready to attend my bidding, I'll e'en start for London directly. So if you can do anything better in

the way of pleasing a lady than ordinary men, write
directly: if not, adieu, Monsieur le Prince.

> *I won't say yours,*
> *By day or night, or any kind of light;*
> *Because you are too impudent.*

It was necessary to put this letter into the post-
office myself, as Lord Craven's black footman would
have been somewhat surprised at its address. Cross-
ing the Steyne, I met Lord Melbourne, who joined
me immediately.

'Where is Craven?' said His Lordship, shaking
hands with me.

'Attending to his military duties at Lewes, my
Lord.'

'And where's my son Fred?' asked His Lordship.

'I am not your son's keeper, my Lord,' said I.

'No! By the bye,' inquired His Lordship, 'how is
this? I wanted to call upon you about it. I never
heard of such a thing in the whole course of my
life! What the devil can you possibly have to say
against my son Fred?'

'Good heavens! my Lord, you frighten me! I
never recollect to have said a single word against
your son as long as I have lived. Why should I?'

'Why, indeed!' said Lord Melbourne. 'And since
there is nothing to be said against him, what excuse
can you make for using him so ill?'

'I don't understand you one bit, my Lord.' (The
very idea of a father put me in a tremble.)

'Why,' said Lord Melbourne, 'did you not turn

the poor boy out of your house as soon as it was dark; although Craven was in town, and there was not the shadow of an excuse for such treatment?'

At this moment, and before I could recover from my surprise at the tenderness of some parents, Frederick Lamb, who was almost my shadow, joined us.

'Fred, my boy,' said Lord Melbourne, 'I'll leave you two together; and I fancy you'll find Miss Wilson more reasonable.' He touched his hat to me, as he entered the little gate of the Pavilion, where we had remained stationary from the moment His Lordship had accosted me.

Frederick Lamb laughed long, loud, and heartily at his father's interference. So did I, the moment he was safely out of sight; and then I told him of my answer to the Prince's letter, at which he laughed still more. He was charmed with me for refusing His Royal Highness. 'Not,' said Frederick, 'that he is not as handsome and graceful a man as any in England; but I hate the weakness of a woman who knows not how to refuse a prince, merely because he is a prince.'—'It is something, too, to be of royal blood,' answered I frankly; 'and something more to be so accomplished: but this posting after a man! I wonder what he could mean by it!!'

Frederick Lamb now began to plead his own cause. 'I must soon join my regiment in Yorkshire,' said he (he was at that time aide-de-camp to General Mackenzie); 'God knows when we may meet again! I am sure you will not long continue with

Lord Craven. I foresee what will happen, and yet, when it does, I think I shall go mad!'

For my part, I felt flattered and obliged by the affection Frederick Lamb evinced towards me; but I was still not in love with him.

At length the time arrived when poor Frederick Lamb could delay his departure from Brighton no longer. On the eve of it, he begged to be allowed to introduce his brother William to me.

'What for?' said I.

'That he may let me know how you behave,' answered Frederick Lamb.

'And if I fall in love with him?' I inquired.

'I am sure you won't,' replied Fred. 'Not because my brother William is not likeable; on the contrary, William is much handsomer than I am; but he will not love you as I have done, and do still; and you are too good to forget me entirely.'

Our parting scene was rather tender. For the last ten days, Lord Craven being absent, we had scarcely been separated an hour during the whole day. I had begun to feel the force of habit; and Frederick Lamb really respected me, for the perseverance with which I had resisted his urgent wishes, when he would have had me deceive Lord Craven. He had ceased to torment me with such wild fits of passion as had at first frightened me; and by these means he had obtained much more of my confidence.

Two days after his departure for Hull, in Yorkshire, Lord Craven returned to Brighton, where he was immediately informed, by some spiteful enemy of mine, that I had been, during the whole of his absence, openly intriguing with Frederick Lamb. In consequence of this information, one evening, when I expected his return, his servant brought me the following letter, dated Lewes:

A friend of mine has informed me of what has been going on at Brighton. This information, added to what I have seen with my own eyes, of your intimacy with Frederick Lamb, obliges me to declare that we must separate. Let me add, Harriette, that you might have done anything with me with only a little more conduct. As it is, allow me to wish you happy; and further, pray inform me, if in any way, à la distance, I can promote your welfare.

CRAVEN.

This letter completed my dislike of Lord Craven. I answered it immediately, as follows:—

MY LORD,

Had I ever wished to deceive you, I have the wit to have done it successfully; but you are old enough to be a better judge of human nature than to have suspected me of guile or deception. In the plenitude of your condescension you are pleased to add that I 'might have done anything with you with only a little more conduct', now I say, and from my heart, the Lord defend me from ever doing anything with you again! Adieu.

HARRIETTE.

My present situation was rather melancholy and embarrassing, and yet I felt my heart the lighter for my release from the cocoa trees, without its being my own act and deed. It is my fate! thought I; for I never wronged this man. I hate his fine carriage, and his money, and everything belonging to, or connected with him. I shall hate cocoa as long as I live; and I am sure, I will never enter a boat again if I can help it. This is what one gets by acting with principle.

Harriette had one point of snobbery which caused her to make an exception to her universal benevolence to the male human race. She was inclined to boast of her father's noble Swiss blood, and in her *Memoirs* she explains her feelings about social distinctions. 'In point of fact, at least in my humble opinion,' she wrote, 'there is no endurable medium between men of the very highest fashion, and honest tradesmen, to those who have once acquired a taste and habit of living with high-bred people.' Tradesmen she treated with a kind of frank familiarity which persuaded them to renew her bills as often as she wished, but the whole respectable middle class were her loathing: perhaps because she never had an opportunity of making acquaintances among them. From the very outset of her career she aimed at the nobility, or if her lovers were not all exactly noble, they were at least extremely rich, and accepted in fashionable circles.

William and Frederick Lamb were sons of a Viscount, both to inherit the title, the elder as the Lord

Melbourne who guided Queen Victoria's early years on the throne, the younger, after a distinguished diplomatic career, to succeed his brother. As such they were eligible for Harriette's affections.

The heir to the throne was also naturally eligible, but whether he ever knew anything about Harriette's invitation is doubtful. It was hinted that Harriette, who was on good terms with Colonel Thomas, his secretary, asked him to write the letter as from the Prince Regent, so that she might use it to make Fred Lamb jealous.

Harriette's position was far from pleasant. Lord Craven had turned her out and there were unkind rumours about Harriette's friendliness with his black servant; she could not and certainly did not wish to return home; Fred Lamb was far away at Hull with his regiment. But before she could make up her mind whom to choose for a temporary protector, her fate was decided for her.

The next morning, while I was considering what was to become of me, I received a very affectionate letter from Frederick Lamb, dated Hull. He dared not, he said, be selfish enough to ask me to share his poverty, and yet he had a kind of presentiment that he should not lose me.

My case was desperate; for I had taken a vow not to remain another night under Lord Craven's roof. John, therefore, the black, whom Craven had, I suppose, imported, with his cocoa trees from the West

Indies, was desired to secure me a place in the mail for Hull.

It is impossible to do justice to the joy and rapture which brightened Frederick's countenance when he flew to receive me and conducted me to his house, where I was shortly visited by his worthy general, Mackenzie, who assured me of his earnest desire to make my stay in Hull as comfortable as possible.

On this Julia Johnstone's acid comment was that Harriette did indeed go to Hull, but there made herself so conspicuous by frequenting the parade ground and flirting with all the officers, that General Mackenzie had to request her to withdraw.

On returning to London Fred Lamb established Harriette in lodgings at Duke's Row, Somers Town. In the early years of last century Somers Town, called after the owner of the land, Lord Somers, now the sordid neighbourhood lying between the Euston Road (then and till a good deal later called the New Road), Hampstead Road, and the present St. Pancras station, was little more than a square and a few streets, separated by fields from Camden Town on the north and Bloomsbury on the south. It was largely populated by the poorer class of French émigré and was never a fashionable quarter. Its most interesting feature was the Polygon, where Harriette at one time lodged, an island of houses built in a square. Clarendon Square still survives, but the Polygon has long ago been pulled down.

Somers Town was in fact a pleasant suburban place,

not too near the temptations of London, and not too
far for Fred Lamb to visit Harriette as often as he
wished. But here Harriette made the lamentable discovery that Lamb cared more for his comfort than her
own. Far from wishing to flaunt his conquest before
an admiring world, he kept her in comparative poverty
and solitude while he pursued his usual life of pleasure.
Harriette, whose pride was piqued by Lamb's coolness,
and whose curiosity had been roused by the stories he
had told her about the Marquis of Lorne, decided in
one of her impulses to write to that nobleman, saying
that if he would walk up to Duke's Row, Somers
Town, he would meet a most lovely girl.

If you are but half as lovely as you think yourself,
was the Marquis's answer, *you must be well worth
knowing; but how is that to be managed? not in the
street! But come to No. 39 Portland Street and ask for
me.*   L.

To this Harriette, probably distrusting the address,
which was not his own, replied:

*No! our first meeting must be on the high road, in
order that I may have room to run away if I don't like
you.*   HARRIETTE.

The Marquis rejoined:

*Well then, fair lady, to-morrow, at four, near the
turnpike, look for me on horseback; and then, you
know, I can gallop away.*   L.

The meeting took place and was so successful that Harriette and Lorne walked together for two hours and made an appointment to meet again on the following day. From this point Harriette usually speaks of him as Argyle. He did not become Duke of Argyle till 1806, but Harriette usually calls her friends by the titles which many of them subsequently inherited. Her irresponsible way of interchanging 'Argyle' and 'Lorne', 'Duke' and 'Marquis', often makes her difficult to follow, but it will be simpler to follow her in her use of her friends' titles and to keep to her spelling of their names. Argyle was an accepted spelling at that time.

A conversation then took place between Harriette and her conscience. Conscience maintained that Lamb was relying in confidence on her honour. Harriette pointed out that his confidence was only the effect of vanity. Conscience replied that the least Harriette could do was to confess to Lamb on his return that she had written to and walked with Argyle, adding rather speciously that her dear mother would never forgive her if she became artful.

Thus encouraged and fortified, Harriette, with the simplicity which was an engaging part of her character, broke the news to Lamb, who with perfect fatuity answered:

'I have the most perfect esteem for my dearest little wife, whom I can, I know, as safely trust with Argyle as Craven trusted her with me.'

With a clear mind Harriette was able to wait for Argyle on the following day, but he did not come. Mortified by his apparent rejection of her advances, she exclaimed, 'He shall not have all the cut on his side neither,' and thereupon wrote him a letter, the final paragraph of which is worth quoting as a model for all young women in similar circumstances.

I have not quite deserved this contempt from you, and, in that consolatory reflection, I take my leave— not in anger, my lord, but only with the steady deter- mination so to profit by the humiliating lesson you have given me, as never to expose myself to the like contempt again.

Your most obedient servant,
HARRIETTE WILSON.

An answer from Argyle came by the twopenny post, making a fresh appointment, which Harriette ig- nored. Meanwhile she was surprised to receive a letter from her old friend Tom Sheridan, asking for an in- terview. As Lamb was away at Brocket Hall, the fam- ily seat in Hertfordshire, Harriette had no hesitation in asking Sheridan to call. He came on a mission from Argyle, to explain that an invitation from the Prince of Wales had kept him from visiting Somers Town at the appointed time, and to beg for forgiveness.

'There is nothing to forgive,' said I, 'if no slight was meant. In short, you are making too much of me, and spoiling me, by all this explanation; for, indeed I had at first been less indignant; but that I fancied His Grace neglected me because—' and I hesitated, while I could feel myself blush deeply.

'Because what?' asked Tom Sheridan.

'Nothing,' I replied, looking at my shoes.

'What a pretty girl you are,' observed Sheridan, 'particularly when you blush.'

'Fiddlestick!' said I laughing; 'you know you always preferred my sister Fanny.'

'Well,' replied Tom, 'there I plead guilty. Fanny is the sweetest creature on earth; but you are all a race of finished coquettes, who delight in making fools of people. Now can anything come up to your vanity in writing to Lorne that you are the most beautiful creature on earth?'

'Never mind,' said I, 'you set all that to rights. I was never vain in your society, in my life.'

'I would give the world for a kiss at this moment,' said Tom; 'because you look so humble and so amiable; but'—recollecting himself—'this is not exactly the embassy I came upon. Have you a mind to give Lorne an agreeable surprise?'

'I don't know.'

'Upon my honour, I believe he is downright in love with you.'

'Well?'

'Come into a hackney-coach with me, and we will drive down to the Tennis Court in the Haymarket.'

'Is the Duke there?'

'Yes.'

'But—at all events, I will not trust myself in a hackney-coach with you.'

'There was a time,' said poor Tom Sheridan, with much drollery of expression, 'there was a time when the very motion of a carriage would—but now!'—and he shook his handsome head with comic gravity—'but now! you may drive with me, from here to St. Paul's, in the most perfect safety. I will tell you a secret,' added he, and he fixed his fine dark eye on my face while he spoke, in a tone half merry, half desponding, 'I am dying; but nobody knows it yet!'

I was very much affected by his manner of saying this.

'My dear Mr. Sheridan,' said I, with earnest warmth, 'you have accused me of being vain of the little beauty God has given me. Now I would give it all, or, upon my word, I think I would, to obtain the certainty that you would, from this hour, refrain from such excesses as are destroying you.'

'Did you see me play the methodist parson, in a tub, at Mrs. Beaumont's masquerade last Thursday?' said Tom, with affected levity.

'You may laugh as you please,' said I, 'at a little fool like me pretending to preach to you; yet I am sensible enough to admire you, and quite feeling enough to regret your time so misspent, your brilliant talents so misapplied.'

'Bravo! Bravo!' Tom reiterated, 'what a funny little girl you are! Pray, miss, how is your time spent?'

'Not in drinking brandy,' I replied.

'And how might your talent be applied, ma'am?'

'Have not I just given you a specimen in the shape of a handsome quotation?'

'My good little girl—it is in the blood, and I can't help it—and if I could it is too late now. I'm dying, I tell you. I know not if my poor father's physician was as eloquent as you are; but he did his best to turn him from drinking. Among other things, he declared to him one day that the brandy, Arquebusade, and Eau de Cologne he swallowed, would burn off the coat of his stomach. Then, said my father, my stomach must digest in its waistcoat, for I cannot help it.'

'Indeed, I am very sorry for you,' I replied; and I hope he believed me; for he pressed my hand hastily, and I think I saw a tear glisten in his bright, dark eye.

'Shall I tell Lorne,' said poor Tom, with an effort to recover his usual gaiety, 'that you will write to him, or will you come to the Tennis Court?'

'Neither,' answered I; 'but you may tell His Lordship that, of course, I am not angry, since I am led to believe he had no intention to humble nor make a fool of me.'

'Nothing more?' inquired Tom.

'Nothing,' I replied, 'for His Lordship.'

'And what for me?' said Tom.

'You! what do you want?'

'A kiss!' he said.

'Not I, indeed!'

'Be it so, then: and yet you and I may never meet again on this earth, and just now I thought you felt some interest about me'; and he was going away.

'So I do, dear Tom Sheridan!' said I, detaining him; for I saw death had fixed his stamp on poor Sheridan's handsome face. 'You know I have a very warm and feeling heart, and taste enough to admire and like you, but why is this to be our last meeting?'

'I must go to the Mediterranean,' poor Sheridan continued, putting his hand to his chest, and coughing.

To die! thought I, as I looked on his sunk, but still very expressive dark eyes.

'Then God bless you!' said I, first kissing his hand, and then, though somewhat timidly, leaning my face towards him. He parted my hair, and kissed my forehead, my eyes, and my lips.

'If I do come back,' said he, forcing a languid smile, 'mind let me find you married, and rich enough to lend me an occasional hundred pounds or two.' He then kissed his hand gracefully, and was out of sight in an instant.

I never saw him again.

It is a pretty and affecting interview, charmingly related, and that Sheridan did not die for another fifteen years or so (in 1817) does not spoil its literary value.

Harriette's wounded pride was healed, Argyle was

restored to her favour, and daily walks took place, though Harriette kept the Duke severely in his place, cutting him for a time when his advances became too passionate.

Horace Beckford and two other fashionable men, who had heard from Frederick of my cruelty, as he termed it, and the Duke's daily romantic walks to the Jew's Harp House, had come upon him, by accident, in a body, as they were galloping through Somers Town. Lorne was sitting, in a very pastoral fashion, on a gate near my door, whistling. They saluted him with a loud laugh. No man could, generally speaking, parry a joke better than Argyle, for few knew the world better : but this was no joke. He had been severely wounded and annoyed by my cutting his acquaintance altogether, at the very moment when he had reason to believe that the passion he really felt for me was returned. It was almost the first instance of the kind he had ever met with. He was bored and vexed with himself, for the time he had lost, and yet he found himself continually in my neighbourhood, almost before he was aware of it. He wanted, as he has told me since, to meet me once more by accident, and then he declared he would give me up.

'What a set of consummate asses you are,' said Argyle to Beckford and his party, and then quietly continued on the gate, whistling as before.

'But r-e-a-l-l-y, r-e-a-l-l-y, ca-ca-cannot Tom She-She-She-Sheridan assist you, Marquis?' said the handsome Horace Beckford, in his usual stammering way.

'A very good joke for Fred Lamb, as the case stands now,' replied the Duke, laughing; for a man of the world must laugh in these cases, though he should burst with the effort.

'Why don't she come?' said Sir John Shelley, who was one of the party.

An odd mad-looking Frenchman, in a white coat and a white hat, well known about Somers Town, passed at this moment, and observed His Grace, whom he knew well by sight, from the other side of the way. He had, a short time before, attempted to address me, when he met me walking alone, and inquired of me when I had last seen the Marquis of Lorne, with whom he had often observed me walking? I made him no answer. In a fit of frolic, as if everybody combined at this moment against the poor, dear, handsome Argyle, the Frenchman called, as loud as he could scream, from the other side of the way, '*Ah! ah! oh! oh! vous voilà, Monsieur le Comte Dromedaire* (alluding thus to the Duke's family name, as pronounced Camel), *mais où est donc Madame la Comtesse?*'

'D——d impudent rascal!' said Argyle, delighted to vent his growing rage on somebody, and started across the road after the poor thin old Frenchman, who might have now said his prayers, had not his spider-legs served him better than his courage.

Fred Lamb was very angry with me for not laughing at this story; but the only feeling it ex-

*The Duke of Argyle whistling and
waiting for H. Wilson.*

cited in me was unmixed gratitude towards the Duke, for remembering me still, and for having borne all this ridicule for my sake.

Fred Lamb grew colder and more selfish every day. He read Milton, Shakespeare, Byron, *The Rambler*, and Virgil aloud to Harriette, but money was not forthcoming. She had been lodging with a 'comical old widow, who had formerly been my sister Fanny's nurse when she was quite a child,' but the old lady, whose house and trade we may be allowed to suspect, now acquainted her that she had not another shilling either to provide her dinner or Harriette's.

Necessity hath no law, thought I, my eyes brightening, and my determination being fixed in an instant. In ten minutes more the following letter was in the post-office, directed to the Marquis of Lorne.

If you still desire my society I will sup with you to-morrow evening in your own house.
                    Yours, ever affectionately,
                                HARRIETTE.

I knew perfectly well that on the evening I mentioned to his grace, Fred Lamb would be at his father's country house, Brocket Hall.

I will not say in what particular year of his life the Duke of Argyle succeeded with me. Ladies scorn dates! Dates make ladies nervous and stories

dry. Be it only known then, that it was just at the
end of his Lorne shifts and his lawn shirts. It was at
that critical period of his life, when his whole and
sole possessions appeared to consist in three dozen of
ragged lawn shirts, with embroidered collars, well
fringed in his service; a threadbare suit of snuff colour, a little old hat with a very little binding left, an
old horse, an old groom, an old carriage, and an old
château. It was to console himself for all this an-
tiquity, I suppose, that he fixed upon so very young
a mistress as myself. Thus, after having gone
through all the routine of sighs, vows, and rural
walks he at last saw me blooming and safe in his
dismal château in Argyle Street.

Joy produced a palpitation which had well nigh
been fatal to— No matter, to be brief—

A late hour in the morning blushed to find us in
the arms of each other, as Monk Lewis, or somebody
else says; but the morning was pale when compared
to the red on my cheek—aye, ladies, pure red, when
I, the very next day, acquainted Fred Lamb with
my pretty, innocent, volatile adventure!

Fred was absolutely dumb from astonishment,
and half choked with rage and pride.

Lamb left her 'in madness and fury,' and she immediately took a furnished house at the west end of
the town to receive her new lover, whose passion for
the time knew no bounds.

Though Harriette had left Fred Lamb, he had by
no means passed out of her life. On the contrary, he

was for a long time one of her assiduous courtiers and more than once made attempts of alarming violence to get possession of her again. Harriette must have reported him with some accuracy, for whenever he appears or speaks it is in character, and we are left with a very fair idea of the man he was, a man whom Greville, who had known him long and intimately, described as follows, after his death in 1853.

'Very handsome in youth, clever, agreeable and adroit, he was much addicted to gallantry and had endless liaisons with women, most of whom continued to be his friends long after they had ceased to be his mistresses, much to the credit of all parties. He was largely endowed with social merits and virtues, without having or affecting any claim to those of a higher or moral character. I have no doubt he was much more amiable as an old man than he had ever been when he was a young one.'

Oh, this tiresome Fred Lamb! [cried Harriette when he had for long been begging and persecuting her to spend a night with him at that well-known halfway house between London and Brighton, The Cock at Sutton.] Oh, this tiresome Fred Lamb! I wonder if any woman alive was ever in love with him, with the exception of the once celebrated Charlotte Windham; who would have taken him into keeping, at least so I have heard, and found him in washing, tea, sugar, and raw eggs, to the end of his natural life, had he not cut her dead, *pour mes propres beaux yeux*. Handsome! clever! young! a

great plenipo, and the recorded son of the Earl of
Melbourne. What would ladies be at? *On ne con-*
noit pas toujours son père, c'est un malheur; on est
sur, cependant, d'en avoir eu un, cela console! as
says Pigault Le Brun. [It is hardly worth going
through the works of that once popular and most
prolific dramatist and *romancier* to verify this delightful quotation.] His passions were most ardent,
he would grind his teeth in bitterness of wounded
pride if you did not happen to be affected with the
same ardour. He is now an ambassador, and just as
well off as ambassadors usually are; yet in my present poverty I have vainly attempted to get a hundred pounds out of him. He has occasionally, indeed, sent me five or ten pounds; but not without
much pressing; and he has not yet paid me my expenses to Hull and back.

Doubtless this is the reason why Harriette is so severe on her second lover. But in her account of the
meeting at The Cock, what she relates does him great
credit. As the evening wore on, the thought of spend-
ing the night with a man whom she had never really
loved became so unendurable that with her usual
frankness she told him so.

Fred Lamb, on this occasion, behaved very well
and very gentlemanlike, much as his pride and feelings were hurt. He ordered out my carriage, and
accompanied me home with friendly politeness, nor

did he make a single unpleasant observation on my refusal to remain there.

It is regrettable to learn that after so many passionate or tender scenes, Fred Lamb called on Harriette's publisher, Stockdale, after the publication of the first parts of her *Memoirs*, 'to threaten him, or us, with prosecution, death and destruction' if his name was allowed to appear again. Luckily for posterity, his threats, unsupported by financial backing, were disregarded.

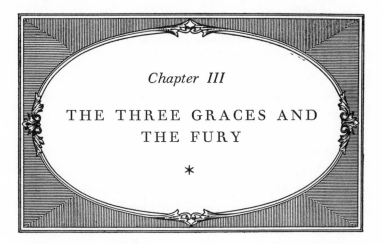

Chapter III

THE THREE GRACES AND
THE FURY

*

WHILE SHE was living in Somers Town, Harriette had made the acquaintance of a mysterious, romantic lady called Mrs. Julia Johnstone, who lived in a villa on Primrose Hill, with five beautiful children. Mr. Johnstone, though he appeared devoted to Julia, seldom made his appearance oftener than twice a week, and came across a retired field to her house, which might have been more conveniently reached by the roadway. Not long afterwards Julia related her history to Harriette, though in her *Confessions* she furiously denied the version that Harriette gives. It is enough to say that she was of good birth, and had been for some years mistress of Colonel Cotton of the 10th Hussars. As he had a wife and seven legitimate children he could not support his Julia in luxury, but her constancy, in spite of a child every eleven months and a very small income, was unshakeable. The name of Josiah Cotton, or Cottin (both spellings are used), appears in the Army List till the year 1799, when he

was a Lieutenant-Colonel, but Harriette's statement
that he was dismissed by the Colonel-in-Chief, the
Prince of Wales, is not substantiated.

Julia was a well-bred, languishing creature, with
exquisite skin, a graceful form, and pretty arms,
hands, and feet, though not regularly beautiful. Of
her character, Harriette, who was an extremely
shrewd judge when not biassed, writes: 'She struck me
as a woman of very violent passions, combined with
an extremely shy and reserved disposition.' It is a not
uncommon type, and such women, when they encourage their hearts to get the better of their heads, are
very unhappy. Too diffident to show their real feelings, except in moments of great stress, they torture
themselves with their own passions, or alienate the
affection of their friends and lovers by revealing them
too openly. Julia and Harriette knew each other intimately for several years, and though each had unkind
words to say about the other, one feels a curious kind
of respect existing between them. In spite of their dis-
similarity of temperament and their occasional rival-
ries there was never any open breach. As professional
demireps they probably knew each other's metal, and
neither cared to strike too deeply a friend who could
strike hard in return.

As Harriette was now a respectable kept mistress in
a good house, she was able to resume relationships
with such of her family as were moving in fashionable society, including her elder sister Fanny. Of
Frances Dubochet, known later and till her death as
Fanny Parker, no one had ever an unkind word to say.

Even Julia Johnstone, once her bosom friend, could find no worse to say of her than this:

> She was a poor, timid, good-natured thing, incapable of doing either harm or good. She scarcely knew the distinction between virtue and vice; whenever she did good, it was from accident; when she committed evil, it was from want of knowing better, and she had a vacant see-saw way of thinking that everything happened for the best. If you could not love her, it was impossible to hate her.

Fanny had run away with a Mr. Woodcock, who could not obtain a divorce from his wife, and lived a steady retired life for seven years with his three children. At his death she came into the world again and was extremely popular among both men and women, being one of those really good-hearted creatures—though not without a spice of gentle malice—who always defend their friends in their absence, and are naturally kind to anyone who is shy or unhappy. Lord Yarmouth, later Marquis of Hertford, known from his name and hair as 'Red Herrings,' was her warm admirer, and always insisted that she was the beauty of the family. He wished to have her portrait painted by Lawrence and place it in his apartment. 'That laughing dark blue eye of hers,' he would say, 'is uncommonly beautiful.' In his behaviour to poor Fanny Parker he showed a side of his character which few would suspect in that cynical, hard-living nobleman; a side which Thackeray did not see in the Marquis of Steyne, though Disraeli may have guessed it in Lord

Monmouth. When Fanny was dying his kindness was incessant, and even Julia Johnstone admitted it.

Fanny, Harriette, and Julia now drifted into an alliance, offensive and defensive. Most people thought they were sisters, and they were called the Three Graces. But as there are not four Graces, Amy, the eldest of the three Dubochets, was outside the magic circle, and was often called one of the Furies. Julia described her as 'a fine dark woman with a Siddonian countenance and a masculine spirit,' while Harriette said much the same, adding the following account of her sister's earlier career :—

It was Amy, my eldest sister, who had been the first to set us a bad example. We were all virtuous girls, when Amy, one fine afternoon, left her father's house and sallied forth, like Don Quixote, in quest of adventures. The first person who addressed her was one Mr. Trench, a certain short-sighted pedantic man, whom most people know about town. I believe she told him that she was running away from her father. All I know for certain is, that when Fanny and I discovered her abode, we went to visit her, and when we asked her what on earth had induced her to throw herself away on an entire stranger whom she had never seen before? Her answer was, 'I refused him the whole of the first day; had I done so the second, he would have been in a fever.'

Amy was really very funny, however spitefully disposed towards me. To be brief with her history :

Trench put her to school again, from motives of virtue and economy. From that school she eloped with General Maddan.

Amy's virtue was something like the nine lives of a cat.

With General Maddan she, for several years, professed constancy; indeed, I am not quite certain that she was otherwise. I never, in my occasional visits, saw anything suspicious, except, once, a pair of breeches!!

It was one day when I went to call on her with my brother. General Maddan was not in town. She wanted to go to the opera. The fit had only just seized her, at past nine o'clock. She begged me to make her brother's excuse at home, as, she said, he must accompany her. 'What, in those dirty boots?' I asked.——'I have got both dress-stockings and breeches upstairs, of Maddan's,' replied Amy; and I assisted at the boy's toilette. In handing him the black pair of breeches, which Amy had presented me with, I saw marked, in Indian ink, what, being in the inside, had probably escaped her attention. It was simply the name of Proby.

'How came Lord Proby's black small-clothes here?' said I.

Amy snatched them out of my hand in a fury, and desired me to go out of the house. *Au reste,* she had often, at that time, three hundred pounds in her pocket at once, and poor Maddan had not a shilling. All this happened before I had left my home.

At the period I now write about, I believe that

Maddan was abroad, and Amy lived in York Place, where she used to give gay evening parties to half the fashionable men in town, after the opera. She never came to me but from interested motives. Sometimes she forced herself into my private box, or teased me to make her known to the Duke of Argyle.

It was General Madden, as the name is more correctly spelt, who remarked once of his temporary sister-in-law that 'I can't abide Harriette, for she is a devil incarnate and always at her window like the sign of Queen Elizabeth over a tavern door, to invite passers-by to walk in.'

Harriette was now launched on the happiest and most untroubled period of her life. Under Argyle's discreet protection she found nothing to desire except that he should not share his affections between her and a 'nasty Lady W— with whom the world said he had been intriguing these nineteen years.' More than once she quarrelled with him over this lady, but she was just enough in love to be easily cajoled into forgiveness. In a year or two she was to have a *grande passion* and suffer so much that she was never again the careless tomboy to whom Lord Rivers said, 'Your little, light feet seem scarcely to touch the earth, as though you could almost fly,' but while her heart was free she had no care for the future, and enjoyed every moment of the day and night.

One of the reasons for her immense popularity, even among men who had no wish to make love to

her, was her inexhaustible vitality. To ride in Hyde
Park, to walk for miles, to dine in company, to visit
the opera, where she entertained dozens of men with
her quick, amusing conversation, to spend two or
three hours at her sister Amy's supper parties, teasing
her admirers and annoying her sister, and then to retire in excellent spirits to 'Argyle's gloomy château'
for the night; all this was only an ordinary day to her.
Never, except when she had been ill, did she mention
the word fatigue. If she did not wish to drive home
with a man, but was anxious to provoke him, she was
capable of walking him from the opera to Camden
Town when she lived there, and then giving him his
congé. More than one of her lovers, or would-be
lovers, was almost walked to death by this indefatigable little creature. Witness Lord Granville Leveson-
Gower, whom in a fit of caprice she invited to meet
her in Regent's Park. As soon as she set eyes upon his
lordship she decided that he was not to her taste, but
having brought him up to Marylebone fields on a
hot summer morning, she thought it would not be fair
or ladylike to dismiss him till she had given his talents
and powers of pleasing a fair trial. Accordingly, she
walked him up to the top of Primrose Hill, on to
Hampstead, and back to Great Portland Street, when
his lordship, entirely exhausted and wiping his face,
begged to be allowed to sit down and rest, apprehend-
ing a fever or sudden death, upon which Harriette dismissed him, telling him that he was not in the least
the sort of person she wanted. Her contempt for him
led her to call him Lord George instead of Lord Gran-

ville, and to apologise for it by remarking that it is difficult to bear in mind the names of those who do not excite in us the least interest. This cavalier treatment was not forgotten.

There is a half-length picture of Harriette, 'my head leaning on my finger, which is my usual attitude as you see in the portrait,' which is the best likeness existing of her.* According to her own and contemporary accounts she was small, with very little feet, of which she was extremely proud. Her eyes were brown, her eyelashes long and dark, and she wore her hair— which must have changed since the days when her sisters called her 'ugly, straight-haired figure of fun'— in a careless mop of curls. While the women of her circle wore elaborate toilettes of satin, silk and lace, and ostentatiously flaunted their jewels, Harriette's invariable dress was a rich figured white French gauze over white satin. She had no ornaments in her curly hair, but sometimes wore long jewelled ear-rings. She had all the impertinence of a charming, petted boy, a Cherubino, and Lord Stewart's name for her, 'little fellow,' fits her far better than the 'Angelick Harriette' of Argyle and other lovers.

The Three Graces, Fanny, Harriette, and Julia, now took a box at the opera. Amy had another near them and gave parties on Saturday nights, to which she was obliged to ask her sisters in order to get the men whom her rather parsimonious suppers did not satisfy. Harriette's own description of a night at the opera gives a lively impression of these evenings, and

* Reproduced facing page 160.

Lord Granville Leveson-Gower fails to give satisfaction.

a few comments on some of the men she mentions will show the varied nature of her friends.

The Duke of Devonshire, the future employer of Paxton, was a mere boy at this time, but his deafness was already a marked inconvenience.

Henry Luttrell, natural son of the Earl of Carhampton and 'father confessor-general' to the Graces, was a man about town and a writer of light verse, of which his 'Advice to Julia' is the best known. He delighted in the life of London society, where his brilliant conversation and turn for epigram gave him the position that his birth denied; his chief aversion was a bore. Gronow spoke of him as 'the most agreeable man I ever met, and the last of the Conversationalists.'

'Fat Nugent' was Lord Nugent, later an M.P. and an ardent supporter of Catholic enfranchisement. His bulk was the theme of many stories. In 1823 he went to Spain to offer his personal help to the Cortes, who had taken the king with them and shut themselves up in Cadiz against the Royalists and the French. This action on the part of a British subject of note was a breach of neutrality which might have provoked unpleasant consequences, but for Canning's treatment of the subject.

'About the middle of last July,' he observed in the House of Commons, 'the heavy Falmouth coach was observed to proceed to its destination with more than its wonted gravity. The coach contained two passengers: the one a fair lady of no considerable dimensions; the other a gentleman who was about to carry

the succour of his person to the struggling patriots in
Spain. Things were at that juncture moving fast to
their final issue. How far the noble lord induced to
the termination by plumping his weight into the sinking scale of the Cortes was too nice a question for him
(Mr. Canning) now to determine.'

The speech convulsed the House, Nugent appears to
have been delighted by this peculiar tribute, and the
serious aspect of the case was forgotten. It was some
time before Nugent could live down his description as
an 'enormous breach of neutrality'.

Lord Alvanley, who succeeded to his title in 1804,
was a well-known character of Regency times. When
Harriette first knew him he had a commission in the
Coldstream Guards, and later served with distinction
in the Peninsular War. He was famous for his wit,
and after Brummell's fall in 1816 was generally given
the credit of all the good or bad sayings from the
clubs, while his good nature was remarkable among
the dandies, whose remarks were too often sour and
spiteful. His habit of insisting that a cold apricot tart
should be served at his table all the year round gave
him a certain reputation for amiable eccentricity. Less
amiable was his habit of reading in bed by the light of
a candle, which he extinguished either by throwing it
on to the floor and taking a shot at it with a pillow, or
putting it, still alight, under his bolster. At the country houses where he often stayed a servant was ordered to sit up in the passage and keep watch over his
room. There is a drawing of him by Dighton, a stout-
ish man in a dark blue coat and tight trousers, yellow

gloves and a high collar, busily walking along the street.

Count Palmella, the Portuguese Ambassador, was as much at home in London society as was the Marquis de Soveral in King Edward VII's time. Much of his diplomatic life was spent in England, and he represented the Queen of Portugal at Queen Victoria's coronation.

Lord Frederick Bentinck, who held a commission in the 1st Foot Guards, appears from time to time in the *Memoirs*, always in character, and always in a very amiable light as the paternal giver of good advice, which Harriette listened to kindly and ignored. His favourite question whenever he met her was, Where she expected to go : a question to which there was no answer.

George Brummell needs no explanation, but it may be interesting here to note what Barbey d'Aurevilly has to say in his *Du Dandysme et de Georges Brummell*.

'Une (femme) seule, à notre connaissance, a laissé sur Brummell de ces mots qui cachent la passion et qui la révèlent, c'est la courtisane Henriette Wilson: chose naturelle, elle était jalouse non du cœur de Brummell, mais de sa gloire. Les qualités d'où le Dandy tirait sa puissance étaient de celles qui eussent fait la fortune de la courtisane.'

That is, Brummell cultivated and exercised in the highest degree the qualities by which alone the courtesan can make and keep her success. Fastidious taste, complete self-assurance, politeness as a duty to himself, deliberate and brutal rudeness to anyone whom he considered presuming, the art of setting the tone and fashion to his world, so that no gathering was complete without him, no fashion correct till he had approved. Harriette, hot-headed, impulsive, careless, could not impose herself as he did, and it is possible that, as d'Aurevilly says, she subconsciously resented his empire over both sexes, though in the end both were bound for the same dingy goal of poverty and exile. If d'Aurevilly analysed her sentiments rightly, a question open to argument, she did not need to envy Brummell after 1816.

The Honourable John William Ward, one of Harriette's especial dislikes, succeeded his father as Lord Dudley in 1823. He was a man of considerable talents, a good scholar, brilliant and sarcastic in conversation, but victim to an absence of mind which finally developed into insanity. His friends maintained that his 'distractions' were not always genuine. In proof of this a story was current that he came out of the House of Lords one night and could not find his carriage. It was late, he was frantically afraid of catching cold, and accepted an offer from a friend to drive him to Dudley House. During the drive he began to talk to himself, a habit which he called 'Dudley talking to Ward', and was heard to say:

'A deuce of a bore! This tiresome man has taken me home, and will expect me to ask him to dinner. I suppose I must do so, but it is a horrid nuisance!'

Upon this his friend closed his eyes and assuming the same sleepy monotonous voice, began to mutter:

'What a dreadful bore! This good-natured fellow Dudley will think himself obliged to invite me to dinner and I shall be forced to go. I hope he won't ask me, for he gives d——d bad dinners!'

Lord Dudley started, looked confused, said nothing, but never forgave his friend, for he prided himself on being a good hater.

Harriette's dislike of him was violent, and may be accounted for by the reason which made Rogers compose the epigram:

> Ward has no heart they say, but I deny it;
> He has a heart, and gets his speeches by it.

The next opera was unusually brilliant. Amy's box was close to ours, and almost as soon as we were seated, she entered, dressed in the foreign style, which best became her, accompanied by Counts Woronzow, Beckendorff [as Harriette always spells Benckendorff], and Orloff. Beckendorff was half mad for her, and wanted to marry her with his left hand.

'Why not with the right?' said Amy.

'I dare not,' answered Beckendorff, 'without the consent of the Emperor of Russia'.

Amy had desired him to go to Russia, and obtain this consent from the Emperor, more than a month before; but still he lingered.

Our box was soon so crowded that I was obliged to turn one out as fast as a new face appeared. Julia and Fanny left me to pay a visit to the enemy, as

Luttrell used to call Amy. Observing me, for an instant, the Duke of Devonshire came into my box, believing that he did me honour.

'Duke,' said I, 'you cut me in Piccadilly to-day.'

'Don't you know,' said thick-head, 'don't you know, *belle Harriette*, that I am blind as well as deaf, and a little absent too?'

'My good young man,' said I, out of all patience, *'allez donc à l'hôpital des invalides:* for really, if God has made you blind and deaf, you must be absolutely insufferable when you presume to be absent too. The least you can do, as a blind, deaf man, is surely to pay attention to those who address you.'

'I never heard anything half so severe as *la belle Harriette*,' drawled out the Duke.

Luttrell now peeped his nose into my box and said, dragging in his better half, half-brother I mean, fat Nugent, 'A vacancy for two! How happens this? You'll lose your character, Harriette.'

'I'm growing stupid from sympathy, I suppose,' I observed, glancing at His Grace who, being as deaf as a post, poor fellow, bowed to me for the supposed compliment.

'You sup with Amy, I hope?' said I to Luttrell. 'And you?' turning to Nugent.

'There's a princess in the way,' replied Nugent, alluding to the late Queen.

'Nonsense,' said Luttrell. 'Her Royal Highness has allowed me to be off.'

'You can take liberties with her,' Nugent remarked. 'You great wits can do what you please.

She would take it very ill of me; besides, I wish Amy would send some of those dirty Russians away. Count Orloff is the greatest beast in nature.'

Lord Alvanly now entered my box.

'*Place pour un,*' said I, taking hold of the back of the Duke of Devonshire's chair.

'I am going,' said His Grace; 'but seriously, Harriette, I want to accomplish dining alone some evening on purpose to pay you a visit.'

'There will be no harm in that,' said I.

'None! None!' answered Luttrell, who took my allusion.

Alvanly brought me a tall, well-dressed foreigner, whom he was waiting to present to me, as his friend.

'That won't do, Lord Alvanly,' said I; 'really, that is no introduction and less recommendation. Name your friend, or away with him.'

'*Ma foi, madame,*' said the foreigner, '*un nom ne fait rien du tout. Vous me voyez là, madame, honnête homme, de cinq pieds et neuf pouces.*'

'*Madame est persuadée de vos cinq pieds, mais elle n'est pas si sure de vos neuf pouces,*' Alvanly observed.

'*Adieu, ma belle Harriette,*' said the Duke, at last taking my hint, and rising to depart.

Julia and Fanny now returned: the latter, as usual, was delighted to meet Alvanly.

'Do you come from the enemy?' Luttrell inquired of them.

'Yes,' replied Fanny, laughing.

'My dear Fanny,' said Luttrell, in his comical, earnest, methodistical manner, 'my dear Fanny, this will never do!'

'What won't do?' inquired Fanny.

'These Russians, my dear.'

'She has got a little Portuguese, besides the Russians, coming to her to-night,' said I. 'The Count Palmella.'

'The ambassador?' Nugent asked.

'God bless my soul!' said Luttrell, looking up to the ceiling with such a face! Tom Sheridan would have liked to have copied it when he played the methodist in a tub at Mrs. Beaumont's masquerade.

'They are only all brought up upon trial,' I observed; 'she will cut the rest, as soon as she has fixed on one of them.'

'Yes, but you see coming after these cossacks is the devil!' lisped Alvanly, with his usual comical expression. 'God bless your soul, we have no chance after these fellows.'

'There is Argyle looking at you from Lady W—'s box,' Nugent said.

The remark put me out of humour, although I did observe that, though he sat in her ladyship's box, he was thinking most of me. Nevertheless, it was abominably provoking.

Lord Frederick Bentinck next paid me his usual visit.

'Everybody is talking about you,' said his lordship. 'Two men downstairs have been laying a bet that you are Lady Tavistock. Mrs. Orby Hunter says you are the handsomest woman in the house.'

Poor Julia, all this time, did not receive the slightest compliment or attention from anybody. At last she kissed her hand to someone in a neighbouring box.

'Who are you bowing to?' I inquired.

'An old flame of mine, who was violently in love with me when I was a girl at Hampton Court,' whispered Julia. 'I have never seen him since I knew Cotton.'

'What is his name?' I asked.

'George Brummell,' answered Julia.

I had never, at that time, heard of George Brummell.

'Do you know a Mr. George Brummell?' said I to Lord Alvanly.

Before his lordship could answer my question, Brummell entered the box and, addressing himself to Julia, expressed his surprise, joy, and astonishment at meeting with her.

Julia was now all smiles and sweetness. Just before Brummell's arrival she was growing a little sulky. Indeed she had reason, for in vain did we cry her up and puff her off, as Lord Carysfort's niece, or as an accomplished, elegant, charming creature, daughter of a maid of honour: she did not take. The men were so rude as often to suffer her to follow us, by herself, without offering their arms to conduct her to the carriage. She was, in fact, so reserved, so shy, and so short-sighted that, not

being very young, nobody would be at the trouble
of finding out what she was.

In the round room we held separate levees. Amy
always fixed herself near enough to me to see what
I was about, and try to charm away some of my
admirers. Heaven knows! Fanny and I had plenty
to spare her; for they did so flock about us, they
scarcely left us breathing room. Argyle looked as
if he wanted to join us, but was afraid of Lady
W—.

'Are you not going home, pretty?' he would say
to me, between his teeth, passing close to my ear.

'Do speak louder, Marquis,' I answered, provoked
that he should be afraid of any woman but myself.
'I am not going home these three hours. I am going first to Amy's party.'

Lorne looked, not sulky nor cross, as Fred Lamb
would have done, but smiled beautifully and said:
'At three, then, may I go to you?'

'Yes,' answered I, putting my hand into his, and
again I contrived to forget Lady W—.

There was all the world at Amy's, and not half
room enough for them. Some were in the passage,
and some in the parlour, and in the drawing-room
one could scarcely breathe. At the top of it, Amy
sat coquetting with her tall Russians. The poor
Count Palmella stood gazing on her at a humble
distance.

The little delicate weak gentlemanlike Portuguese was no match for the three cossacks. I do not
believe he got in a single word the whole evening

but once; when Amy remarked that she should go the next evening to see the tragedy of Omeo.

'What tragedy is that, pray?' drawled out the Honourable John William Ward, starting from a fit of the dismals, just as if someone had gone behind him and, with a flapper, reminded him that he was at a party, and ought to *faire l'aimable aux dames*.

'You may laugh at me as much as you please,' answered Amy, 'and I must have patience and bear it, ight or ong; for I cannot pronounce the letter *r*.'

'How very odd!' I remarked. 'Why, you could pronounce it well enough at home!' I really did not mean this to tease her; for I thought, perhaps, lisping might grow upon us, as we got older, but I soon guessed it was all sham by the gathering storm on Amy's countenance. The struggle between the wish to show off effeminate softness to her lovers, and her ardent desire to knock me down, I could see by an arch glance at me from Fanny's laughing eye, and a shrug of her shoulder was understood by that sister, as well as by myself. Fanny's glance was the slyest thing in nature, and was given in perfect fear and trembling.

'Harriette's correctness may be, I am sorry to say—,' and she paused to endeavour to twist her upper lip, trembling with fury, into the shape and form of what might be most pure and innocent in virtuous indignation!

Count Beckendorff eyed me with a look of pity and noble contempt, and then fixed his eyes with rapture on his angel's face!

Joking apart, he was a monstrous fool, that same Count Beckendorff, in the shape of a very handsome young cossack.

'Where's the treaty of peace?' said Nugent, dreading a rupture which would deaden half the spirit of the little pleasant suppers he wished to give us, at his own rooms in the Albany. 'No infringement, we beg, ladies. We have the treaty, under your pretty hands and seals.'

'Peace be to France, if France in peace permit it!' said I, holding out my hand to Amy, in burlesque majesty.

Amy could not for the life of her laugh with the rest; because she saw that they thought me pleasant. She, however, put out her hand hastily, to have done with what was bringing me into notice: and, that the subject might be entirely changed, and I as much forgotten, she must waltz that instant with Beckendorff.

'Sydenham!' said Amy, to one of her new admirers who, being flute-mad, and a beautiful flute-player, was always ready.

'The flute does not mark the time enough for waltzing,' said he, taking it out of a drawer; 'but I shall be happy to accompany Harriette's waltz on the pianoforte, because she always plays in good time.'

'Do not play, Harriette,' said Amy, for fear it should strike anyone that I played well; 'if I had wished her to be troubled I should have asked her myself. The flute is quite enough'; and she began twirling her tall cossack round the room. He appeared charmed to obey her commands, and sport his really graceful waltzing.

'I do not think it a trouble in the least,' I observed, opening the instrument without malice or vanity. I was never vain of music; and at that early age so much envy never entered my head. I hated playing too; but fancied that I was civil in catching up the air and accompanying Colonel Sydenham.

'Harriette puts me out,' said Amy, stopping, and she refused to stand up again, in spite of all Sydenham could say about my very excellent ear for music.

'*Madame a donc le projet d'aller à Drury Lane, demain?*' said the Count Palmella at last, having been waiting with his mouth open ever since Amy mentioned Omeo for an opportunity of following up the subject.

Amy darted her bright black eyes upon him as though she had said, *Ah! te voilà! d'où viens tu?* but without answering him, or perhaps understanding what he said.

'*Si madame me permettra,*' continued the Count, '*j'aurai l'honneur de lui engager une loge.*'

'*Oui, s'il vous plaît, je vous en serai obligée,*' said Amy, though in somewhat worse French.

The celebrated beau, George Brummell, who had been presented to Amy by Julia, in the round room at the opera, now entered, and put poor Julia in high spirits. Brummell, as Julia always declared, was, when in the 10th Dragoons, a very handsome

young man. However that might have been, nobody could have mistaken him for anything like
handsome, at the moment she presented him to us.
Julia assured me that he had, by some accident,
broken the bridge of his nose, and which said broken
bridge had lost him a lady and her fortune of
twenty thousand pounds. This, from the extreme
flatness of it, of his nose, I mean, not the fortune,
appeared probable.

He was extremely fair, and the expression of his
countenance far from disagreeable. His person, too,
was rather good; nor could anybody find fault with
the taste of all those who, for years, had made it a
rule to copy the cut of Brummell's coat, the shape of
his hat, or the tie of his neckcloth: for all this was
in the very best possible style.

'No perfumes,' Brummell used to say, 'but very
fine linen, plenty of it, and country washing.'

'If John Bull turns round to look after you, you
are not well dressed; but either too stiff, too tight, or
too fashionable.'

'Do not ride in ladies' gloves, particularly with
leather breeches.'

In short, his maxims on dress were excellent. Besides this, he was neither uneducated nor deficient.
He possessed, also, a sort of quaint dry humour, not
amounting to anything like wit; indeed, he said
nothing which would bear repetition; but his affected manners and little absurdities amused for the
moment. Then it became the fashion to court Brummell's society, which was enough to make many

seek it who cared not for it, and many more wished to be well with him, through fear, for all knew him to be cold, heartless, and satirical.

Amy gave us merely a tray-supper in one corner of the drawing-room, with plenty of champagne and claret. Brummell, in his zeal for cold chicken, soon appeared to forget everybody in the room. A loud discordant laugh from the Honourable John Ward, who was addressing something to Luttrell at the other end of the table, led me to understand that he had just, in his own opinion, said a very good thing; yet I saw his corner of the room full of serious faces.

'Do you keep a valet, sir?' said I.

'I believe I have a rascal of that kind at home,' said the learned ugly scion of nobility with disgusting affectation.

'Then,' I retorted, 'do, in God's name, bring him next Saturday to stand behind your chair.'

'For what, I pray?'

'Merely to laugh at your jokes,' I rejoined. 'It is such hard work for you, sir, who have both to cut the jokes and to laugh at them too!'

'Do, pray, show him up, there's a dear creature, whenever you have an opportunity,' whispered Brummell in my ear, with his mouth full of chicken.

'Is he not an odious little monster of ill-nature, take him altogether?' I asked.

'And look at that tie!' said Brummell, shrugging

up his shoulders and fixing his eyes on Ward's neck-cloth.

Ward was so frightened at this commencement of hostilities from me, that he immediately began to pay his court to me, and engaged me to take a drive with him the next morning, in his curricle.

'Go with him,' whispered Brummell in my ear. 'Keep on terms with him, on purpose to laugh at him.' And then he turned round to Fanny to ask her who her man of that morning was?

'You allude to the gentleman I was riding with in the Park?' answered Fanny.

'I know who he is,' said Alvanly. 'Fanny is a very nice girl, and I wish she would not encourage such people. Upon my word it is quite shocking.'

'Who did you ride with to-day, Fanny?' I inquired.

'A d—d sugar baker,' said Alvanly.

'I rode out to-day,' replied Fanny, reddening, 'with a very respectable man, of large fortune.'

'Oh, yes!' said Alvanly, 'there is a good deal of money to be got in the sugar line.'

'Why do not you article yourself then to a baker of it,' I observed, 'and so pay some of your debts?' This was followed by a laugh, which Alvanly joined in with great good humour.

'What is his name?' inquired Luttrell.

'Mr. John Mitchel,' answered Fanny. 'He received his education at a public school, with Lord Alvanly.'

'I do not recollect Mitchel,' retorted Alvanly; 'but

I believe there were a good many grocers admitted at that time.'

Fanny liked Lord Alvanly of all things, and knew very little of Mr. Mitchel, except that he professed to be her very ardent admirer; yet her defence of the absent was ever made with all the warmth and energy her shyness would permit. 'Now, gentlemen,' said Fanny, 'have the goodness to listen to the facts as they really are.' Everybody was silent, for everybody delighted to hear Fanny talk.

'That little fat gentleman there'—looking at Lord Alvanly—'whom you all suppose a mere idle, lazy man of genius, I am told, studies *bons mots* all night in his bed. (A laugh.) Further, I have been led to understand that, being much lower down in the class than Mitchel, though of the same age, his lordship, in the year eighteen hundred and something or other, was chosen, raised, and selected, for his civil behaviour, to the situation of prime and first fag to Mr. Mitchel, in which said department, his lordship distinguished himself much by the very high polish he put upon Mr. J. Mitchel's boots and shoes.'

There was not a word of truth in this story, the mere creation of Fanny's brain; yet still there was a probability about it, as they had been at school together, and which, added to Fanny's very pleasing odd mode of expression, set the whole room in a roar of laughter. Alvanly was just as much amused as the rest; for Fanny's humour had no real severity in it at any time.

'But, Fanny, you will make a point of cutting this grocer, I hope?' observed Brummell, as soon as the laugh had a little subsided.

'Do, pray, Fanny,' said I, 'cut your Mitchels. I vote for cutting all the grocers and valets who intrude themselves into good society.'

'My father was a very superior valet,' Brummell quickly observed, 'and kept his place all his life, and that is more than Palmerston will do,' he continued, observing Lord Palmerston, who was in the act of making his bow to Amy, having just looked in on her from Lady Castlereagh's.

'I don't want any of Lady Castlereagh's men,' said Amy. 'Let all those who prefer her Saturday night to mine stay with her.'

'Who on earth,' said Luttrell, with his usual earnestness, 'who on earth would think of Lady Castlereagh when they might be here?'

'Why, Brummell went there for an hour, before he came here,' said Alvanly.

'Mr. Brummell had better go and pass a second hour with her ladyship,' retorted Amy, 'for we are really too full here.'

'I am going for one,' I said, putting on my shawl; for I began to think it would not do to neglect Argyle altogether. I made use of one of the Russian's carriages, to which Brummell handed me.

'To Argyle House, I suppose?' said Brummell, and then whispered in my ear, 'You will be Duchess of Argyle, Harriette.'

I found Argyle at his door, with his key, a little

impatient. I asked him why he did not go to Amy's.

'I don't know your sister,' answered his Grace, 'and I dislike what I have seen of her. She makes so many advances to me!' I defended my sister as warmly as though she had really treated me with kindness, and felt at that time seriously angry with the Duke for abusing her.

The next morning, from my window, I saw Amy drive up to my door, in the Count Palmella's barouche. She wants me to write a copy of a letter for some of her men, thought I, well knowing that affection never brought Amy to visit me.

'Are you alone?' asked Amy, bouncing into the room.

'Yes,' said I.

'Then tell that count downstairs, he may go home,' addressing my servant.

'Poor little man!' I remarked, 'how terribly rude! I could not be rude to such a very timid gentlemanly man as that!'

'Oh, he makes me sick,' said Amy, 'and I am come to consult you as to what I had better do. I like liberty best. If I put myself under the protection of anybody I shall not be allowed to give parties and sit up all night; but then I have my desk full of long bills without receipts!'

'I thought you were to marry Beckendorff and go to Russia,' I observed.

'Oh, true, I have come to tell you about Beckendorff. He is off for Russia this morning to try to obtain the consent of the Emperor and that of his own

family. There was no harm in sending him there,
you know! for I can easily change my mind when
he comes back if anything which I like better occurs.
He wished our brother George to be his aide-de-
camp, but George would not go.'

'Is not Beckendorff a general in the service of the
Emperor?' I asked.

'Yes, yes! but never mind Beckendorff,' answered
Amy, impatiently. 'I want two hundred pounds directly. It spoils all one's independence and one's consequence to ask Englishmen for money. Palmella
wishes to have me altogether under his protection.
He is rich; but—but I like Colonel Sydenham best.'

'Sydenham has no money,' said I. 'Palmella seems
disposed to do a great deal for you, and he is very
gentlemanlike: therefore, if a man you must have,
my voice is for Palmella!'

'Well,' said Amy, 'I cannot stop! I do not much
care. Palmella makes me sick too. It cannot be
helped. You write me a copy directly to say I consent to enter into the arrangement, as he calls it,
which he proposed: namely, two hundred pounds a
month, paid in advance, and the use of his horses
and carriage.' This letter was soon dispatched to His
Excellency Palmella; and Amy shortly afterwards
took her leave.

The London season was now drawing to a close, and
Argyle prepared to pay his usual visit to his Scotch
estates. He suggested that Harriette should accompany
him, though in a decent and obscure way, but she was

not disposed to leave London. She was getting into debt and indulging in melancholy reflections on the brevity of life and her own lack of principle. Such stirrings of conscience always meant that her heart was not fully occupied by the lover of the moment, and though she was not exactly looking out for a new lover, she was not unwilling to make a change.

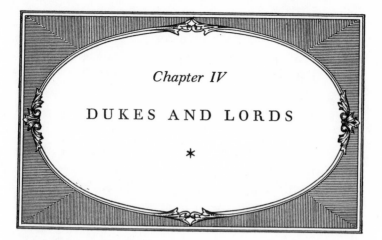

Chapter IV

DUKES AND LORDS

*

ALTHOUGH HARRIETTE had still a merely amateur status, some of the professionals had looked upon her with an appraising eye. While she was still living in Somers Town, a certain Mrs. Porter of Berkeley Street had called upon her. Mrs. Porter exercised the amiable trade of procuress, and among her protégées had been the lovely Emma Hart, afterwards Lady Hamilton. The reason of her call was to bring proposals from General Walpole, who desired the honour of Harriette's acquaintance. Harriette accepted the offer, and promised to meet the general at Mrs. Porter's house on a given evening, but although she was in need of money her courage failed her at the prospect of a lover of over sixty, and she sent the old nurse, disguised under a thick veil, to take her place. The general swore and raved, and left Mrs. Porter's house, closely followed by his elderly charmer, vowing never to patronise the establishment again. The estimable Mrs. Porter did not, however, bear Harriette any grudge, and soon after Argyle had left London, she paid a second call, to make advances on behalf of another admirer. Harriette, romantically hoping that it might be a very good-looking man with a large Newfoundland dog who had been occupying her whole mind of late, insisted on knowing his name. Mrs. Porter confessed that it was Lord Wellington, who anxiously wished to see her, 'as his situation prevented the possibility of his getting regularly introduced.' Harriette consistently speaks of him as the Duke, but his title was not conferred till 1814.

Under ordinary circumstances Harriette was extremely particular about introductions. Both then and later no man was allowed in her house or opera box unless he had been regularly introduced by one of her friends, and anyone who presumed to infringe this rule was unmercifully snubbed and made to look very foolish in public. But Wellington was an exceptional person. Debts were mounting, Argyle was in Scotland, and Harriette 'badly needed a steady sort of friend of some kind in case the bailiff should get hold of me,' so she consented to receive him. Punctually to the moment the duke arrived. Harriette found him sadly deficient in drawing-room conversation, and went so far as to say that when he called at night wearing his broad red ribbon of the Bath, he looked like a rat-catcher, but the oddly assorted pair struck up a friendship from the first meeting.

'I wonder,' said Wellington one morning, 'I wonder you do not get married, Harriette.'

(By the bye, ignorant people are always wondering.)

'Why so?'

Wellington, however, gives no reason for anything unconnected with fighting, at least since the convention of Cintra; and he, therefore, again became silent. Another burst of attic sentiment blazed forth.

'I was thinking of you last night after I got into bed,' resumed Wellington.

'How very polite to the Duchess,' I observed. '*Apropos* to marriage, Duke, how do you like it?'

Wellington, who seems to make a point of never answering one, continued, 'I was thinking—I was thinking that you will get into some scrape when I go to Spain.'

'Nothing so serious as marriage, neither, I hope!'

'I must come again to-morrow to give you a little advice,' continued Wellington.

'Oh, let us have it all out now and have done with it.'

'I cannot,' said Wellington, putting on his gloves and taking a hasty leave of me.

I am glad he is off, thought I, for this is indeed very uphill work. This is worse than Lord Craven.

Not long afterwards the Duke called to take his leave before going to Spain.

'I am off for Spain directly,' said Wellington.

I know not how it was, but I grew melancholy. Wellington had relieved me from many duns, which else had given me vast uneasiness. I saw him there perhaps for the last time in my life. I had been in bad spirits all the morning and strange, but very true, and he remembered it still, when I was about to say God bless you, Wellington! I burst into tears. They appeared to afford rather an unusual unction to his soul, and his astonishment seemed to me not quite unmixed with gratitude.

'If you change your address,' said Wellington, kissing my cheek, 'let me find your address at Thomas's Hotel as soon as I come to England; and if you want anything in the meantime, write to Spain; and do not cry; and take care of yourself; and do not cut me when I come back. Do you hear?' said Wellington, first wiping away some of my tears with his handkerchief, and then kissing my eyes, he said 'God bless you!' and hurried away.

It was hardly kind of Harriette after this and many other real kindnesses from the Duke to laugh at his cotton night-cap (but she had had a particular aversion to these things since seeing Lord Craven's), and to exhibit him, dripping with wet, standing opposite her street door at midnight, bawling up at the window.

Good news!! Glorious news! Who calls? said Master Puff, the newsman. Not that anybody called the least in the world; but Wellington was really said to have won a mighty battle, and was hourly expected. Cannons were fired and much tallow consumed in illumination. His Grace of Argyle came to me earlier than usual on that memorable eve-

ning; but being unwell and love-sick, he found me
in my bed-chamber when, catching me in his arms,
he swore by his brown whiskers that this night
at least he would be a match for mighty Wellington.

'*Quelle bizarre idée vous passe par la tête?*' said
I. 'Surely you have forgotten the amiable duchess,
his bride, and all the fatigue his grace has encoun-
tered, enough to damp the ardour of any mighty
hero or plenipotentiary, for one evening, at any
rate; therefore, trust me, Wellington will not dis-
turb us to-night.'

At this very moment a thundering rap at the
door was heard.

'*Vive l'amour! Vive la guerre*,' said Argyle. '*Le
voilà!*' And hastily throwing my dressing-gown over
his shoulders, and putting on one of my old nightcaps, having previously desired the servant not to
let anybody in, hastily put his head out of my bedroom window, which was on the second floor, and
soon recognised the noble chieftain, Wellington!
Endeavouring to imitate the voice of an old duenna,
Argyle begged to know who was at the door?

'Come down, I say,' roared this modern Blue
Beard, 'and don't keep me here in the rain, you old
blockhead.'

'Sir,' answered Argyle in a shrill voice, 'you
must please to call out your name, or I don't dare
to come down, robberies are so frequent in London
just at this season, and all the sojers, you see, coming home from Spain that it's quite alarming to
poor lone women.'

Wellington took off his hat and held up towards the lamp a visage which late fatigue and present vexation had rendered no bad representation of that of the knight of the woeful figure. While the rain was trickling down his nose, his voice, trembling with rage and impatience, cried out, 'You old idiot, do you know me now?'

'Lord, sir,' answered Argyle, anxious to prolong this ridiculous scene, 'I can't give no guess; and do you know, sir, the thieves have stolen a new water-butt out of our airy, not a week since, and my missis is more timbersome than ever!'

'The devil!' vociferated Wellington, who could endure no more, and muttering bitter imprecations between his closed teeth against all the duennas and old women that had ever existed, returned home to his neglected wife and family duties.

That's all!!

Harriette's passion for the unknown with the New-foundland dog now began to oppress her spirits and make her quite tiresome to her friends. She haunted Hyde Park and the banks of the Serpentine, where she had previously seen him, but with no success. At last one evening at the opera she saw the pale expressive face of the unknown and pointed him out to Julia, who recognized him as Lord Ponsonby. She told Harriette that he had formerly been engaged to a girl who adored him, but had broken off the marriage at the last moment, with the excuse that his father would not give his consent. The girl was now Lady Conyng-

ham, and Ponsonby had since married Lady Fanny
Villiers, daughter of Lady Jersey. Harriette resolved
not to make any advances to become acquainted with
Lord Ponsonby, and on the following evening she
fortified herself in this resolution by passing his house
in Curzon Street at least fifty times. 'I saw and examined the countenances of his footmen, and the colour
of his window-curtains; even the knocker of his door
escaped not my veneration, since Lord Ponsonby must
have touched it so often.' By dint of following her
prey everywhere, which is one way of not making
advances, she succeeded in making him notice her.
One day when at her window ('like the sign of Queen
Elizabeth over a tavern door, inviting passers-by to
walk in') she saw Lord Ponsonby riding up the street.
As he passed the house he looked up at the window and
blushed. The following morning brought a letter
from him, Harriette flew to her ready pen in reply,
and an impassioned correspondence followed, probably
based on real letters and touched up by Harriette in
later years. Harriette's infatuation for Lord Ponsonby
seems to have blinded her to the fact that he was, even
in her partial narrative, a prig of the first water,
flattered by the admiration and outspoken passion of a
notorious woman, but determined in no way to compromise his name or comfort. The rather ostentatious
thoughtfulness of his love was such that even the loving Harriette was occasionally provoked.

One night, about a week from the day Ponsonby
first visited me, when I did not expect him till mid-

night, I retired to bed and fell fast asleep, which said long nap neither Ponsonby nor anyone else had disturbed. When I awoke the sun was shining through my curtains. My first waking thoughts were always on Ponsonby, and I recollected, with a deep feeling of disappointment, that he had promised the night before to come to me by midnight, and I had desired my maid to send him up into my room as soon as he arrived. I felt for his little watch, which I always placed under my pillow; judge my astonishment to find attached to it a magnificent gold chain of exquisite workmanship. I began to think myself in the land of fairies! and still more so when I observed a very beautiful pearl ring on one of my fingers. I rubbed my eyes and opened them wide to ascertain, beyond a doubt, that I was broad awake. A very small strip of writing paper, which I had drawn from under my pillow, with my watch, now caught my attention, and I read, written with a pencil in Ponsonby's small, beautiful characters: *Dors, cher enfant, je t'aime trop tendrement pour t'éveiller.*

It was very sentimental and affectionate, for Ponsonby knew how much I required rest. I was very grateful, and yet I thought it altogether exceedingly provoking! How could I be so stupid as not to awake, even when he had his hand under my pillow in search of my watch! I rang my bell, and inquired of my maid how long she thought Lord Ponsonby had stayed with me the night before.

'More than an hour,' was the reply.

'Dear Ponsonby,' said I, as soon as she had quitted the room, while I bestowed a thousand eager kisses on the beautiful watch and chain, 'you are the first man on earth, who ever sacrificed his own pleasure and passions to secure my repose!'

For nearly three years the affair flourished, kept alive by the difficulties of meeting. As Harriette was living in her own house, it was not easy for Lord Ponsonby to visit her publicly. For once in her life Harriette's sense of humour deserted her and she showed a passion and abandon worthy of her friend Julia. When Ponsonby called on her in the evening she used to drive with him in a hackney-coach to the House of Lords and wait outside the door half the night for the pleasure of driving home with him to his door and receiving one more kiss. It was all slightly cloying for an ambitious, fashionable man, who had been betrayed by his own vanity into a liaison which he wanted the courage to end.

Such a liaison can never be kept secret for long, and as the whole polite world knew about it, it was inevitable that it should come, sooner or later, to the ears of Ponsonby's wife. Lady Ponsonby was noted for her beauty, and though an attack of scarlet fever when a girl had left her rather deaf, this misfortune did not prevent her having and encouraging many admirers. Lord Ponsonby's behaviour to his wife appears to have been no more engaging than his behaviour to his mistress. 'Lady Ponsonby,' wrote Lady Granville Leveson-Gower, 'is beautiful beyond description, and an engaging, affectionate, gentle person, with an understanding crushed by his affected contempt and brutality, for I am convinced he is in fact desperately in love with her all the time. They have, I hear, come to an understanding. He is to give up Miss Wilson and all that sort of thing, and she is to renounce her little manœuvres round the ring, in the opera. Lord Ponsonby is very affected and agreeable, for his affection is not offensive—and therefore, as far as society goes, there is no cause of complaint.'

Lord Ponsonby had now found the excuse for which he had been waiting. After filling Harriette with apprehensions by his continued gloom and depression, he gave her, after a peculiarly melancholy evening spent in her company, a sealed letter, which she imagined to be a promise to provide for her. As such letters are always the *coup-de-grâce* from a man to a mistress of whom he is tired, Harriette promptly tore it up and threw it out of the window of the coach in which they were making their usual excursion to the House of Lords. On the following evening, while she was expecting his visit, she received a letter stating that Lady Ponsonby had discovered the intrigue, and they must part for ever.

Poor Harriette, supported only by her sense of the dramatic, tied on her bonnet, lay on her face on the floor, swallowed lavender drops, wrote twenty pages wet with tears, roamed wildly through the streets, was assisted half-fainting into a hackney-coach by a benevolent old Jew, went to bed, and had a high fever. Her sister Fanny nursed her back to life, though not to health. Her first act when she could hold a pen was to write to Lord Ponsonby one of those long, moralising, romantic, tearful, rambling letters which are barely readable by an infatuated lover, irritating and revolting to a man who no longer loves and has but little heart. No answer came, her money was exhausted, the low fever was preying on her constitution, when one morning Wellington walked in, having just arrived from the Continent the night before.

'How do you do? what have you been about?' asked His Grace: then, fixing his eyes on my pale, thin, careworn face, he absolutely started, as though he had seen the ghost of some man he had killed, honestly of course!

'What the devil is the matter?' inquired Wellington.

'Something has affected me deeply,' answered I, my eyes again filling with tears, 'and I have been ill for more than two months.'

'Poor girl!' said Wellington, as though he really would have pitied me, had he but known how, and then added, 'I always dreaded your getting into some scrape. Do you recollect I told you so? How much money do you want?' said this man of sentiment, drawing near the table, and taking up my pen to write a draft.

'I have no money,' I replied, 'not a single shilling; but this is not the cause of my sufferings.'

'Nonsense, nonsense,' rejoined Wellington, writing me a check. 'Where the devil is Argyle? Why

do not you make him pay your debts? I will give
you what I can afford now, and you must write to
me, as usual, at Thomas's Hotel, if this is not sufficient.

'Good God! how thin you are grown! Were you
sorry I left you? I remember you shed tears when
I told you I was off for Spain. I am a cold sort of
fellow. I dare say you think so, and yet, I have
not forgotten that either: because there is no hum-
bug about you; and, when you cry, you are sorry,
I believe. I have thought of you, very often, in
Spain; particularly one night, I remember, I
dreamed you came out on my staff.'

Wellington consoled me as well as he could, and
sat with me nearly three hours. His visit made no
impression on me, except that I was grateful for
his kindness in leaving me the money I wanted.

Once more she wrote to Ponsonby, once more she
roamed the streets and lingered nightly outside his
house, now at the corner of Park Lane and Upper
Brook Street. At last the long-expected answer came
—'very short and not particularly sweet'; in fact, the
letter of a man who is thoroughly bored and wishes
to be rid for good of an importunate woman.

Meanwhile Amy had been doing her best to secure
Argyle for herself, and had succeeded to her sister's
position. She was expecting a child which she averred
to be the duke's, though he would not admit anything,
and had entirely ungrounded hopes of becoming
Duchess of Argyle. Harriette's nerves were also in a

deplorable state, so it is hardly surprising that the two sisters, when they met, had a furious quarrel in the best Dubochet tradition. Harriette locked the door to prevent Amy getting away and 'looked round for some instrument to execute vengeance.' Amy, as a rule famed for her ungovernable temper, was so terrified by Harriette's violent behaviour that she threw open the window and called out to a boy in the street that a wicked woman who was no better than she should be had locked her in.

'I shouldn't wonder,' answered the boy, laughing and running away. 'A pair of you, no doubt!' I by this time was heartily ashamed of having been thus surprised into temporary madness, owing to the extreme irritability of my nerves.

'Go out of the house,' said I, 'for God's sake; there is something too indelicate and disgusting in your pity. You are very welcome to live with Argyle, if you can endure the idea. I certainly felt the loss of a friend in my present low nervous state; but His Grace knows well that I have been in love with another for three years, one on whom your soft circular effusions made not the slightest impression, unless of disgust.'

I hastened out of the room, and locked myself into my bed-chamber. Amy's visit, I afterwards found, was in consequence of the anxiety Argyle had expressed concerning my health, and Amy guessed that she must show off sisterly affection, or Argyle would dislike her!

Argyle called on her once more. His old flame, Lady W— had died, and he was expressing his grief by omitting to shave. Harriette did not invite him to repeat his visit. Not long afterwards he married Lady Anglesey, who had divorced her husband in Scotland, and Amy's hopes were at an end, though she determinedly called her son Campbell.

Harriette's feelings for Lord Ponsonby were deep and real at the time. In a letter to Lord Byron, written a good many years later, she spoke of the 'agony of mind' that she endured for two years after Ponsonby left her. She was then a middle-aged woman, writing confidentially to Byron, with no particular reason to play to the gallery. But time wears down the finest feelings, and in after years Harriette had no hesitation in making use of her former lover, with his 'godlike head, mouth of perfect loveliness, and peculiarly intellectual beauty.' She attempted blackmail by sending a copy of her *Memoirs* to Lady Ponsonby. There is no evidence that Ponsonby ever tried to buy her off, and finding her plan unsuccessful, she took her revenge. Lord Ponsonby had continued to be on very good terms with Lady Conyngham, his early flame, much to the annoyance of George IV. In 1826 the question arose of sending an envoy to Buenos Aires, and Ponsonby was appointed Envoy Extraordinary and Minister Plenipotentiary by Canning. It is recorded that His Majesty, who was out of health at the time and transacting government business in his sick room, stated that he 'felt much better' after an interview with Canning on this subject. There was a piece of gossip current at the time that the king's jealousy of Ponsonby had been re-awakened by some letters between Ponsonby and Lady Conyngham, which had come years ago into Harriette Wilson's possession and been sold by her in order to implicate him; a sordid end to the romance of twenty years before.

It is a relief to turn to some of Harriette's lighter moods. As she said of herself, to seize upon the ludi-crous points of any subject was her forte or calling, and tragedy became wearisome in her hands. It was in conversations that she excelled. She had a poor invention, but was a born reporter, quick to seize the salient points in a character, to parody or mimic a style of speech. Not one of her fashionable friends speaks out of character. Some, notably Lord Alvanley and Lord Frederick Bentinck, are introduced again and again, each time with a fresh touch that under-lines what we already know and adds to the complete portrait of the man. Nor was she less successful with her sketches of the lower orders.

As an example of her brilliant, mock serious mimi-cry, there are few scenes better than the interview with Sir William Abdy. This unhappy gentleman's wife had eloped with Lord Charles Bentinck. His mar-riage was annulled in 1816, when the lady married Lord Charles, but Harriette chose to place the scene during her liaison with Ponsonby.

One day she was surprised by a visit from Sir William, whom she knew but slightly, and it struck her as strange that he should pay visits so immediately after his wife's elopement, which had caused a good deal of gossip in which Sir William, as the outraged husband, had naturally come off badly.

'I have called upon you, Miss Harriette,' said Sir William, almost in tears; 'in the first place, because you are considered exactly like my wife (my likeness to Lady Abdy had often been thought very striking), and, in the second, because I know you are a woman of feeling!!'

I opened my eyes in astonishment.

'Women,' he continued, 'have feeling, and that's more than men have.'

I could not conceive what he would be at.

'You know, Miss Harriette, all about what has happened, and my crim. con. business, don't you, miss?'

'Yes.'

'Could you have thought it?'

'Oh, yes!'

'And yet, I am sure, Charles Bentinck is worse than I am.'

'In what way, pray?'

'Why, a worse head,' said Sir William, touching his forehead, 'and I don't pretend to be clever myself.'

'Is that all? But I would not be so very demonstrative as to touch my forehead, if I were you.'

'That Charles Bentinck,' said he, half angry, 'is

the greatest fool in the world; and in Paris we always used to laugh at him.'

'But,' said I, 'why did you suffer his lordship to be eternally at your house?'

'Why, dear me!' answered Abdy, peevishly, 'I told him in a letter, I did not like it, and I thought it wrong; and he told me it was no such thing.'

'And therefore,' I remarked, 'you suffered him to continue his visits as usual?'

'Why, good gracious, what could I do! Charles Bentinck told me, upon his honour, he meant nothing wrong.'

This man is really too good! thought I, and then I affected the deepest commiseration of his mishap.

'Why did she run away from you?' said I. 'Why not, at least, have carried on the thing quietly?'

'That's what I say,' said Abdy.

'Because,' I continued, 'had she remained with you, sir, you would have always looked forward with hope to that period when age and ugliness should destroy all her power of making conquests.'

'Oh,' said Abdy, clasping his hands, 'if any real friend, like you, had heartened me up in this way, at the time, I could have induced her to have returned to me! But then, Miss Wilson, they all said I should be laughed at, and frightened me to death. It was very silly to be sure of me, to mind them; for it is much better to be laughed at, than to be so dull and miserable, as I am now.'

'Shall I make you a cup of tea, Sir William?'

'Oh! miss, you are so good! tea is very refreshing, when one is in trouble.'

I hastened to my bell, to conceal the strong inclination I felt to laugh in his face, and ordered tea.

'Green tea is best, is it not, miss?' said Sir William.

'Oh, yes,' answered I, 'as green as a willow leaf: and, in extreme cases, like yours, I am apt to recommend a little gunpowder.'

'Just as you please, miss.'

I asked him, after he had swallowed three cups of tea, whether he did not feel himself a little revived?

'Yes, miss, I should soon get better here; but you know my house is such a very dull house, and in such a very dull street too! Hill Street is, I think, the dullest street in all London, do you know, Miss Wilson.'

'True, Sir William! would not you like to go to Margate?'

'Why, I was thinking of travelling, for you know, in Hill Street, there is her sofa, just as she left it.'

'Very nervous indeed,' said I, interrupting him. 'I would burn the sofa, at all events.'

'And then there is her pianoforte.'

'Lady Abdy was musical then?'

'Oh, very. She was always at it! I used to be tired to death of her music, and often wished she would leave off: but now she is gone, Miss Wilson,

I would give the world to hear her play Foote's minuet!'

'Or, "Off She Goes," ' added I.

'What is that, pray, miss?'

'A very lively dance,' I answered.

'True, miss, I recollect my wife used to play it.'

'Dear me, Sir William, how could she be so foolish as to run away? I dare say you never interfered with her, or entered her room without knocking.'

'Never, upon my honour.'

'Well, I always heard you were a very kind, obliging, good-natured husband.'

'Yes, and sometimes, when I used to knock latterly, Lady Abdy would not open the door!'

'That was wrong,' said I, shaking my head, 'very wrong.'

'And how could that nasty, stupid fellow seduce her, I cannot think!'

'There was good blood in her veins, you know, by the mother's side. Besides, to tell you the truth, I don't think Charles Bentinck did seduce Lady Abdy from you.'

'Oh! dear, Miss Wilson, what do you mean?'

'Shall I speak frankly?'

'Oh Lord a mercy! pray do! I am quite in a fright!'

'I think Fred Lamb was one of her seducers; but how many more may have had a finger in the pie, I really cannot take upon myself to say.'

'Oh, Lord! oh, Lord! Miss Wilson!' said Sir

William, grasping my arm with both his hands, 'you do not say so? What makes you think so?'

'I have seen Fred Lamb daily, and constantly, riding past her door. I know him to be a young man of strong passions, much fonder of enjoyment than pursuit; and further, my sister Fanny, one of the most charitable of all human beings, told me she had seen Fred Lamb in a private box at Drury Lane with your wife, and her hand was clasped in his, which he held on his knee.'

'Oh, la, miss!!'

'Come, do not take on so,' said I, in imitation of Brummell's nonsense, and striving to conceal a laugh, 'leave your dull house in Hill Street, and set off to-morrow morning on some pleasant excursion. Be assured that you will find fifty pretty girls, who will be so delighted with you, as soon to make you forget Lady Abdy.'

'But then,' said Sir William, 'I cannot think how she came to be in the family-way: for I am sure, Miss Wilson, that during all the years we have lived together, I always—'

'Never mind,' interrupted I, 'go home now, and prepare for your journey, and be sure to write to me, and tell me if your mind is easier.'

'Thank you, Miss Wilson! you are all goodness. I'll be sure to write, and I mean to set off to-morrow morning, and I'll never come back to that nasty, dull, large house of mine again.'

'Get the sofa removed,' said I, 'at all events.'

'Yes, miss, I will, thank you; and the pianoforte.

So good-bye, miss'; and then returning, quite in a whisper, he said, 'perhaps, Miss Wilson, when you and I become better acquainted, you'll give me a kiss!'

I only laughed, and bade him take care of himself, and so we parted.

Harriette's views about honest tradesmen have been already mentioned. One of these, Mr. Smith, a haberdasher of Oxford Street, was almost a particular friend of hers. He held several promissory notes for large amounts, but did not press her for the money, because he was afraid that by offending her he would lose the custom of the many rich young men whom she introduced to his shop. Her description of a business visit from Smith is an excellent piece of Low Life above Stairs.

Smith the haberdasher of Oxford Street, was the next person announced to me. He is a short, thick-built man, with little twinkling eyes, expressive of eager curiosity, and a bald head. This man had known me when I was quite an infant, having served my mother, I believe, before I was born, and often talked and played with us all while children. As I grew up, his extreme vulgarity, and the amorous twinkle of his little eyes, furnished me with so much real sport and amusement, that, in gratitude for his being so very ridiculous, I had, by degrees, lost sight of all my usual reserve towards these sort of people; and once, when I was eleven years of age, this man caught me in the very act of mimicking his amorous leers at our maidservant. I was close behind him, and he saw me in the look-ing-glass.

'Oh, you rogue!' said Smith; and from that day, good-bye all serious reserve between Smith and me. I would have cut him, only nobody sold such good gloves and ribbons. I often took people to his shop to amuse them, while I encouraged Smith to be as ridiculous as possible, by affecting to be rather flattered by his beautiful leering and his soft speeches.

Smith was as deaf as a post, and never spoke without popping his ear against one's mouth, to catch the answer, and saying, hay! hay! long before one's lips could move to address him.

I guessed at the motive for his visiting me on this occasion; for I knew that two of my promis-sory notes of hand, for fifty pounds each, had been returned to him on that morning, as they had also been three months before, when I made him renew them. Not that I was in any sort of difficulty during the whole period I remained with Lord Ponsonby, who always took care of me, and for me; but Smith's scolding furnished me with so much enter-tainment, that I purposely neglected his bills, know-ing his high charges, and how well he could afford to give long credit. He came into the room with a firmer step than usual, and his bow was more stately.

'Your sarvant, miss.'

'Smith,' said I, 'those bills were paid to-day, I hope?'

Smith shook his head. 'Too bad, too bad, miss, upon my word!'

I laughed.

'You are a pretty creature!' said Smith, drawing in his breath, his amorous feelings, for an instant, driving the bills out of his head, and then added hastily, with an altered expression of countenance, 'But you really must pay your bills!'

'You don't say so?'

'If,' continued Smith earnestly; 'if you had but ha' let me ha knode, you see; but, in this way, you hurt my credit in the city.'

'What signifies having credit, in such a vulgar place as that?'

'You talk like a child,' exclaimed Smith, impatiently.

'Come,' said I, 'Smith, hand out your stamps.'

'And, miss, do you expect me to find you in stamps too?'

I laughed.

'But,' continued Smith, growing enthusiastic all at once, 'you look so beautiful and charming, in your little blue satin dress. You bought that satin of me, I think? Ah, yes, I remember—you do look so pretty, and so tempting, and so, so—oh, Lord.'

'Mr. Smith, I really will speak to Mrs. Smith, if you will go into these sort of raptures.'

'Beg your pardon! beg your pardon! Have got a curious little article here to show you (pulling something from his breeches pocket, which proved to be some embroidered, covered buttons). Beg your pardon, but bless you!!! You are so well made, you see about here (touching his own breast). There is never a one of your sisters like you about here. I always said it. Hay? hay? I was a saying so, you see, to my young man, yesterday, when you came into the shop. Now, there's Miss Sophy, pretty creature too! very, but oh, Lord! you beat them all, just about here.'

'Mr. Smith, I really must send a note to your wife to-morrow.'

'Oh, no! I am sure you won't. You would not be so hard-hearted.' He then proceeded, in a whisper, 'The fact is, there's never a man in England as don't have a bit of frolic; only they doesn't know it you see. Pretty hair!!—'

'Mr. Smith, if you meddle with my hair, I shall seriously be angry, and ring for my servant.'

'Beg pardon—thousands of pardons—it's the worst of me, I'm so imperdent, you see!—can't help it—been so from a child—never could keep my hands off a fine woman! and Mrs. Smith is confined, you see: that's one thing! hay? hay? but it shan't happen again. Now, about these here bills? If I draw you up two more, now, will you really give me your word they shall be paid?'

'No,' answered I.

'You won't?'

'No!'

'Then I'll tell you what, miss! I can't say as you

treat me exactly like a lady, and—now don't laugh—oh, you sly, pretty rogue!—hay? hay? beg pardon—it's my only fault, you see. So very imperdent! Come, I'll draw up these here bills.'

He began writing, and I laughed at him again. He shook his head at me. 'Sad doings, miss, these here bills being returned.'

'It's the worst of me,' said I, mimicking his manner. 'It's the worst of me, that I never do pay my bills. Have been so from a child!'

Lord Ponsonby's well-known rap at the door occasioned Smith to be bundled into the street, bills and all, without the slightest ceremony.

Mr. Smith's next visit was equally unsuccessful, when he came with some more returned bills.

Angels defend us! said I, what am I to say to him this time? I looked in the glass, settled my head-dress as becomingly as possible, and trusted to my charms and soft speeches for subduing his anger, as usual.

As I entered, I caught a full view of my friend Smith, in the glass; he was pacing the room with sturdy firmness, as though preparing himself for a desperate attack. His brow was knit, and, in his hand, he held the fatal black pocket-book, which I had no doubt contained my bills, six or seven times returned on his hands. *Avec tout mon savoir faire, je craignais de ratter le procureur*, as Laura says in Gil Blas; I therefore returned to my bedroom unseen, and desired my faithful housekeeper, Mrs. Kennedy, to declare that her mistress had been seized with a fit, on her way downstairs, and that, during the last attack of this sort, with which she had been afflicted, she had actually bitten her nurse's thumb clean off.

'Will you like to step up, and see her?' added Kennedy.

'No, no, I thank you,' answered Smith, putting on a pair of his thickest beaver gloves, as though to defend his thumbs. 'Some other time, if you please. My compliments'; and he was hurrying away.

'You will oblige me by stepping upstairs,' said Kennedy, 'as I really am frightened out of my wits; and Miss Wilson requires at least three persons to hold her when in these fits, and our William is just gone out with a letter to Sir Henry Mildmay's.'

'Very sorry to hear it,' replied Smith, running downstairs. 'I regret that I have such a particular engagement that I cannot stay another instant,' and he immediately gained the street door, which he took care to fasten safely, as soon as he was on what he now conceived the right side of it.

Mr. Smith appeared again in a letter purporting to be from Fanny Parker to her sister Harriette, but in reality a most impudent concoction of Harriette's own making.

MY DEAR HARRIETTE,

Who do you think I met at Cowes? No less a per-

*sonage than your friend and kind creditor, Mr. Smith
of Oxford Street. I recognised him by his voice, as he
was addressing a little fat friend of his. We were sitting on a bench, near enough to hear every word they
said.*

*'Mr. Smith,' said the little fat man, holding out his
hand, 'mercy on me! Smith! Is it really you? What
in the name of wonder can have brought you to
Cowes?'*

*'Vy, Lord!' answered Smith, 'vat but the vinds
and the vaves could bring me here, hay? I've been
down to Margate since I seed you. Bless your life, I'm
on a tower.'*

'What might that be, pray?'

'Vy, a tower, man. Don't you know vat a tower is?'

'Not I, indeed.'

*'Vy, you stupid! A tower is a kind of circular jour-
ney, gallivanting from this here place to that are place,
for a month or two, merely to pleasure it, like.'*

*'And pray, what might you call pleasure, Mr.
Smith?'*

*'Pleasure?' answered Smith, 'vy, I calls pleasure
getting up at six in a morning, and taking a dip into
the sea, and then a hearty good breakfast of hot rolls
and butter, and coffee and eggs.'*

'And what then?' said the little fat man.

*'Vat then? You ere a bachelor too, and ask vat then?
And all these ere beautiful nice, plump, dear lasses
about? Bless their dear souls! I'm a-going to take one
of 'em to the play to-night.'*

'Oh, you rogue and a half,' said the little fat man, giving Smith a punch on the breast.

The rest of this sprightly letter consisted of a very detailed account of a proposal made to Fanny by Mr. Blore, a stone-mason of Piccadilly, and an old friend of the family, the proposal being invented by Harriette to get money from Blore.

A more sinister note of comedy is struck in the story of Lord Scarborough's visit. Harriette had a servant, Will Halliday, in whose peculiarities she took a certain pride.

Apropos of that same Mr. Will Halliday, who, though always in print, never expected the honour of being published, everybody wished to know why I kept such a clockwork, stiff, powdered, methodistical-looking servant, with a pig-tail? whom one might have taken for Wilberforce himself, instead of Will Halliday; and yet that piece of mechanism with his eyes turned towards the ceiling, and his hair to match, used to steal my wine, as though he had forgotten all about his commandments; and when I reproached him with it, he declared that it was impossible, 'because,' to use his own words, 'I am the most particlerst man as is'; and, because I preferred losing my wine to being talked to, I submitted.

'Mr. Will,' I used to say, 'yes and no are all I want to hear from any footman; if they will say more to me than this, I shall wait upon myself.'

Will would console himself, on these occasions, with a young companion of mine, while she remained with me, whenever he could find her disengaged, or she had the misfortune to be in the parlour while he was laying the cloth.

'Miss Hawkes,' he would begin, to her great annoyance, 'Miss Hawkes, now you see my missis don't like a sarvent to say nothing but yes and no. Now sometimes, as I says, Miss Hawkes, yes or no won't do for everything. Missis was very angry about my speaking yesterday; but if I haddunt a-told her I was the most particlerst man as is, she might a thort I drinkt her wine, because I keeps the key of the cellar; and then again, Miss Hawkes, respecting o' my great coat; I wants to tell Missis as how it's a mile too wide in the back: for you see, miss, Missis don't observe them ere things. Will you be so good, miss, as to mention that I wants to show her how my great coat sets behind?'

'I will go and tell her directly,' said Miss Hawkes, delighted with an excuse to get away.

'Well then,' said I, in answer to what Miss Hawkes told me, 'I will look at the man's coat after dinner, only I am sure I shall laugh if he is to walk about the room sporting his beautiful shape.'

Having thus for once given Will liberty of speech, I was in dread of its consequences all dinner-time. As soon as he had withdrawn the cloth, and placed the dessert upon the table, he began to cough, and place himself in an attitude of preparation. Now it is coming! thought I, and I saw Miss

Hawkes striving to restrain her inclination to laugh out loud, with all her might.

Will began sheepishly, with his eyes and his fingers fidgeting on the back of a chair; but he grew in height, and in consequence, as he went on. 'I was a-saying to Miss Hawkes, madam, that respecting o' your commands, that yes and no won't do for everything. Now, ma'am, respecting o' my great coat—'

'You had better put it on, William,' said I, holding down my head, that I might not look at Miss Hawkes.

'Yes, ma'am; sartanly, ma'am,' said Will, bustling out of the room, and returning in an instant, equipped in a drab great coat, so very large behind, that it made him look deformed; but did not, in the least, alter his usual way of strutting about the room, like a player.

> Whose conceit
> Lies in his hamstring, and doth think it rich,
> To hear the wooden dialogue and sound,
> 'Twixt his stretch'd footing, and the scaffoldage.

So, between my horror of making free with John Bull, and my wish to laugh at my footman, I was in perfect misery.

'Take it off, William,' said I, faintly, and without venturing to raise my head, feeling that another glance at Will, eyeing his person all over, with his sharp little ferret-eyes, would have finished me. 'Take it off, and carry it to the tailor's.'

But Will, having once received a *carte blanche* for more than his usual yes and no, was not so easily quieted.

'Thank you, ma'am, you are very good, ma'am. I'll step down to-night with it; for the other evening, ma'am, when you sent me to carry back that are pheasant, my Lord Lowther's servant brought you, I says, says I, to Sally, "as it is such a wet night, Sally, I won't put on my laced hat, so I claps on an old plain one; and, when I comed to St. James's Street, there was a bit of a row with some of they there nasty women at the corner, and you see, ma'am, this ere coat sticking out, in this ere kind of a way behind, and with that large cane of mine, there was a man says, says he to me, here, watchman! why don't you do your duty?" '

It was now all over with our dignities. Will, in finishing his pathetic speech, appeared almost on the point of shedding tears. We both, in the same instant, burst into an immoderate fit of loud laughter, when Will had the good sense to leave us.

After dinner, Will told me that a strange gentleman begged to be allowed to speak to my *femme-de-chambre*, Mrs. Kennedy.

I desired Kennedy to attend me.

She returned to say that the gentleman sent me word, in confidence, that he was Lord Scarborough, who had been so long, and so very desirous to make my acquaintance—and regretted the impossibility of getting presented, since he was not a single man.

'Go and tell him,' I answered, 'that the thing is

quite impossible, more men being regularly introduced to me by others, and of the first respectability, than I liked.'

He entreated Kennedy to come up to me again.
She declared that she could not take such a liberty
with me. Lord Scarborough having, as she afterwards confessed, softened her heart by a five-pound
note, induced her to carry me up his watch, with
his arms on the seal, that I might be certain who
he was.

I was in a great passion with Kennedy, and
down she went, declaring she had lost her place.

I rang the bell, it having just struck me that the
man ought to pay for putting me in a passion and
giving all this trouble; therefore, 'Tell him,' I said,
when Kennedy returned, 'that a fifty-pound note
will do as well as a regular introduction, and, if
he leaves it to-night, I will receive him to-morrow
at ten.'

He hesitated—wished he could only just speak
to me, and give me the draft himself.

'Do as you like,' Kennedy replied. 'Miss Wilson
is not at all anxious for you or your fifty pounds;
but she has company, and will not be disturbed
to-night.'

'Well,' said my lord, 'I think you look like an
honest, good sort of woman, who will not deceive
me.'

'Never,' said Kennedy, with earnestness; and he
wrote a draft for me, for fifty pounds, begging she
would herself be at hand to let him in when he

should arrive the next night. 'I will be very punctual,' continued his lordship.

'So will I too,' repeated Kennedy; 'I will wait for you in the passage': and with this they took leave, and I immediately rang my bell for Will Halliday.

'William,' said I, 'that gentleman will be here at ten to-morrow, and he will, probably, again ask for Kennedy. Can you look quite serious, and declare to him you never heard of such a person?'

'As grave as I do now, ma'am.'

'Very well, that is quite enough; but he will, no doubt, proceed to ask for me, by my name. Can you still be serious, while declaring that you have no mistress, and that your master is, you know, well acquainted both with his lordship and his lady wife?'

'Most certainly, ma'am,' said Will, as seriously as though he had been at vespers; 'I will just clap your directions down in my pocket-book; so you need not be afraid of me, ma'am; because you see, as I told you before, I'm the most particlerst man as is.'

'But suppose he insists, William?'

'Oh, ma'am! I'll tell him I've got my knives to clean, and shut the door, very gently, in his face.'

'Thank you, William. I shall feel obliged to you.'

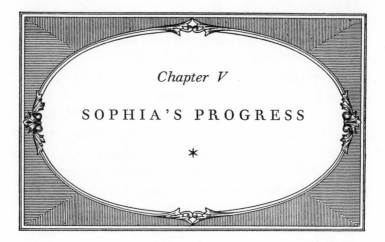

Chapter V

SOPHIA'S PROGRESS

∗

THE OTHER graces and the fury were also pursu-
ing their mounting career. Julia and Fanny had
set up a joint household, and Mr. Johnstone, alias
Colonel Cotton, was beginning to think his Julia un-
necessarily gracious to George Brummell, though
he need not have been anxious, for Brummell was
entirely indifferent to women except as part of society. Amy had changed her name to Mrs. Sydenham
and was living under the protection of her flute-
playing Colonel, who found her eternal evening
parties so little to his taste that he had to go to Brighton and help Lord Wellesley (for whom Harriette
had no liking at all) to take care of Moll Raffles—a
person whose name precludes the necessity of further
description. Another sister, Sophia Dubochet, was
now ready for public life. Mrs. Dubochet paid a visit
to Harriette to complain that Lord Deerhurst was
following Sophia in the streets and paying her attention. He had also written to her and sent her cheap

jewellery in old boxes from Love and Wirgman, the fashionable jewellers.

On hearing this news, Harriette went to call on her sister Fanny, where she found Colonel Armstrong, a man of fashion and A.D.C. to the Duke of York. He was known as an excellent soldier, and had his regiment of the Coldstream Guards in such a high state of discipline, particularly his N.C.O.s, that it was said that all the adjutants of the line regiments were trained by him. Though he was not a martinet, it was his boast that only two men had ever been flogged while he had the regiment.

After some general conversation, Colonel Armstrong suggested that they should pay a surprise visit to Amy.

'Do you propose dining with her?' said I.

'Why not?' inquired Colonel Armstrong.

'I hope she will treat you better than she does her own sisters, when we try her pot-luck.'

'I am not at all particular,' said Armstrong.

'I never saw but one man,' retorted I, 'among all Amy's train of admirers, whom she did not contrive to cure of their temerity in intruding themselves to dinner.'

[This was the Baron Tuille (or de Tuyll, as it is more correctly written), who had emigrated from Holland in the troubled years at the beginning of the century, and became popular in London society. It was probably his commission in the 7th Light

Dragoons which procured him the entrée to Amy's parties.]

'The Baron Tuille's ardent love was, for six months, proof against Amy's bill of fare. Amy used to sit and sit, till hunger would not permit her to fast any longer, and, at last, she would say, "Baron! I am going down to dinner; but I have nothing to offer you but a black pudding!"

' "Note!!" the Dutchman always answered, "Note! noting I like so vel!" '

'What,' said Armstrong, 'does she never have anything but black pudding?'

'Oh! yes,' I replied, 'sometimes toad-in-a-hole, or hard dumplings; but black pudding takes the lead.'

Fanny, with all her good nature, began to laugh as she related the following little anecdote, which had occurred while I was at Salt Hill, apropos to Amy's penchant for a black pudding. My little sister Sophia had been permitted to go and dine with Amy one day, having been particularly invited a week before. Nevertheless, when she arrived, Amy appeared to start, as though surprised, and said, 'Oh! by the bye, I forgot to order my dinner, and my maid and man are both out with letters and cards of invitation. However, I can soon manage to get a black pudding broiled. You will not mind running to South Audley Street for a pound of black pudding? Shall you, my dear?'

'Oh, no!' replied Sophia, reddening up to the eyes at the vile proposal, having lately become a coquette, from being told that she was an angel, and being really a very ladylike girl at all times; and just now she wore her smartest dress. However, she always said yes to whatever people asked her, wanting courage or character to beg leave to differ from anybody's opinion.

The said black pudding, then, was put into her hand by the vulgar, unfeeling pork-butcher, enveloped only by a small bit of the dirty *Times* newspaper just sufficiently large for her to take hold of it by, in the middle.

Sophia, being a remarkably shy, proud girl, felt herself ready to sink as she walked down South Audley Street, at that very fashionable hour of the day, with such a substitute for a reticule, flourishing, quite bare in her hand, as a greasy black pudding! She tried hanging down her arm; but rose it again in alarm, lest she should spoil her gay new frock. Then a ray of good sense which shot across her brain, her head I mean, induced her, with an effort of desperation, to hold the thing naturally, without attempting to conceal it; but, oh luckless fate! at the very moment poor Sophia had obtained this victory over her feelings, who should she bolt against, all on a sudden, in turning down South Street, but the first flatterer and ardent admirer of her young grace's, Viscount Deerhurst!!!

The black pudding was now huddled up into the folds of her new frock: then she rued the day when pocket-holes went out of fashion. Deerhurst now holding out his hand to her, her last desperate resource was to throw down the vile black pudding, as softly as possible, behind her, and she then shook hands with his lordship.

'Miss! Miss!' bawled out at this instant a comical-looking, middle-aged Irish labourer, who happened to be close behind her, and had picked up the delicate morsel at the instant of its fall.

Thrusting forward the spectral lump, 'Miss! Miss! how comed you then, dear, to let go o' this and never miss it? Be to laying hold of it at this end, honey! It's quite clean, dear, and sure and you need not be afeard to handle it at the same end,' added Pat, giving it a wipe with the sleeve of his dirty ragged jacket.

Deerhurst who, it must be allowed, possesses a great deal of natural humour, could stand this scene between Pat and Sophia no longer, and burst into an immoderate fit of laughter, while poor Sophia, almost black in the face with shame and rage, assured the man she had dropped nothing of the sort, and did not know what he meant—and then she ran away so fast that Deerhurst could not overtake her, and she got safe home to her mother's, leaving Amy to watch at her window the arrival of her favourite black pudding.

Colonel Armstrong was absolutely delighted with this account; but said he should decline her potluck, as it is vulgarly called. He nevertheless wished us, of all things, to accompany him to her house, and which we agreed to.

We found Amy in the act of turning over the

Sophia and the black pudding.

leaves of Mr. Nugent's music-book, and Mr. Nugent singing an Italian air, to his own accompaniment, ogling Amy to triple time.

The man commonly called King Allen, now Lord Allen, appeared to be only waiting for a pause of harmony in order to take his leave.

[Lord Allen, the 6th Viscount, was a noted Regency character. As an ensign in the Foot Guards, he showed marked gallantry at Talavera. Later in life he is described as *grognon chez lui, comme ailleurs;* a tall, stout, pompous-looking personage, with an invariably new-looking hat and well-polished boots. His only exercise and usual walk was from White's to Crockford's and from Crockford's to White's. He greatly resembled in later life an ancient grey parrot, both in the aquiline outline of his features and in his peculiar mode of walking, with one foot crossed over the other in a slow and wary way.]

'Ha! how do you do?' said Amy, and Nugent arose to welcome us with his everlasting laugh.

'Well, Harriette,' said Amy, 'you are come back, are you? I have heard that you went into the country with your whole library in your carriage, like Dominie Sampson; and let me see, who was it told me you were gone mad?'

[Amy's allusion to Dominie Sampson shows a gift for prophecy, as *Guy Mannering* was not published till 1815, some years later.]

'Your new and interesting admirer, His Grace of Grafton, perhaps, for I have heard that he is matter-of-fact enough for anything.'

'It is a pity, my dear Harriette, that you continue to have such coarse ideas!' retorted Amy, *en faisant la petite bouche* with her usual look of purity, just as if she had not been lately receiving the sly hackney-coach visits of the old beau.

'A-a-my! A-a-my! was Grafton nice?' I asked, mimicking her patting admirer, Hart Davis.

Armstrong, seeing her rising fury, changed the conversation, by telling her that he had some idea of intruding upon her to dinner the next day.

'Oh, I really shall give you a very bad dinner, I am afraid,' said Amy, having recovered from her growing anger towards me, in real alarm.

'My dear Mrs. Sydenham,' replied Colonel Armstrong earnestly, 'I hate apologies, and indeed am a little surprised that you should pay yourself so poor a compliment as to imagine for a moment any man cared for dinner, for vile, odious, vulgar dinner, in your society. Now, for my part, I request that I may find nothing on your table to-morrow but fish, flesh, fowl, vegetables, pastry, fruit, and good wine. If you get anything more I will never forgive you.'

Amy's large round eyes opened wider and wider, and so did her mouth, as Armstrong proceeded; and before he had got to the wine she became absolutely speechless with dismay. Armstrong, however, appeared quite satisfied, remarking carelessly that he knew her hour and would not keep her waiting.

'Is anybody here who can lend me two shillings to pay my hackney-coach?' said Allen.

'No change,' was the general answer, for everybody knew King Allen!

The beaux having left us, Amy opened her heart, and said we might partake of her toad-in-a-hole if we liked; but that she must leave us the instant after dinner.

'What for?' Fanny inquired.

'Nothing wrong,' answered Amy, of course.

'Very little good, I presume,' said I, 'if we may judge from his appearance; however' (taking up my bonnet) 'I do not want to run foul of the Duke of Grafton since he votes me mad'; and I took my leave.

'Now, gentle readers,' says Harriette at the end of this scene, 'after this long digression, you shall hear of the shocking seduction of the present Viscountess Berwick by Viscount Deerhurst.'

Before embarking upon the adventures of Sophia Dubochet, it should be stated that Berwick, a barony dating from 1784, has never been a Viscounty. But it sounds better. As for Lord Deerhurst, later Lord Coventry, his character is so torn to pieces by Harriette, that it is only just to say that he was noted for his wit and his devotion to his father, who was blind. 'Persons are still living,' writes Captain Gronow, 'who remember this nobleman hastening down Piccadilly after some pretty girl or other. He was distinguished for his good looks and manly bearing; but he always seemed in a hurry; his habits and appearance were in other respects singular.' In fact, his peculiarities may be accounted for by the beginnings of insanity. He was found by a friend 'in a strange drivelling state of rage, jealousy, friendliness and tears' about the fancied misconduct of one of his mistresses, and eventually became quite insane.

'She is off! Sophia is off! run away, nobody knows where,' was the cry of all my sisters one fine morning.

Harriette and her family immediately wrote to Deerhurst, and Sophia was sent home again, but an attempt was made to force him to make a provision for her. After some wrangling, carried on in a manner discreditable to both parties, Deerhurst consented to set Sophia up 'in a very miserable lodging, consisting of two small dark parlours near Grosvenor Place; but then to make her amends he sent her in six bottles of red currant wine, declaring to her that such wine was much more conducive to health than any foreign wine could possibly be.' He also consented to pay her £300 a year, to be reduced to £100 at the first sign of inconstancy. Here Sophia set up a little court of her own.

When I called on Sophia, I generally found two or three beaux talking nonsense to her. Sophia appeared to dislike Lord Deerhurst of all things, and complained that he was unusually sparing of soap and water at his toilette.

'He dresses completely,' said Sophia, 'before he touches water; and, being equipped, he wets a very dirty hair-brush and draws it over his head; and this is what he calls washing it—and then, having thus washed his hands and face, he says that he feels fresh and comfortable.'

One day Deerhurst insisted on my accompanying him and Sophia in his curricle to go out of town somewhere to dinner.

'Three in a curricle?' said Sophia.

'Oh, it is no matter at this time of the year,' Deerhurst replied.

I inquired where we should dine?

Deerhurst named some small place about eight miles from town, but I have forgotten what he called it. He took us to a common village pothouse, where nothing could be put on the table besides fried eggs and bacon.

'Most excellent!' exclaimed Deerhurst; 'an exquisite dish—and so very rural!'

Our rural dinner was soon dispatched; and, as I could not endure the strong smell of tobacco which issued in copious fumes from the tap-room, I proposed returning to town as fast as possible.

Sophia, who always agreed with everybody, was asked first by Deerhurst if eggs and bacon were not a delightful dish?

She answered, 'Very much so indeed.'

I then asked her if it were not enough to make us sick on such a hot day?

To which her reply was, 'I am quite sick already.'

In coming home Deerhurst put his horses all at once into a full gallop as we drew near the turnpike, bent on the noble triumph of cheating—I will not use the technical word—the man of twopence!! The lord of the gate, in a fury, ran after Deerhurst, and with some difficulty contrived to catch hold of his whip.

'Let go my whip!' vociferated Deerhurst.

'You sneaking b—kg—d!' said the man, still holding fast by one end of the whip; 'this is not the first time you have attempted to cheat me.'

'Let go my whip and be d—d to you!' bawled Deerhurst.

The man, however, refused and, in the struggle, it was broken.

'Now, d—n your soul,' said Deerhurst, darting from the curricle, without the least regard to our fears, and leaving us to manage two spirited horses how we could. In an instant he had stripped off his coat, and was hard at it with the fat, dirty turnpike-man.

'Oh!' ejaculated I in despair, 'that ever I should have ventured out in such disgusting society!'

'Very disgusting indeed,' echoed Sophia.

Once Deerhurst was down; but we soon discovered that the fat turnpike-man was undermost, and 'Go it, my lord! you a lord? a rum lord!' burst from a Babel-like confused world of voices.

The Honourable Arthur Upton happened to be passing at this moment. I called out to him by his name, and he came up to the curricle. I told him that we were frightened almost to death at the scene which presented itself; and our peculiar situation, having no proper dresses nor shoes for walking, and requested that he would make somebody stand at the heads of the horses.

He did so, and afterwards obligingly made his way to Lord Deerhurst. He begged his lordship would excuse the liberty he took, adding, 'We know each other personally, Lord Deerhurst, and I cannot help feeling hurt and grieved to see you so engaged, particularly with two young ladies under your immediate protection. I feel myself bound, seeing so many blackguards against you, to stand by you as long as you choose to keep me in this very disgraceful situation.'

'What,' cried out the many-mouthed-mob, 'you are another lord, I suppose? Here's rum lords for you! cheating a poor man out of twopence and then stopping to fight in the road. My sarvices to you, my lord! Who would not be a lord?'

'Out of respect for you, Mr. Upton,' said Deerhurst, 'I will pay this fellow'; and thus, after knocking the poor man about till he was black and blue, his lordship being possessed of all such skill as his friends Crib [sic] and Jackson had taught him, he paid him the twopence which was originally his due, and was hissed and hooted till he drove out of sight.

When he rejoined us his nose and fingers were covered with blood.

'Did you ever see such an impudent rascal, my dear Sophia?' said Deerhurst to her.

'Never in my life,' prettily repeated Sophia in her own cuckoo-strain.

Some days after this interesting rural party I called, with Fanny, to see Amy, and found the door of her drawing-room locked.

'Good gracious,' said Amy, as she opened it, after keeping us some time, 'why does not John send the locksmith to this vile door, as I have so constantly desired him! It's quite a nuisance, being obliged to lock it in order to keep the wind out.'

I shall not easily forget the figure Arthur Upton cut. When we entered, his powder and pomatum was rolling down his face in large drops! I can't conceive what it could all mean!

But beg security to bolt the door,

as Lord Byron somewhere has it.

'Amy,' said I, 'I have news for you of your sighing, waltzing Beckendorff.'

'Oh, Lord!' answered Amy, 'I am sorry the poor fool is returned; for I really cannot marry him now.'

'I do not think you can,' answered I, and then related what I had heard.

'He is the fox and I am the grapes,' said Amy; 'for no doubt he has heard I am Mrs. Sydenham.'

'Alias Upton,' continued I.

'Harriette judges of other people by herself,' retorted Amy; 'but being innocent these things never wound my feelings.'

About this time Sophia had a fancy to console herself with Colonel William Fitzhardinge Berkeley for Deerhurst's dirtiness and neglect. This Colonel Berkeley was the eldest son of the Earl of Berkeley, and a first cousin of Berkeley Craven. Though his father had not married his countess till after the birth of four children, Colonel Berkeley had been brought up as the heir. He made determined attempts to claim the earldom, but there was no proof of an earlier marriage, and his very dubious methods of pressing his claim did not improve his social position. He was well-bred, a good dancer and singer, spoke French well, and had agreeable manners and conversation, but he had a distaste for good society, and mixed so entirely with second-rate and raffish circles that many of his acquaintance were forced to cut him. Though he never succeeded to the earldom, he inherited a large fortune and his father's interest in Gloucestershire, and was made Baron Segrave and Earl Fitzhardinge. Julia says that Harriette, in her artless way, usually addressed him as Bastard. Harriette herself, it may be added, was for some time known to her circle by the endearing appellation of 'Sich-a-liar.'

Harriette, always anxious for her sister Sophia's interest, paid her a call to inquire after her health one evening, and found Colonel Berkeley.

He was very lively and agreeable, which I think was generally the case with him. The man bears an indifferent character, and perhaps with some reason; but I have always seen him pleasant, and I never knew or heard of his breaking his word. His fancy for Sophia did not prevent his being polite and attentive to me, as often happens with ill-bred young men of the present day.

In less than half an hour after Colonel Berkeley's arrival, in bounced Lord Deerhurst, in an agony of tears!!

'Oh, Sophy! Sophy!' exclaimed his lordship, blubbering and wiping his eyes with a very dirty, little, old red pocket-handkerchief—'Oh, Sophy, I never thought you would have used me in this way!!'

Sophy declared herself innocent, which was indeed the fact, as far as regarded Colonel Berkeley.

'I cannot bear it,' continued Deerhurst, rushing out of the room like the strolling representative of a tragic king in a barn, and seating himself on the stairs near the street door to sob and blubber more at his ease.

Colonel Berkeley looked at his lordship in utter astonishment, exclaiming, 'My good fellow, what the devil is the matter?'

'Why! did you not—' he paused.

'Did he not what?' I asked.

'Oh, Lord! oh, dear!' roared out Deerhurst.

'Don't take on so, my lord,' interposed Sophia's fat landlady, offering his lordship a glass of water.

Deerhurst accepted it with apparent gratitude, as though quite subdued.

'Could you have believed it, madam?' said he. 'Did you believe that young creature was so depraved?'

'What do you mean by depraved?' I asked. 'Why, I can answer for it, Sophia has never given Colonel Berkeley the slightest encouragement, and beyond a mere yes or no, she never opens her lips to him.'

'Oh! don't tell me! don't tell me!' still blubbered his lordship, the big tears rolling down his cheeks.

'This is incredibly astonishing!' ejaculated Colonel Berkeley, in a very natural tone of surprise.

'What is incredibly astonishing?' I asked. 'I am determined to understand this. In fact, I think I have guessed already. Lord Deerhurst, by the restoration of his annuity, will put two hundred pounds a year into his pocket on Sophia's first act of infidelity. You are his friend, and have done nothing but express your astonishment at his lordship's tears and apparent jealousy ever since he came blubbering into the room; therefore, since his arrival so quickly succeeded yours, I will lay my life you two desperate *mauvais sujets* came here together.'

'Nonsense!' replied Colonel Berkeley, laughing.

'I am now sure of it,' added I.

Colonel Berkeley slyly nodded assent to my remark.

Deerhurst was smelling a bottle of hartshorn, which Sophia's landlady held fast, to the end of his nose. Berkeley addressed Sophia in a whisper. Deerhurst jumped up like a madman and was leaving the room.

'My good fellow,' said the Colonel, taking Lord Deerhurst by the arm, for this excellent acting had really deceived even Berkeley himself, whom his lordship had brought to Sophia's door in his own carriage, for the express purpose of taking her off his hands, 'if you really are annoyed at my visit, if you have changed your mind—only say so, and I give you my word I will not call on Sophia again. Be a man! don't make this noise and bellowing; but tell me frankly what you wish. You and I are old friends.'

Deerhurst said that his feelings were wounded and his heart-strings cracked; therefore he must go home and get them mended: and he darted out of the house.

'What the deuce can all this mean?' said Berkeley. 'The man really is unhappy. I must go after him.'

'Take me with you,' I said, 'just to gratify my curiosity.'

'With all my heart,' replied Berkeley, 'if my carriage is at the door.'

'Did not you drive here in it?'

'No,' whispered he, 'Deerhurst brought me with him, and I desired my coachman to follow with my vis-à-vis.'

We found it at the door, and were set down at Lord Deerhurst's house in Half Moon Street.

We were shown into the drawing-room where,

after waiting about five minutes, his lordship half opened the door of his bedroom, which was the one adjoining, and showed us such a merry-looking face, *qu'il n'étoit plus réconnoissable.*

'Glad to see you both,' said his lordship, wiping his hands with a very dirty towel. 'Will you come in? But you must excuse the disorder. You know it is a mere bachelor's room,' continued he, lighting a long tallow-candle by a short piece, which was burning in a broken candlestick.

'Why don't you ride and tie regularly with your two muttons,' said I, 'when you want to be economical? and then no one would know they had not been allowed to burn on together with an equal flame, like you and Sophia.'

'Oh, Lord!' said Deerhurst, laughing, 'I can't cry any more at this moment, for I have just washed my face.'

'But seriously,' Colonel Berkeley observed, 'I have followed you because, upon my soul, I do not understand you. I want to know whether my attentions to Sophia are really disagreeable; for I don't see how a man could command so many tears to flow at pleasure.'

'Oh! there was a boy at Westminster could cry a great deal better than I can,' said Deerhurst.

'I won't believe you,' retorted Berkeley, laughing, 'unless you'll sit down on that chair and favour me with another cry; and first ring for some proper candles, will you? How came these stinking butchers' candles in your room?'

'Bachelor, you know, bachelor!' said Deerhurst, grinning.

'What the devil has that to do with it?' exclaimed Berkeley.

Deerhurst excused himself, declaring that tears, even sham ones, must be spontaneous; 'and yet,' said he, sinking into an arm-chair and again taking out the self-same dirty little red calico pocket-hand-kerchief, 'and yet, though I appear a wild, profli-gate, hardened young man, I never think of that sweet girl Sophia without its bringing tears into my eyes': and he blubbered aloud, and again the big tear rolled down his cheeks.

'This would melt a heart of stone,' I observed, putting on my cloak, 'so I am off.'

Undeterred by this failure, Colonel Berkeley ar-ranged a water party for Harriette and Sophia. After a pleasant day Berkeley began to blame Sophia for trifling with him, telling her flatly that, if she meant to refuse him after all, she ought not to have admitted him so often.

Sophia began to hint, with proper delicacy and due modest blushes, that her living with him or not must depend on what his intentions were: in other words she gently intimated that as yet she was igno-rant what settlement he meant to make upon her. The gay handsome Colonel Berkeley's vanity being now so deeply wounded he in his sudden rage en-tirely lost sight of what was due to the soft sex, at least to that part of it which had been so hard upon him.

'Do you fancy me then so humble and so void of taste as to buy with my money the reluctant embraces of any woman breathing? Do you think I cannot find friends who have proved their affection by the sacrifices they have made for me, that I should give my money to buy the cold-blooded being who calculates, at fifteen years of age, what the prostitution of her person ought to sell for?'

Sophia was frightened and shed tears.

'Colonel Berkeley,' said I, 'we are your visitors and wish to retire immediately from such unmanly insult as you have offered to us. Will you procure us some safe conveyance? no matter what.'

After which fine display of moral feeling on both sides they all shook hands and went home; but Colonel Berkeley avoided Sophia for the future.

Deerhurst continued to be a source of considerable annoyance to Harriette, who disliked him excessively, but did not wish Sophia to jeopardise her annuity by any imprudent act. One evening, when Sophia, with the young Duke of Leinster and Harry de Roos, were dining with Harriette, Lord Deerhurst called, and in spite of Harriette's broad hints that the company did not wish to see him, insisted on introducing himself to Leinster. The obliging Sophia protested in one breath that she was glad to see him, in the next that it was too bad of him to intrude. The arrival of Luttrell put it into Harriette's head to try to make Deerhurst ashamed of himself: vainly, as the event proved.

After dinner Luttrell called to say that Amy gave her first party since her confinement on this evening, and had permitted him to say that, as it was a mutual convenience that we should meet civilly at parties and neither friendship nor intimacy was necessary for that purpose, she was ready to ratify the engagement made between us a few years back, to offer me no insult, and desired I would go to her in the course of the evening, and bring as many of my male friends as I pleased.

I asked Leinster and de Roos if they would like to take me to Amy's with them?

'Most willingly,' was their answer.

'Make no apologies for not asking me,' said Deerhurst, 'for, with all my impudence, I do not think I could face that tartar of a sister of yours without a special invitation.'

'Are you fond of looking at jewellery?' I asked Luttrell.

'Very,' answered Luttrell, 'and I believe I am rather a good judge too.'

'Then,' said I, 'Sophia, my dear, if you have brought your jewels with you, pray ask Mr. Luttrell's opinion of their value.'

Sophia drew from her reticule two smart jewel-boxes of Love, the jeweller's. 'These are the jewels which were presented to my sister by Viscount Deerhurst,' said I, as I handed them to Mr. Luttrell.

The box contained a necklace of large green glass beads, set in yellow metal. There was a leaden ring with a blue bead in it, a small Tunbridge-ware tooth-pick case with

'When this you see, remember me'

superscribed on it, and two brass seals, one with the name of Sophia on it, the other with a little winged figure, evidently meant for a cupid or a parrot; but it was very difficult to decide which it most resembled. Everybody laughed heartily, but the loudest laugher of our party was Viscount Deerhurst.

'And then,' said Deerhurst, trying to recover himself, 'and then, having won the young lady by dint of these valuable jewels, Robinson, the attorney of Bolton Street, first draws up an agreement to secure to her an annuity of three hundred a year, and the next day tells you his agreement is not worth sixpence!!'

There was only one of our society who carried politeness so far as to seem amused at such disgusting profligacy.

Luttrell looked with unqualified contempt on his lordship. Leinster and de Roos, considering themselves too young to set an example, or reform the age, fixed their eyes steadily on the carpet, while de Roos's fair cheek was tinged with a deep blush. Sophia alone joined Lord Deerhurst in his laugh; declaring that it was very funny to be sure.

'Lord Deerhurst,' said I, 'Sophia is my sister and

if she chooses to submit to insult and ill-usage from
you, it shall not be in my house, where you were not
invited.'

Sophia immediately worked herself up into a passion of tears, declaring that she did not want to be
insulted, and would much rather not return to Lord
Deerhurst, who, she was sure, was a very nasty man
indeed, and hardly ever washed his head.

Deerhurst carelessly declared himself quite ready
to support the dire calamity, and wished, of all
things, Sophia would live with her sister Harriette.

'The man is not worth a thought, much less a
tear,' said I to Sophia. 'You are welcome to my
house as long as I have got one to share with you;
in the meantime let us drive to Amy's.' Sophia did
not accompany us; but retired with Lord Deerhurst,
who had remarked in her ear that I was jealous and
wanted him myself.

'I think Harriette is a little jealous really, so I'll
go home with you to make her mad,' said Sophia.

And off they went.

Amy's drawing-room was quite full. She looked
very well, and fairer, as well as less fierce, than before her confinement. Fanny appeared unusually
lovely, dressed in a pale pink crape dress, which set
off her rosy, white, delicate skin, to the greatest advantage; and with her unadorned bright auburn
curls, waving carelessly around her laughing dark
blue eyes and beautiful throat, she seemed the most
desirable object in the room. Julia was very fair too;
perhaps her skin was whiter than Fanny's, and of

quite as delicate a texture; but it had not the vermilion tinge, and the blue veins were less defined. Both were of the highest order of fine forms. They were also of the same height, which was that best adapted to perfect symmetry; their feet and ankles were alike models for the statuary's art, and Fanny's shoes fitted Julia as well as her own; but Fanny's hair was dark and more glossy than Julia's. Fanny's teeth were beautiful, while Julia's, though strong, were uneven; and Fanny's smile was infinitely more attractive than Julia's, whose countenance was, in fact, as I think I have before mentioned, rather harsh than pleasing. Yet there was such a decided resemblance in their *tout ensemble* that everybody mistook Julia for Fanny's eldest sister.

This evening Julia, I suppose with a view to outshine us all, wore a dress of white silvered lama, on gauze, and a Turkish turban of bright blue, fringed with gold. There was a voluptuous and purely effeminate languor about Julia's character, which was well adapted to the eastern style of dress. The large, straight, gauze sleeve did not at all conceal the symmetry of her beautiful arm. Fanny's dimpled arms were quite uncovered, and encircled with elegant but simple bracelets, composed of plaited hair, clasped with a magnificently brilliant ruby. They were both infinitely graceful. Fanny would lay her laughing face on her folded arms, reclining on a table, while she made some odd reflections; or she would fasten her pocket-handkerchief or her shawl across her head and ears when she felt the air affect her head, without inquiring of her glass whether she had thus added to or diminished her attractions: yet everything became her; or rather all were determined to think faultless her in whose beautiful eyes shone the warmest philanthropy, whose every word and action proved the desire she ever felt to make others appear to advantage.

Julia's attitudes, though graceful, were studied and luxurious, but always modest and effeminate.

Amy wore a yellow satin dress fastened round the waist with a gold band. Her profuse raven locks were entirely unadorned, and her neck, arms and fingers were covered with glittering jewels of every colour. A Mrs. Armstrong, whom Amy had lately patronised, was of the party. She was the *chère amie* of Colonel Armstrong, an aide-de-camp of the Duke of York.

This evening was set apart for dancing, and Fanny and Julia, being the very best dancers in the room, were in their glory.

All the world were, or wished they were there, but many could not get farther than the passage, the whole house being so crammed. Among others was the man they call the dancing Montgomery [noted for having taken part in the first quadrille at Almack's in 1815, when the dance was introduced from France by Lady Jersey], although perhaps I do him too much honour by putting him in print; he was such a slovenly unlicked cub, of what particular family I am ignorant; but it was clear this

man had originally been designed by nature for a
lout, only he went to Paris, and came home a dancer,
every inch of him, below the girdle. As for his
shoulders and arms, they continued as before;
Frenchmen cannot work miracles, like German
princes! but they converted into a fop this ready-
made clown, to the utter discomfiture of our gauzes
and India muslins, which were sure to suffer as
often as we ventured to employ him to hand us tea,
negus, or orgeat.

'Would you like to dance?' said George Brummell to Mrs. Armstrong, *en passant*.

'I have only just left off,' answered she, rising
and curtseying with much politeness; 'but I am
never tired of dancing.'

'You have a dancing face,' Brummell quietly observed, fixing his eyes steadily on her countenance
for a second or two, and then passing on.

Poor Lucy, she afterwards declared to us, was
never so ashamed and humbled since she had been
born.

All this time Montgomery's thick straight locks
were steadily beating time on his watery forehead,
as he trod the mazy dance with all his might, footing it away most scholastically. He did indeed dance
famously; but then he was always out at the elbows,
which appeared to have no connection whatever
with his feet, particularly on this eventful night,
when one of his elbows came in such neighbourly
contact with the eye of the poor Duc de Berri, who
was just entering the room, while Montgomery was

swinging short corners near the door, as sent His Royal Highness reeling backwards.

Tout le monde fut au désespoir!!

'*Mon Dieu! Quel malheur, monsieur le duc!*' said Amy.

'*Rien, rien du tout,*' answered the good-natured Duc de Berri, holding his handkerchief to his eye.

'*Il y a tant de monde ici, ce soir, et la salle n'est pas grande, comme vous voyez, monsieur,*' said Fanny to His Highness; as usual endeavouring to excuse and conciliate all parties.

'*Ma fois! je n'y vois goutte!*' said the duke, laughing, with his handkerchief still before his eyes.

Montgomery came forward to express his regrets; but it was plain from his manner that he did not at all attribute the accident to anything like awkwardness on the part of himself or his elbows, of which he seemed not a part. However, I do not mean to depreciate Mr. Montgomery's dancing, in the least; only do but give him elbow-room and he will astonish you!

[The duc de Berri, second son of the comte d'Artois, later Charles X, emigrated at the Revolution and served with the army of Condé. He came to England in 1806, and was assassinated in Paris in 1820.]

I think it was on this evening I saw Colonel Parker for the first time. He appeared to have seriously attached himself to my sister Fanny. He was an officer in the Artillery, and a near relation to

Lady Hyde Parker, I believe. I was anxious to see
poor Fanny comfortably settled; and her tastes being all so quiet and her temper so amiable, I knew
that riches were by no means necessary to her felicity. Colonel Parker possessed a comfortable independence, and was very anxious to have Fanny entirely under his protection. 'She shall bear my
name, and I will show her all the respect a wife can
require, and she shall always find me a gentleman,'
said he. I could not, however, help thinking that
Fanny, with her strictly honest principles, her modest, amiable character, and her beauty, ought to
have been Parker's wife instead of his mistress, and
therefore I did not advise her to live with him. His
person was elegant; fine teeth and fine hair was,
however, all he had to boast of, in the way of
beauty; but Fanny did not like handsome men, and
appeared very much to admire and esteem Colonel
Parker. I do not exactly know what aged man he
was; but I should think him under thirty.

But I am tired of this party of Amy's, therefore
my kind readers will permit me to change the subject.

Amidst all these distractions, literature was not neglected. Harriette had always fancied herself as a stu-
dent, and indeed set up what must be a record by
reading in three weeks the history of Greece, of Rome,
and of England, Voltaire's *Charles the Twelfth*, Rous-
seau's *Confessions*, Racine's tragedies, Boswell's *Life
of Johnson*, and most of Shakespeare. Many people,

she had heard say, found some passages of Shakespeare obscure, but to her all the beauties were so clear and plain that the little obscurities were not worth puzzling over—perhaps quite a good way of regarding the matter. Harriette's views on celebrated authors were as downright as most of her opinions. Lady Mary Wortley Montagu's style she found very unequal, now paltry and ungraceful, now elevated; some of the letters appeared to her most indecent and profligate, while others showed extreme refinement and delicacy. As for Byron's *Don Juan*, she professed to take violent exception to it, giving herself the trouble of writing to scold him for making a mere coarse old libertine of himself.

Her first essay in authorship was in the dramatic line. She put together a few pages of a comedy which George Lamb, Fred Lamb's younger brother, himself a dramatist in a small way—his two act opera, *Whistle for It*, ran for three nights at Covent Garden in 1807 —criticised kindly, saying that though it was long and deficient in stage tact, there was no lack of quiet good humour about it. Encouraged by these words and true to her principle of aiming high, Harriette wrapped herself up in her large cloak, put her unfinished MS. into her reticule, and ventured in fear and trembling to wait upon the great Mr. Murray.

Murray looked on me with as much contempt as though Ass had been written in my countenance. Now I know this is not the case. He said, with much rudeness that I might put the manuscript on his table and he would look at it, certainly, if I desired it.

I asked when I should send for it.

Whenever you please, was his answer; as though he had already recorded his decision against me, and made his mind up not to look at it. I promised to send for it the next evening. I did so, and the manuscript was returned without an observation.

The undaunted authoress then submitted it to Messrs. Allman of Princes Street, Hanover Square, who offered to publish the work, sharing the expenses and profits with her.

On the receipt of this note, which I have now in my possession, I got into a rage with old purblind Murray. I wish, thought I, I wish I could make rhymes! I would send him a copy of verses to thank him. The worst of it was, I had never made a single rhyme in my life, and when I had tried to make two lines jingle together, everybody said they had the merit of being infinitely below par; but even that I considered very much better than vile mediocrity, in poetry. In short, there was no rhyme about them, and very little reason. However, I thought that anything would do for Murray, who had been so rude to me; therefore, in a few minutes, I managed to compose and seal up the following state of the case—which said composition my reader cannot say I have encouraged him to lose time in perusing.

The Maiden Effort of a Virgin Muse!

I never thought of turning poet,
And all my friends about me know it,
Till t'other day. I'll tell you why.
Alas! the story makes me sigh!
I tried, in prose, a few light sketches,
Of characters—pats, players, and such wretches,
Which my own folks said were pretty:
In fact, I thought them downright witty;
And, for the good of future ages,
I sallied forth, with these few pages,
To a publisher's, in such hurry,
As to arrive too soon for that beau-thing, Murray,
Who coolly kept the lady waiting.
An old beau must have time for prating.
At last he came. Oh, mercy! Oh, my stars!
What an appalling beau-costume he wears!
A powder'd bob, spectacles, and black coat!
I wish to heaven I had never wrote!
Or ta'en my book, so not here, any where.
Sure this won't do! The man's a bore or bear!
My charms to him were nought: nor my oration:
But what care I for Murray's admiration?
If I had penn'd some Quarterly cupidity,
He would have gladly borne with its stupidity.
At length, Sir, cried I, in a fuming rage,
Pray, just peruse, at least, a single page.
With a most supercilious kind of glance,
Hum, drawl'd out Murray, you've not the slightest chance.
Pray, Sir, must one come here in a bob-wig?
Cried I, in my turn, striving to look big;
And then went home to mourn my waste of paper,
Pens, ink, time, and e'en my last wax taper.
Prosers, methought, require an education;
But poets gain, by birth, their own vocation.

The house of Murray has no record of this incident.
Some years later Harriette finished her play. It was

taken from Molière's *Malade Imaginaire,* and as she had only submitted a few pages of her unfinished work, Mr. Murray's refusal to consider it appears far from unreasonable. 'It was by no means a literal translation,' she states. 'I reduced it to three acts, and altered what I conceived was too coarse and indecent for an English audience'; a statement at which one can but marvel.

This work was sent through a friend to Charles Kemble, who replied that he did not think it calculated to forward the interests of the stage. She then offered it to Elliston, the well-known actor, for many years manager of Drury Lane, but they quarrelled, and he never returned it. If it ever existed it must have been destroyed long ago, and was probably a poor piece of work.

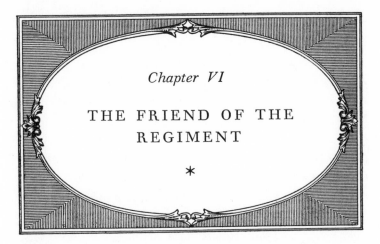

Chapter VI

THE FRIEND OF THE
REGIMENT

*

HARRIETTE, MEANWHILE, found leisure to attend to the affairs of her sister Fanny, now known as Mrs. Parker, a name which she bore for the rest of her life. She had two or three children by her first lover; the boy, George Woodcock, being a high-spirited child, quite out of place in the world of women. His mother was unable to pay for his schooling, so Harriette good-naturedly offered to pay the bills and have him to stay with her for part of the holidays. Before the week was out he had broken open her jewel box, stolen her money, kissed her housemaid, and half killed her footman, so that it was with the greatest pleasure that she drove him down to Leytonstone, assuring him in the presence of his schoolmaster that if she heard any complaints she would have him sent to sea. One letter of his, which was preserved by his aunt, certainly reads like every boy's letter since the beginning of the world.

My Dear Aunt,

I hope you are well, as this leaves me at present. Excuse this bad writing, as I am so very bad, and my head aches fit to split; but I am ordered, this very moment, before the post goes out, to acquaint you with my accident, as Monsieur Codroie says, perhaps, you may wish me to come to town, to have the rest of my teeth put to rights; the fact is, then, to be short, I was running just now, and I hit my face against another boy's head, and broke out my two front teeth.

Your affectionate nephew,

George Woodcock.

P.S. Pray deliver the enclosed to William, in answer to a long stupid sermon he has written to me, about five shillings he says I bor-rowed of him.

George's enclosure was merely poor Will Halliday's laboured epistle turned inside out, with these eloquent words written on the seal:

> Five and four makes nine,
> Mind your business and I'll mind mine.

Once more he appears, staying with his aunt in Paris:

a fair, fresh-coloured, remarkably strong, active boy, with white, thick, curly hair, dressed in a light blue jacket and trousers, with a small ruff round his throat. He did not know one single word of French; nay, more, was such a complete John Bull as to declare upon his word and honour that he would take all the care he possibly could not to learn it. All he feared and dreaded was that the vile jargon should come to him by itself, in spite of all he could do to prevent it.

After this delightful description of a human boy, it is sad to learn from Julia that George became a midshipman, was turned out of the navy for theft, and eventually became a pirate, in which profession he died fighting. Of the other two Woodcock children, nothing is known.

Julia's time was now divided between Sir Harry Mildmay, whom she adored, and Napier, who had money, but required her entire faithfulness and more when she needed twenty pounds. Amy was making love to Mildmay to annoy Julia. Sophia, feeling 'neglected and uncomfortable and disgusted' in her lodgings, had gone to board with Julia.

Harriette had plenty of admirers, among them the young Duke of Leinster, towards whom she was not ill-disposed. One evening, in her box at the opera, Julia asked the Duke how he liked Oxford.

'Delighted with it,' replied the Duke. 'Apropos of Christchurch. Do you know that Brummell is cut amongst us, and who do you think sets the fashions there now?'

'Yourself, perhaps.'

'No, nothing is asked, but whether Harriette Wilson approves of this or that? Harriette likes

white waistcoats—Harriette commends silk stockings, etc. I asked my friend, the young Marquis of
Worcester, why he did not curl his straight locks?
Harriette considers straight hair the most gentlemanlike. On my asking him if he knew Harriette,
the Marquis owned that he had never seen her, adding, "I ran up three times to the Opera on purpose;
but she did not make her appearance. Will you present me to her? I shall be much indebted to you."
"Not I, upon my honour," was my answer, "and I
am the only young man at Oxford acquainted with
you." '

Harriette was interested by this mention of a new
admirer, little suspecting how large a part he was to
play in her life for the next three years. Next time she
went to the opera she found the Duke of Leinster again
in her box.

'I am glad you have no men with you,' said his
grace, with something like agitation of manner;
'for I want to speak to you. Do you know, my
friend, of whom I spoke to you, is come up from
Oxford on purpose to try to get introduced! I know
he must return to college to-night, and I am, I confess, rather anxious that he should be disappointed.'
    'Nonsense,' said Julia. 'Who is it, pray?'
    'The Marquis of Worcester,' replied his grace.
    'Is he handsome?' I inquired.
    'Not a bit of it,' said the Duke.
    'What is he like?' Fanny asked.

'I do not know anybody he is like, upon my honour, unless it be his father. He is a long, thin, pale fellow, with straight hair.'

'You need not be alarmed,' said I; 'I shall not be presented to your friend, if I can help it. I always tell everybody I know not to bring men here, without first coming up to ask my permission.'

'I know you do,' said Leinster; 'since this is the answer Lord Worcester has received from several of your friends, to whom he has applied.

'There he is!' continued Leinster, leaning towards the pit. 'Do not you observe a very tall young fellow, in silk stockings, looking steadfastly up at this box. Upon my honour, he won't wear trousers or curl his hair, because he heard that you dislike it.'

'It is very flattering,' said I, eagerly looking out for him with my opera glass, an example which was followed by Julia and Fanny.

The young Marquis was, at that time, too bashful to stand the artillery of three pair of fine eyes at once, and turned away from our eager gaze! but not till I had satisfied myself that he would not do for me one bit better than his uncle, Lord G. L. Gower, and, in the next five minutes, I had forgotten his existence.

Lord Frederick Bentinck now came and asked me when I meant to keep my promise of accompanying him to Vauxhall?

'Oh, we shall never get to Brighton,' said Fanny,

who doted on donkey-riding. 'Harriette will keep us in town all the summer, as she did last year.'

'Summer!' interposed George Brummell, entering in a furred greatcoat. 'You do not mistake this for summer, do you? A little more of your summer will just finish me,' pulling up his fur collar.

'Upon my honour, I think it very hot,' said Leinster. 'It must be hot, you know, because it is August.'

'I never know the difference, for my part,' Fred Bentinck observed. 'The only thing that ever makes me cold, is putting on a greatcoat; but then I have always a great deal to do, and that keeps me warm. Once for all, madam, will you go to Vauxhall on Monday night? If you will, I will put off my sister, and accompany you.'

I assented, in spite of everything Fanny and Julia could say to prevent me; for Fred Bentinck always made me merry.

Lord Deerhurst now entered, accompanied by a tall young man. 'I do not often introduce gentlemen to ladies,' said his lordship, 'and perhaps I am taking a liberty now; yet I hope you can have no objection to my making you known to the Marquis of Worcester.'

I bowed rather formally; because I had before desired Deerhurst not to bring people to me without my permission. However, the young Marquis blushed so deeply, and looked so humble, that it was impossible to treat him with incivility; but, having taken one good look at my conquest, and thus convinced myself that I should never love him, I conversed indifferently, on common subjects, as people do who happen to meet in a stage-coach, where time present is all they have to care about. Deerhurst was lively and pleasant; the Marquis scarcely spoke; but the little he did find courage to utter was certainly said with good taste, and in a gentlemanly manner.

Leinster was infinitely bored and annoyed, though he tried to conceal it.

'What do you think of him?' asked Leinster, whispering in my ear.'

'I will tell you to-morrow,' I replied; and, the better to enable myself to do this, I examined the person of the young Marquis for the second time. It promised to be very good, and his air and manners were distinguished; but he was extremely pale, and rather thin; nevertheless, there was something fine and good about his countenance, though he was certainly not handsome.

Deerhurst invited the Duke of Leinster to go into the pit with him.

Leinster hesitated.

I understood him. 'Do not be afraid,' said I in his ear. 'Of course, having already engaged you to take me to my carriage, I shall neither change my mind, nor break my word.'

Leinster gratefully grasped my hand; but fixed his eyes on Worcester, still hesitating. Not that it was in his grace's nature to break his ducal heart for any woman, and still less, perhaps, for me; but a

man's school-fellow pushing himself forwards, and
trying to cut him out, where he had formed high
expectations, is always a bore, even to the coldest
man alive.

'Of course my sister Amy will be happy to see
Lord Worcester to-night,' said I, aloud, in answer
to what I read in Leinster's countenance.

Lord Worcester bowed, and looked rather more
confused than pleased.

'Do come, my lord,' said Fanny, who liked what
she had seen of his lordship, extremely.

To Leinster's joy, and our astonishment, Lord
Worcester said, he must really decline my very polite offer, grateful as he felt for it.

'Nonsense!' exclaimed Deerhurst. 'What a very
odd fellow you are! I really cannot make you out. I
give you my honour, Harriette,' continued his lordship, 'that, not an hour ago, he declared he would
give half his existence to sit near you, and talk to
you for an hour; and now you invite him to pass
the evening in your society, he appears to be frightened to death at the idea!'

'You are all alike; a set of cruel wicked deceivers,'
said I, carelessly; being really indifferent as to the
impression it made on Lord Worcester, who, in his
eagerness to exculpate himself from this charge of
caprice, blushed deeply, and evinced considerable
agitation.

'No, indeed, I beg, I do entreat that you will not,
you must not imagine this. I have a particular reason for not going to your sister's; but it would be

impertinent in a stranger, like me, to take up your time by an explanation: only pray acquit me. Do not send me away so very unhappy; for, you must know, I am sure you must, that the indifference of which you accuse me would be impossible, quite impossible, to any man.'

'What is the matter with you, young gentleman?' said I, looking at him with much curiosity, 'and why do you lay such a stress on trifles light as air?'

'To you, perhaps,' observed Worcester, trying to laugh from a fear of seeming ridiculous.

'There is a pretty, race-horse little head for you!' said Deerhurst, touching my hair.

'I never saw such beautiful hair,' Worcester remarked timidly.

'Put your fingers into it,' said Deerhurst. 'Harriette does not mind how you tumble her hair about.'

'I should richly deserve to be turned out of the box, were I to do anything so very impertinent,' interrupted his lordship.

'Oh, no,' said I, leaning the back of my little head towards Worcester, 'anybody may pull my hair about. I like it, and I am no prude.'

Worcester ventured to touch my hair, in fear and trembling, and the touch seemed to affect him like electricity. Without vanity, and in very truth, let him deny it if he can, I never saw a boy, or a man, more madly, wildly, and romantically in love with any daughter of Eve, in my whole life.

'Come with me,' said Deerhurst to Leinster.

'Remember your promise,' Leinster whispered to me as he unwillingly followed his lordship.

'May I,' said Lord Worcester eagerly, as though he dreaded an interruption, 'may I, on my return to town, venture to pay my respects?'

'Certainly,' answered I, 'if I am in town; but we are going to Brighton.'

True love is ever thus respectful, and fearful to offend. Worcester, with much modesty, conversed on subjects unconnected with himself or his desires, apparently taking deep interest in my health, which, I assured him, had long been very delicate.

Just before the curtain dropped, Worcester seemed again eager to say something on his refusal to accompany me to Amy's.

'Leinster is coming to take you to your carriage, I know,' said he, 'and I wish—'

'What do you wish?'

'That you would permit me to explain something to you, and promise not to call me a conceited coxcomb.'

'Yes! I'll answer for her,' said Fanny, 'so out with it, my lord. Why be afraid of that great black-eyed sister of mine, as if she were of so much consequence?'

'Well then,' continued Worcester, blushing deeply, 'Lord Deerhurst told me that your sister treated you unkindly, and that you never allowed your favourites to visit her. Upon my honour, I

Harriette Wilson

A Morning Gallop at Brighton
(Lord Melbourne and Harriette Wilson)

The Duke and the Duenna

Emotional Evening in Upper Brook Street

*The Marquis of Worcester, lacing
Harriett Wilsons stays &c.*

LISTER. PINX.   PAGE. SCULP.

Amy

From an admired Picture in Possession of a Noble Duke.

JULIA.

would rather never see you again, than pay my
court to anybody who has behaved ill to you.'

Before I could reply, Leinster came hurrying and
bustling into the box, as the curtain dropped.

'You return to Oxford to-night, I believe?' said
his grace to Worcester, who replied that he must
start at six in the morning.

I advised him to take a few hours' rest first.

'That will be quite impossible,' Worcester answered in a low voice.

The young Marquis's pale face certainly did
grow paler, as he looked wistfully after Leinster,
whose arm I had taken.

First love is all powerful, in the head and heart
of such an ardent character as Worcester's; and
there really was an air of truth about him which
not a little affected me, for the moment; therefore,
turning back to address him, after I had drawn my
arm away from Leinster:—'Perhaps,' said I, in a
low, laughing voice, 'perhaps, Lord Worcester, it
may be vain and silly in me to believe that you are
disposed to like me; but, as I do almost fancy so, I
come to wish you a good night, and to assure you
that I shall remember your taking up my quarrels,
against my unkind sister, with the gratitude I always feel towards those who are charitable enough
to think favourably of me.'

Worcester began to look too happy.

'But do not mistake me,' I continued, 'for I am
not one bit in love with you.'

Worcester looked humble again.

'In fact,' said I, laughing, 'my love-days are over.
I have loved nothing lately.'

'Not the Duke of Leinster?' inquired his lordship
whose anxiety to ascertain this had overcome his
fears of seeming impertinent.

'No, indeed,' I rejoined, and Worcester's countenance brightened till he became almost handsome.

Leinster approached us, with a look of extreme
impatience.

'Good night, my lord,' said I, waving my hand,
as I joined his grace. Worcester bowed low, and
hastened out of sight.

'If Leinster were not my friend,' said Worcester
to a gentleman, who afterwards repeated it to me,
pointing to Leinster and myself as we stood in the
round room, waiting for his grace's carriage—'if
that young man were not my friend, I would make
him walk over my dead body, before he should take
Harriette out of this house.'

Oh, this love!! this love!!

The season was now closing, so Harriette and Fanny
left town for Brighton, where they had hired a house.

'Well,' said Lord Frederick Bentinck [who had
ridden ten miles of the way with them, and offered
to drive Harriette all the way, with his own horses,
but on certain conditions relative to a night on the
road, which she declined]; 'Well,' he said in his
loud, odd voice, as he took his leave at The Cock at
Sutton, 'I really do hope you will soon come back. I

don't, as you know, make speeches, or pretend to be in love with you. I might have been, perhaps; but the fact is, you are a loose woman, rather, and you know I hate anything immoral. However, you may believe me when I say that I am sorry you are leaving London.'

'And what becomes of you?' I asked. 'Do you mean to remain all your life in town?'

'Oh! I have a great deal to do, and my business, you know, is at the Horse Guards.'

'God bless you, Frederick Bentinck,' said I, as my carriage was driving off. *'Portez-vous bien,* although you are certainly enough to make me die of laughter.'

'And do,' said his lordship, with his half-laughing, half-cross, but very odd countenance, 'pray do conduct yourself with some small degree of propriety at Brighton.'

Brighton, under the patronage of the Prince Regent, was a centre of brilliant social life, often described. With the aristocratic society whose headquarters was the Pavilion, Fanny and Harriette did not, and could not, mix. Their circle was almost exclusively military, being largely recruited from the 10th Hussars. This crack regiment had a distinguished record. It was raised in 1715 and fought in the Seven Years' War, earning glory at Minden, but from the outbreak of the war with France in 1793 it had never left England, which earned it some envy, and some unmerited contempt, from the rest of the army. In 1793 the regiment was gazetted as 'the 10th, or Prince of Wales' Own Regiment of Light Dragoons,' and in 1796 the prince was appointed colonel-in-chief.

Its dress was gay, and attractive to the female heart. Though it had been wearing the Hussar uniform as early as 1803, it was not officially so equipped till 1806, when the men were dressed in pelisses, relic of the sheepskin worn over the shoulders by the Hungarian Hussars and Polish Uhlans, sashes, fur caps, leather pantaloons, and Hessian boots. They were ordered to wear moustachios on the upper lip. The full dress of the officers was magnificently laced jackets, yellow boots, and red breeches with gold fringes. These breeches gave rise to the army joke of 'Cherubim', which was always a success with any regiment but one of the Hussars. In 1811 the Prince added Royal to their name which was changed to Hussars, so that the full title was 'The Prince of Wales' Own Royal Regiment of Hussars.'

The cavalry has always been the favourite branch for young men of good family, and this regiment had a number of officers of noble birth, though the commander, Colonel Quinten, Quinton, or Quintin (all three spellings occur in the Army List) was not one of them. Among them was the duc de Guiche, known then as comte de Grammont, or Gramont, son of the émigré duc de Guiche. He had risen from a cornet and *'le traitement de son grade fournit aux frais de son éducation.'* Gronow says, 'He spoke English perfectly, was quiet in manner, and a most chivalrous, high-minded and honourable man. His complexion was very dark, with crisp, black hair curling close to his small, well-shaped head. His features were regular, some-what aquiline, his eyes large, dark and beautiful; and his manner, voice and smile were considered by the fair sex to be perfectly irresistible.' He was known later as duc de Guiche, and on his father's death took the title of duc de Gramont. He married a sister of the comte d'Orsay.

Harriette had much the same opinion of him, ex-cept that she says his English was 'very good for a Frenchman, although with somewhat of the foreign accent and idiom. He was very handsome, possessed a quick sense of honour, and ever avoided even the shadow of an obligation; I need not add that he, through strict economy, kept himself at all times out of debt. As an officer he was severe and ill-tempered; but well versed in military business; as a Frenchman he was fonder of flirting than loving; and with regard to his being a fop, what could a handsome young Frenchman do less.' It would be possible to read a story between the lines here, remembering an outburst of propriety from Harriette against the count's romping with Lady Charles Somerset's daughters; it is never pleasant for a spoilt woman to find one man who is in-different to her.

I was already acquainted with the present Duc de Guiche, and several other officers. A very fine young man, who had joined only a month previous, was present, and I remember that nobody said a single word to him; but I have entirely forgotten his

name. I inquired his history, and was told that he
was a man of good fortune, but of no family, as
they denominate those who cannot boast recorded
ancient blood in their veins. However, instead of
complaining to the Prince, or calling out the
Colonel, he put a good face on the thing, and always
came into the messroom whistling. He was a very
fine young man, and, while he carefully avoided
any appearance of making up to his proud brother-
officers, was ever ready to prove, by his politeness in
handing them salt, bread, wine, or whatever happened to be near him at table, that he was not sufficiently wounded by their cutting to be sulky with
them, neither was his appetite at all impaired by it.
Of this fact, nobody in their senses could entertain
the smallest doubt.

The Duc de Guiche and Fitzgerald joined us,
and while we were conversing together, the young
cornet galloped past us: I allude to the one who had
been universally cut, ever since he joined, merely, I
believe, because no one knew him, and all were certain that his birth was rather mechanical. The
young man rode a very fine horse, and appeared to
manage him with tact and spirit. I think his name
was Eversfield, or something a good deal like it.

'What a beautiful horse that lad is riding!' said
the Duc de Guiche. 'I wish I knew whether he
would like to sell it, and what he would ask for it?'

'I have a great mind to gallop after him and inquire,' observed young Fitzgerald.

'Pray do not,' said Lord Worcester, 'as he will

certainly be offended. It will, indeed, be much too cool a thing to do, to a stranger to whom none of us have yet spoken.'

'Oh, never mind,' said young Fitzgerald, 'he is a good-natured fellow, I dare say. I spoke to him yesterday, to inquire who made his tilbury'; and off he galloped after Mr. Eversfield, who, in less than a fortnight from this time, became on excellent terms with them all: which proves that, with perfect evenness of temper, and good-nature combined, a man of high independent spirit cannot fail to gain the goodwill of everybody around him.

This anecdote, in no way more remarkable than the story of many young men who have to make their footing good in new and unfavourable surroundings, is interesting as giving us for once an exact date. The names of the Marquis of Worcester and Charles Eversfield first occur in the Army List of 1812 as lieutenants in the 10th Hussars. They had both been gazetted in August of the previous year. Eversfield was never a cornet in that regiment. The Marquis is mentioned once or twice in local newspapers in 1811 as having been present at the theatre and bespeaking plays.

How different from the obliging Mr. Eversfield was Captain Fitzclarence.

The Duke of Clarence's and poor Mrs. Jordan's eldest son, Captain Fitzclarence, I remember, had a forfeit, or a fine to pay, for coming to dinner in dirty boots, or something of that kind. He was indeed voted, by the whole mess, a very dirty fellow in his person, and one who evidently conceived himself so much the better than his brother-officers, from being the bastard of the Duke of Clarence. Everybody acknowledges him to be brave; but I certainly should take him to be about as heartless as any man need be, in order to make his way in the world. He had a trick or two which used to make the officers sick, and he ate so voraciously, that he well nigh bred a famine in the messroom. On one occasion, poor Captain Roberts, who happened to come in later than Fitzclarence, got nothing but bubble-and-squeak, in the dog-days.

This visit was only the prelude to a longer visit to Brighton in the following year. There were several reasons which attracted Harriette to Brighton. The 10th Hussars were stationed there; her new adorer, Lord Worcester, had joined the regiment, hoping, he said, that the regimentals would influence her favourably, and was beginning to press her to live under his protection until the regiment was ordered abroad; though protection is a ridiculous word to use when Worcester was about nineteen, and six years younger than Harriette, besides being dependent on his father. Also her sister Sophia had acquired a new admirer, who might be induced to follow his lady and declare himself if she ran away to Brighton.

'I've some news for you,' said Fanny. 'Sophia has made a new conquest of an elderly gentleman, in a curricle, with a coronet on it. He does nothing on earth from morning till night but drive up and down before Julia's door. Julia is quite in a passion about it, and says it looks so very odd.'

'Talk of the devil,' said Alvanly, as Julia and Sophia entered the room.

'Well, Miss Sophia, so you've made a new conquest?' said Fanny.

'Yes,' answered Sophia, 'but it is of a very dowdy, dry-looking man.'

'But then, his curricle!' I interrupted.

'Yes, to be sure, I should like to drive out in his curricle, of all things.'

'It is very odious of the fright to beset my door as he does,' Julia said.

'So it is, quite abominable; and for my part, I hate him and his curricle too,' good-natured Sophia replied.

His lordship was only forty at the time, but to these volatile young women he doubtless appeared an elderly monster.

Viscount Berwick was a nervous, selfish, odd man, and afraid to drive his own horses. Lord William Somerset was an excellent whip; but he had no horses to whip. Lord Berwick, like Lord Barrymore, wanted a tiger; while Somerset required a man whose curricle he could drive, and whose money he could borrow. The bargain was struck; and Tiger Somerset had driven Lord Berwick some years, when his lordship, after having for more than a fortnight been looking at my sister Sophia, at her window, one day addressed the tiger as follows:

'I have, at last, found a woman I should like to marry, Somerset, and you know I have been more than twenty years upon the lookout.'

'Who is she?' said Somerset, in some alarm.

Berwick told him all he knew, and all he had seen of Sophia.

'I think I know who you mean,' said Tiger, 'since you mention the house; because it belongs to Miss Storer, Lord Carysfort's niece, who has, I know, a fine young girl staying with her, whom Lord Deerhurst seduced.'

'Seduced already! you do not say so?'

'Most true, my lord,' said Tiger Somerset; 'besides, I've often seen her, when Deerhurst used to take her out last year. She has no eyebrows, and—'

'I don't care for that, I love the girl, and will have her,' was his lordship's knock-down argument; and Lord William Somerset, having obtained permission from Julia, presented Lord Berwick to Sophia on the following morning.

Sophia would not hear of such a very nasty, poking, old dry man, on his first visit; but the second day, she was induced to drive out in his barouche. On the third, she declared his lordship's equipage the easiest she ever rode in; but then he wore such a large hat! In short, she could not endure him, even to shake hands with her. I never knew Sophia evince so much decided character, since she was born, as in her dislike of Lord Berwick; though she condescended to enter his barouche, and dine with him, accompanied by Julia or myself, yet no persuasion of Lord Berwick, no prayers that his lordship had wit to make, could prevail on her to trust herself, for an instant, in his society.

Harriette had her hands full at the moment. Worcester was becoming more tearfully affectionate every day, while the Duke of Leinster, whose regiment was about to go to Spain, was jealous of Worcester, who remained behind. Harriette, always ingenious in having her cake and eating it, compromised by giving her word to Leinster that so long as he was in England she would not see his rival, and promising Worcester to be his as soon as the Duke had gone; an arrangement which appears to have satisfied all parties. Julia and Sophia took a house together, while Worcester prepared to receive Harriette in Rock Gardens, on the East Cliff. Lord Berwick at the same time took a house at Brighton to be near his adored Sophia, who placidly continued to accept his jewels, drive in his curricle, and eat his dinners, without considering herself in any way in his debt.

Viscount Berwick, in a magnificent equipage, drawn by four milk-white horses, or four of raven black, I forget which, led the way towards Brighton followed by the more humble vehicles containing his cook, his plate, his frying-pans and other utensils. Soon afterwards, Julia and Sophia started in a neat little chariot, drawn by two scraggy black horses, *parce que* Mademoiselle Sophia *vouloit faire paroitre les beaux restes de sa vertu chancelante.*

Worcester's passion for Harriette now increased to such an extent that he repeatedly missed parade, declaring that no matter what might be the consequence, he could not and never would leave her again. The consequences were twofold and surprising. In the first place Colonel Palmer told Worcester that he would 'scold him if it happened again'; in the second place Harriette got up early and was at the barracks, accompanied by Worcester, at half-past eight every morning, dressed in a blue riding habit, an embroidered jacket or spencer worn over it, trimmed and finished after the fashion of the officers of the 10th, and a little grey fur stable cap with a gold band. When Worcester had been reprimanded by the senior officer commanding, Colonel Quintin, whose wife was on excellent terms with the Regent, Harriette was invited to the officers' mess. Colonel Palmer told Harriette that if Worcester again missed drill, he feared Colonel Quintin would 'act in a way to disgust Lord Worcester with the army altogether.'

What with love, duty, and his social obligations, Worcester was fully occupied; deeply resenting the regimental duties that kept him from Harriette, furious at the Prince's invitations which he could not decline. On an occasion when he went, very sulkily, to a dinner given at the Pavilion for the officers of the

10th, he was able to give a striking proof of his devotion to his Harriette.

'The Prince's band,' said he, 'was so very beautiful, that it would have been impossible for me, who love music to excess, not to have enjoyed it; therefore, as I abhor the idea of enjoying anything on earth of which you cannot partake with me, I went into a corner, where I was not observed, to stop my ears and think only of you.'

On another occasion, when Harriette was obliged to have a back double-tooth drawn, he turned as pale as death, being absolutely sick with fright, and long afterwards wore the tooth hung round his neck. He took upon him all the cares of the house, ordering the dinner because he once heard Harriette say that she did not like to know what she was going to eat. He laced her stays for her, and would get out of bed to make her morning toast with his own hands, believing that she would fancy it more if the footman had not touched it.

Harriette, in spite of the stocking-mending, had never learnt to sew, so if the housemaid was not about Worcester would struggle with his own buttons, sewing them with a very large needle and some coarse thread, while he sang in a melancholy voice the following popular song, which he said was peculiarly suited to sewing on buttons:

> Broken-hearted I vanders,
> Broken-hearted I vanders,
> For my jolly light-horseman
> Vas slew'd in the vars.

Had I vings like a heagle,
Had I vings like a heagle,
I vould fly to the spot
Vere my true love doth lie.

Sophia had by now graciously accepted Lord Berwick's offer of a well-furnished house in Montagu Square with the use of a handsome equipage, reserving payment for the present. Julia had received several hundred pounds in ready money from Lord Berwick for having persuaded Sophia to take this step.

'Well,' said I, sighing, 'you have a large family, and I suppose it is what we must all come to. However, I conceive myself as yet, rather young to take up this new profession of yours, Julia.'

Julia defended her conduct, by assuring me she had not taken it up but for my sister's real interest: as a proof of which, she declared that she had strong reason to believe it was Lord Berwick's intention to marry Sophia.

Her experienced judgment was not at fault, for Lord Berwick soon made a serious offer of marriage, much to the pleasure of Mr. Dubochet, who suddenly appears once more in these pages, never afterwards to be heard of again.

The next day, Lord Berwick received Sophia's permission to write to her father, stating his wish to become his son-in-law, and further begging my father to be present at the ceremony, which with his permission, was to take place on the following day, for the purpose of giving his daughter away, that fair lady being under age.

It may be assumed that Lord Berwick's request for his father-in-law's company at church was due less to a wish to include him in the family circle, than to the fact that Sophia was a minor, and required a father's sanction for her marriage. Harriette cannot have known very much about the wedding herself, for it took place not at St. George's, but at Marylebone Church. Mr. Dubochet subsequently settled in Switzerland, persuaded thereto by his family and son-in-law.

Lord Berwick, as well as many more, has often declared himself to have been much struck with that noble air for which my father was particularly distinguished.

The good gentleman was, of course, flattered, on his own account, and probably thought, with the man in Bluebeard, that

'Tis a very fine thing to be father-in-law
To a rich and magnificent three-tailed Bashaw.

But I do not mean to say he did not rejoice in his daughter's welfare for his daughter's sake too, as that would be to decide harshly of any father, much less of my own. We will therefore, take it for granted that, on this day, at least, *monsieur mon papa trouvait d'une forte belle humeur*; nay, my little sisters have since informed me that, when one of them, having had the misfortune to upset a box full of playthings, which made a violent noise in the room where he was, as usual, puzzling over a problem, just as they expected little short of broken heads, and were all running into the most remote corners of the room, until of the opposite wall they seemed a part, he surprised them, to the greatest possible degree, by saying, '*N'importe, petits imbeciles, venez m'embrasser!*'

Sophia was to be married at St. George's Church.

My father had a neighbour, who once insulted him with remarks about the profligacy of his daughters, and though the man had made very humble apologies, and my father had shaken hands with him, yet he never forgot it. This neighbour was a tradesman in a large way of business, and who lived in a very respectable style of comfort. He had several daughters, the ugliest, perhaps, that could possibly come of one father. There was no such thing as getting these off, anyhow, by hook or by crook, by the straight paths of virtue or the intricate road of vice. Not that I mean to say the latter had been attempted; but of this I am certain, if it had been, it must have been ineffectual.

On the eve of Sophia's marriage, as soon as my father had received Lord Berwick's polite invitation, he went to pay his good neighbour a visit.

'How do you find yourself this evening, my very excellent neighbour?'

'Purely, purely, thank you.'

'And your amiable daughters? Any of them married yet? Any of them thinking of it, hey?'

G— shook his head. 'Husbands, as you well know, are not so easily procured for girls of no fortune.'

'Indeed, sir, I am not aware of any particular difficulty. You know my daughter Paragon has long been respectably married to a gentleman of family; and, as for my daughter, Sophia, I shall, please God I live, witness her wedding to-morrow morning, before my dinner.'

'Who is she to marry, pray?' asked G— with eager curiosity; and which my father answered by putting Lord Berwick's letter into his hands, to his utmost astonishment; and, before he had at all recovered from his fit of envy and surprise, my father took his leave, saying that he had many preparations to make for the approaching marriage.

The next morning, as my father was stepping into the carriage which was to convey him to Lord Berwick's house, in Grosvenor Square, well dressed and in high spirits, he was gratified by the sight of his neighbour, who happened to pass his door at that very moment.

This man, naturally envious, and having hitherto looked down with pity on my father's misfortunes in having such handsome daughters, or, at least, he affected to do so, although in his heart, perhaps he had not despised his children the more, supposing it had been the will of heaven to have bestowed on them countenances less forbiddingly ugly, this man,

I say, could not, under the pressure of existing circumstances, help giving some vent to his spleen, exclaimed—'Don't hurry! don't break your neck!' and then passed on, ashamed, as well he might be, at the littleness of his envy.

Just before Sophia's marriage, Lord Berwick spoke to her, to this effect:

'My beloved Sophia, you are about to become an innocent, virtuous woman, and therefore you must pass your word to cut your sisters dead, for ever and at once. I allude, particularly, to Fanny and Harriette.'

'Yes—certainly—very well,' was Sophia's warm-hearted answer.

'And you will oblige me by neither writing to them, nor receiving any letters from them.'

'Very well; then I will give them up altogether,' said Sophia, with much placidity.

Of Sophia's further career there is little to add. Harriette admits that she sent money and presents to their mother. 'I mention this circumstance, merely as a matter of justice to an uninteresting little being whom I rather dislike than otherwise, and will repeat it as often as I have opportunity to do so.' Her extravagance appears to have involved her husband in money difficulties. She gradually broke off intercourse with her family after Fanny's death, and retired into private life. Lord Berwick died in Naples in 1832, and his widow removed to Leamington, where she died in 1875.

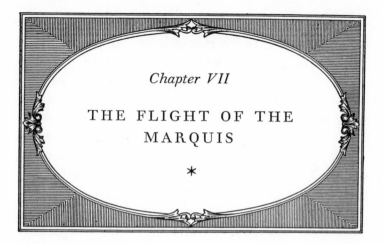

Chapter VII

THE FLIGHT OF THE
MARQUIS

*

HARRIETTE WAS now about twenty-five, and had
had as many lovers, all of them noble and many
of them rich, as is reasonable for any woman to expect. The profession of a courtesan is no inheritance,
except for the very few hard-headed, hard-hearted
Sophias. No serious offer of marriage had ever been
made to Harriette by any of her numerous admirers,
and she began to think of the future with some appre-
hension. Marriage with Worcester was impossible, as
he was under age and would not be his own master till
the beginning of 1813. He was at the time fully determined to make Harriette his wife. All his letters to
her were 'wives and angels, eternal constancy and
eternal despair.' He let the regiment know that whoever did not treat her with the respect due to the future Duchess of Beaufort would incur his resentment.
His parents were not unnaturally alarmed at this infatuation for a notorious woman, several years his
elder, and put pressure upon him to give her up, which

of course increased his romantic ardour. He had also got into the hands of money-lenders, to satisfy Harriette's extravagance. From this entanglement he was rescued by the Duke of Beaufort who, discovering at what interest his son was borrowing money, came down in a very disconcerting way upon the money-lenders with a threat of prosecution for fraud on a minor, if they did not at once send a receipt for the bare amount lent.

When Worcester's troop was ordered to a small country village near Portsmouth, Colonel Quintin obligingly offered him the choice of changing his troop, but Worcester, with more sense of duty than might have been expected, said he would rather not leave it. Accordingly his beloved Harriette consented to share his exile (an exile which included the duc de Guiche and Lord Arthur Hill), and rode with them, in her regimentals, refusing to make use of Worcester's travelling carriage. When they arrived they found no lodging but a 'deplorable pot-house, with plenty of sand on the floor, and plenty of wine-glasses, toothpicks and cruets on the sideboard'; from which one may gather that village inns were very much then what they are now. Here they had to use one room as bedroom and parlour, dining with the other officers in a room smelling of beer and tobacco. The rain was incessant, the wind blew night and day, but all this did but increase Worcester's ardour, if that were possible.

Here Worcester, once upon a time, laid his lordly head upon a large mahogany table, after wiping away the sour beer which fantastically varied its surface, and, with infinite enthusiasm, delivered himself to me in such soft words as, 'Oh, Harriette, my adored, delicious, lovely, divine Harriette, what perfect happiness is this! passing, thus, every minute of the day and night, in your society!! God only knows how long I shall be permitted to enjoy all this felicity; but it is too great, I feel, to last. Nobody was ever thus happy long. They will make my going abroad a point of honour; but even then, my beloved angel-wife will accompany me! yet alas! how dreadful it will be to see you exposed to the dangers and inconveniences of war!'

I had a real tenderness and sisterly affection for Worcester, at that time. I should otherwise have been the most ungrateful, callous, and inhuman creature breathing; and I really was about to make a very tender, warm, and suitable reply; but, at that critical moment, the woman brought in a large platter of ill-dressed veal cutlets and bacon, followed by the Duc de Guiche, and the fat Lord Arthur Hill.

After our sumptuous dinner, Lord Arthur proposed our driving over to Portsmouth, to see the play.

We went accordingly, and having hired a large stage-box, and seated ourselves in due form, all the sailors in the gallery began hissing and pelting us with oranges, and made such an astounding noise that, out of compassion for ourselves, as well as the rest of the audience, we were obliged to leave the theatre before the first act was over, and we were

followed by a whole gang of tars, on our way to the
inn. They called us Mounseers—German moustache rascals, and bl——dy Frenchmen.

Not to digress too long, being all four hissed out
of Portsmouth with much *éclat*, we returned to our
humble village, looking rather wise at each other;
and, for the next two months, or thereabouts, that
we remained in that part of the world, we confined
ourselves to our quarters, *parceque les plaisirs du
village valaient, pour le moins, ceux dont on nous
regalait à la ville.*

The Duke of Beaufort now summoned Worcester to
Badminton, to discuss his future. Worcester, being
again badly in debt, was obliged to obey his father's
commands. From Badminton he wrote piteous letters
to Harriette, declaring that he had been tormented by
his parents till he could neither eat nor sleep. Finally
he begged his angel to disguise herself as a country
woman and come by coach to Oxford, where they
might, without fear of detection, pass one night together at an inn which he named.

At about three o'clock on the day after I had received this letter from Lord Worcester, as my sister
Fanny was standing at her window, pleasing herself with her pretty little daughter Louisa, a hackney-coach stopped at her door, and out of it sprung
a lightfooted spruce damsel, clad in a neat coloured
gown, thick shoes, blue stockings, blue check apron,
coloured neck-handkerchief, cloth cap, and bright

cherry-coloured ribbons. In the next minute, this bold young woman had given both Fanny and her daughter Louisa a hearty kiss!

'Good gracious! my good woman,' exclaimed Fanny, pushing me gently aside, and, in the next instant hearing a loud laugh in the room, for I had not observed Julia and Sir John Boyd sitting at the other window, till they joined in our merriment.

'Lord help the woman,' said Julia, 'what can have put it into her head to appear, this beautiful weather, in such a costume?'

'It is a new style of travelling dress,' said I, 'and I am going to introduce the fashion. What do you think of my cap? It cost eighteen pence, and my blue stockings? but I can't stay gossiping with you fine ladies, or I shall lose my place in the stage. However, do just look at my nice little brand-new red cloak.'

'You don't seriously and really mean to say you are going to travel that figure, and in the broad face of day too?' said Fanny.

'I must! I must! Worcester says, if I don't want to be beaten to a mummy by papa Beaufort, I must go to Oxford in disguise.'

'Disguise, indeed!' said Julia.

'If Fred Bentinck meets a woman of my loose morals in this dress, *il croira que c'est la belle Madéline!*'

'But where is your bonnet?' asked Sir John Boyd.

'Oh! I cannot afford to buy a bonnet; that would

be only half-and-half, a mere vulgar, shabby-genteel, Cockney kind of a maidservant!'

'You will be found out by your taper-waist, and large bosom.'

'Why, what is the matter with it, Sir John? is it not very decently covered by this smart coloured handkerchief?'

'Yes; but it's all too pretty, and your stays are too well made.'

Julia's maidservant, who had not recognised me as I flew past her up the stairs, now entered the room, with a message from my hackney-coachman, who was waiting at the door.

'The coachman, ma'am, desires me to tell the young woman, that he shall expect another sixpence if she does not come down directly.'

'Oh laws! a mighty! and here I hasn't got a sixpence in the world, more than what's tied up here, in this here bag, on purpose for to pay my fare to Oxford,' said I, holding up a small red bag.

Julia's maidservant looked in my face, and seeing everybody ready to laugh, found it impossible to resist joining them.

'Why, the Lord defend me! Miss Harriette, is it really you?' she asked, opening her eyes as wide as possible.

'You see, Sir John, the delicacy of my shape has not stood the least in my way with the coachman, who did not discover the *air noble* under this costume! but I must be off directly.'

'Good-bye! God bless you, mind you write to me

directly, and tell me everything that happens to you,' said Fanny.

They all gave me a kiss, round, for the form of kissing a woman in blue stockings and a check apron, and I was soon seated in the stage-coach, which was being loaded at the door of the Green Man and Still, or as the Frenchman dated his letter, *chez l'homme vert et tranquil.*

'You're not apt to be sick, are you my dear?' inquired a fat-faced merry-looking man, with a red handkerchief tied over his chin, who had already, with a lady whom I fancied might be his wife, taken possession of the two best seats.

I assured them that I was a very good traveller.

'Because my dear, you see, many people can't ride backwards; and there's Mrs. Hodson, my wife, as is one of them.'

'Oh, the young woman is not particler, I dare say,' said Mrs. Hodson, with becoming reserve.

In short, not altogether liking the words, my dear, as they had been applied to me by her husband, she thought it monstrous vulgar.

A lady in a green habit, who was standing near the coach door, now vowed and declared her travelling basket should be taken out of the boot, where it had been thrown by mistake, before she would take her seat.

The coachman in vain assured her it was perfectly safe.

'Don't tell me about its safety,' cried the angry

lady, 'I know what your care of parcels is before to-day.'

'Come, come, my good lady,' said Mr. Hodson, whom I recognised as a London shoemaker of some celebrity, 'come, come, ma'am, your thingumbobs will be quite safe. Don't keep three inside passengers waiting, at a nonplush, for these here trifles!'

'Trifles!' burst forth the exasperated lady, 'are females always to be imposed upon in this manner?'

'*Monsieur Le Clerc!*' continued the lady, calling to a tall thin Frenchman, in a light grey coat, holding under his arm an umbrella, a book of drawings, an English dictionary, and a microscope, '*Monsieur le Clerc*, why don't you insist on the coachman's finding my travelling basket?'

'Yes, to be sure, certainly,' said the Frenchman, looking about for the coachman.

'*Allons, cocher, madame demande son panier. Madame* ask for one litel something, out of your boots, directly.'

'Did I not desire you to mention, *Monsieur Le Clerc*, when you took my place, that the basket was to go inside?' demanded the lady.

'Yes, *oui*,' answered the Frenchman eagerly. 'I tell you, Mr. *Cocher*, dis morning, six, seven, ninety-five times, madame must have her litel— vat you call—over her knee.'

'I'm sorry for the mistake, sir; but it would take a couple of hours to unload that there boot, and I must be off this here instant.'

'Come now, aisey there, aisey,' bawled out a

queer poor Irishman with a small bundle in his hand, running towards the coach in breathless haste. 'Aisey! aisey! there, sure and I'm a match for you, this time anyhow in life,' continued he, as he stepped into the coach, and then took out his handkerchief to wipe the perspiration from his face. He was so wretchedly clothed that Mrs. Hodson eyed him with looks of dismay, while drawing her lavender-coloured silk dress close about her person that it might not be contaminated. I was indeed surprised that this poor fellow could afford an inside place.

The lady and her French beau, seeing no remedy, ascended the steps of the carriage in very ill humour, and they were immediately followed by a man with much comic expression in his countenance. He wore a would-be dashing threadbare green coat with a velvet collar; and his shirt collar was so fine and so embroidered and so fringed with rags, that I think he must have purchased it out of the Marquis of Lorne's cast wardrobe. His little Petersham hat seemed to have been *remit de nouveau* for the third time at least.

'Lord! Mr. Shuffle, how do you do? Who would a thort of our meeting you in a coach?' inquired Mr. and Mrs. Hodson, addressing him in a breath.

'Delighted to see you both,' said Shuffle, shaking hands with them.

'And now, pray, Mr. Shuffle, if I may be so bold, what might have brought you up to London? What antics might you be up to, hey? Are you stage-struck as usual, or struck mad by mere accident?'

'Thereby hangs a tale,' said Shuffle.

'What! a pigtail? I suppose you're thinking of the shop.'

'Not I, indeed,' Shuffle observed. 'I've done with wig-making these two years; for really it is not in the nature of a man of parts to stick to the same plodding trade all his life, as you have done, Hodson.'

Hodson replied that he knew his friend Shuffle had always been reckoned a bit of a genus, and for his part he always knode a genus half a mile off by his threadbare coat and his shoes, worn down at the heels.

'*Aprepo!*' said Mrs. Hodson, 'by the bye, Mr. Shuffle, you forgot to settle for that there pair of boots before you left Cheltenham six months ago.'

'Very true, my dear lady,' answered Shuffle, 'all very true: everything shall be settled. I have two irons in the fire at this time, and very great prospects, I assure you; only do pray cut the shop just now and indulge me with a little genteel conversation.'

'A genteel way of doing a man out of a pair of boots,' muttered Hodson; 'but I'll tell you what, Mr. Shuffle, you must show me a more lasting trade, or one with more sole in it, before you succeed in making me ashamed of being a shoemaker.'

'And pray,' continued Hodson, 'where's the perpetual motion you were wriggling after so long?

and then your rage for the stage, what's become of that? Have you made any money by it?'

'How is it possible,' answered Shuffle, 'for a man to make money by talents he is not permitted to exert? "Sir," said I to the manager of the Liverpool theatre, "I have cut my trade of wig-making dead, and beg to propose myself to you as a first-rate performer."—"Have you any recommendations?" inquired the manager, eyeing me from head to foot. —"Yes, sir," I replied, "plenty of recommendations. In the first place, I have an excellent head." '

'For a wig! a good block, I reckon,' interrupted Hodson.

' "In the second place," Shuffle continued, "I have the strongest lungs of any man in England." '

'That is, unfortunately, the case of my good woman here,' again interrupted Hodson.

' "And as for dying, sir," still continued Shuffle, "I have been practising it for these two years past." '

'Upon red and grey hair, I presume?' said the incorrigible Hodson.

' "Sir," said the Liverpool prig, so Shuffle went on, "Sir, our company happens to be at this moment complete." Fifty managers served me the same. At last, however, I got a hearing, and as I suspected would be the case, was immediately engaged. The play-bills mentioned the part of Romeo by a gentleman, his first appearance on the stage; but it was a low company and beggarly audience, which accounts for my having been pelted with oranges and hissed off the stage!!'

Hodson here burst into a very loud fit of laughter, declaring this was the best joke he ever heard in his life.

Shuffle, without at all joining in his friend's mirth, declared that he had now resigned all thoughts of a profession, the success of which must often depend on a set of ignorant blockheads, and turned his thoughts to love and experimental philosophy.

'I say,' was Hodson's wise remark, looking very significantly at his friend.

'Well, sir, what have you to say?' Shuffle inquired.

'Blow me, Shuffle, if you aren't a little—' Hodson paused and touched his forehead.

'Don't meddle with the head, friend, that's not your trade. Oh, by the bye,' Shuffle continued, 'talking of heels, I want to consult you about a new sort of elastic sole and heel, after my own invention: one that shall enable a man to swim along the river, like a goose, at the rate of fifteen miles an hour!! I have just discovered that the goose owes its swiftness to the shape of its feet. Now my water-shoe must be made to spread itself open when the foot is extended and close as it advances.'

'Well done, gentlemen,' interposed the poor Irish traveller, 'this bates the cork jackets anyhow in life!'

'Who the devil are you, sir?' asked Shuffle, 'and what business have you to crack your jokes?'

'The only little objection that I see to your contrivance,' continued Pat, 'is that the patent shoe will be just after turning into a clog as soon as it gits under water, good luck to it.'

'The devil take me if that warn't a capital joke! so well done, Master Pat,' said Hodson.

'Is that an Irish wig you have got on your head, Pat?' Shuffle asked, by way of being even with him.

'For God's sake, sink the shop, Shuffle, and let's have a little genteel conversation,' said Hodson, imitating Shuffle's late affectation of voice and manner.

'Pray what do you Irish know about wig-making?' asked Shuffle, disregarding Hodson.

'And may be you would not approve, nather, of their nate compact little fashion of breaking a head, perhaps?' inquired Pat very quietly.

'Come, come, my comical fellow,' said Hodson, 'don't be so hot. Mr. Shuffle only meant to remark that it was a pity to wear a red wig over your fine head of hair.'

'Arrah, by my sowl! and is it under it you'd have me wear it?' asked the Irishman.

'You're a funny chap! but I loves to see a man in good spirits,' Hodson remarked.

'Is it in good spirits then you reckon me? Sure and you're out there anyhow in life; for the devil a drop of spirits have I poured into me, good, bad, or indifferent, since yesterday, worse luck to me!'

'What, are you out of employment then?' Mrs. Hodson inquired.

'No, my lady, in regard to my being employed just now, looking out for work.'

Shuffle inquired how long he had left Ireland?

'Not more than a month, your honour; and four weeks out of that time have I been wandering about the great gawky village of London, up one strate and down the tother, in search of a friend; and sorrow bit of the smallest intelligence can I gain, anyhow in the world, of poor Kitty O'Mara.'

'And is that absolutely necessary?' I asked.

'And did I not promise Mistress Kitty, the mother of him, that I would stick by her darling till the breath was clane out of his body? and then, after our death, wasn't it by mutual agreement between Kitty and me, that we should dig each other nate, tight bit of a grave, and bury each other in a jontale, friendly manner? so that, what with disappointment, fatague, and the uncommon insults which have been put upon me lately, sure and I'm completely bothered!'

'And pray, Pat, what takes you over to Oxford?' Hodson asked.

'Sure and I'm just going there to come back again by the marrow-bone stage.'

'But what reason have you for making the journey?' said Shuffle.

'Is it what rasin had I? Haven't I paid for my place more than a week ago, and haven't I lost a good sarvice in them parts by missing the coach by a trifle of half an hour's oversleeping myself? and did not the proprietor of this same coach promise me the first vacant sate?'

'Well but, having lost your place, why trouble

yourself to go down when it is too late?' Hodson inquired.

'And you'd have me chated and diddled out on the fare as well as the sarvice? bad luck to me!' added Pat with comic gravity.

'Blow me if you ain't a funny one,' said Hodson, as the coach stopped to set him down in a small village between London and Oxford, 'and since you've put me into spirits I must put spirits into you, so here's a shilling for you, Pat. In for a penny, as I says, in for a pound. Good-bye, Shuffle, and I shall thank you to call and settle for that there pair of boots. Come, my good woman, give us your hand. Good-bye, my pretty lass,' nodding to me, as he and his better half quitted the coach.

Nothing of very great interest occurred during the remainder of our journey except that Shuffle seemed disposed to hire Pat as his servant. The Frenchman found fault with everything at table, drank *eau sucré*, and studied in his dictionary. The lady in the green habit scorned to address even a single syllable to a person in the humble garb I wore, and I never once opened my lips till we arrived at Oxford, and I was set down at a little inn nearly a mile distant from the one where Worcester promised to wait for me. It was almost one o'clock in the morning, it poured with rain, and there was not a star to enliven a poor traveller!

Here she was lucky enough to find an honest guide who for a small sum agreed to conduct her to the

Crown Inn. Worcester was anxiously awaiting her at the door. She ran up to him and took his arm, but so bedraggled did she look that Worcester, who was not expecting her to arrive on foot, pushed her away.

'My dear Mr. Dobbins,' said I, for that was the name we were to go by at the Crown, where he believed he was not personally known. 'Mr. Dobbins! Don't you recognise your dear Mrs. Dobbins?'

'Good God, my love! how came you alone, this miserable night?' was Worcester's reply. Supper with good claret, fruit, coffee, and everything that could be desired was quickly served.

The night passed happily, but by great ill-luck Harriette was seen and recognised next day, on her return journey, by one of Worcester's uncles. Lord Edward Somerset lost no time in telling the Duke and Duchess of this suspicious circumstance, rashly adding that Harriette was both deformed and ugly, to which Worcester, wisely avoiding the main issue, replied that his aunt, Lady Edward, was so hideous that the man who had chosen her for a wife must for ever give up all pretensions to taste; so the affair blew over.

The Duke of Beaufort now made another determined attempt to detach his son from Harriette. Through an attorney, one Robinson, 'a notorious swindler who has since been confined in chains for forgery,' is Harriette's explanation, he offered Harriette a reasonable compensation if she would give up every letter or copy of a letter that she had received from Worcester.

Harriette, on taking counsel's opinion, found that the letters were, in the eyes of her legal adviser, Mr. Treslove, worth at least £20,000. Here she was faced by a dilemma. Should she retain the letters and blackmail the Duke for as much money as she could get; or should she try the effect of a noble gesture, which might lead her nearer to marriage. She decided on the latter course and sent to the Duke a packet containing certain letters of Worcester's and a pathetic appeal for consideration, declaring that it was her doing that Worcester had not already married her, and that all she asked was a little less ill-will from his parents. To this letter she received no reply.

The Duke meanwhile had been active in other quarters and had obtained for his son an appointment to Wellington's staff. The 10th were not to go out till the following year, 1813, but Worcester was to precede them and take up his duties at once.

It now struck me very forcibly that Worcester had deserved all my devoted attachment, and that I had not been half grateful enough to him. That he would lose his life in Spain, I felt convinced, and that since his regiment remained in England, I should have his blood on my head. What was to be done? My crimson velvet pelisse, trimmed with white fur, and also my white beaver hat, with the charming plume of feathers, were spread out in my dressing-room, ready for Hyde Park and conquests!!

and poor Worcester, perhaps, might soon be numbered with the dead! food for worms!!

After a second flood of tears!! on went the red pelisse and charming white hat and, in less than half an hour, behold me standing at the Duke of Beaufort's street door, awaiting the answer to my humble, single rap, with a little note in my hand, containing these few words, addressed to the Duke.

I earnestly entreat your grace to permit me to speak a few words to you before you attend the levee this morning.

Your most obedient, humble servant,

HARRIETTE WILSON.

After some delay, due to the curiosity and impertinence of his grace's staff, who wished to see what Miss Wilson was like, she met the Duke of Beaufort face to face. High moral feeling was shown on both sides and the Duke himself conducted her to the door after a short lecture on the disadvantages of unequal marriages. Neither side had gained anything, or given anything away. Worcester begged Harriette to accompany him to Spain, but the objections were many and obvious. Harriette handsomely offered to retire to the country while her lover was away, to relieve his not unnatural anxiety as to her fidelity, while he on his side declared that 'her last kiss was to be virgined on his lip,' and that at the end of a year he would return and make her his own.

'If ever you prove false to me, or I to you, may all

inconstant men be called Ponders, and all false women Cressids,' were his parting words; which variation on a respectable name seems to add sanctity to the oath.

The separation, of a heart-rending nature, with abundance of tears from both lovers, was followed by a visit from Mr. Robinson, empowered to offer on the Duke's behalf an allowance for life, paid quarterly, if she would promise never to speak or write to Worcester again, but Harriette still would not commit herself.

A few days later, about three o'clock in the day, my servant announced a gentleman, who refused to send up his name, merely saying that he lived in Grosvenor Square, and wanted to speak to me.

I was about to insist on knowing who my visitor was before I admitted him, when the idea struck me as just possible, and I requested he might be shown upstairs.

It was the Duke of Beaufort!

I was surprised at receiving a visit from His Grace, and still more so when I found that he really had nothing particular to say to me. He hesitated a good deal, looked rather foolish, and wished, for my own sake as well as his son's, that I would abandon all hopes and leave off corresponding with his son.

'Duke,' said I, interrupting him, 'was it not your first and most anxious wish that Worcester should go abroad?'

'It was.'

'Well then, Lord Worcester positively and abso-lutely refused to leave London until I had pledged myself in the most solemn manner to continue faithfully his, and not place myself under the protection of any other man for one twelve-month from the day he should leave England. Do you still ask me to break my oath?'

The Duke, from very shame, perhaps, was silent, and stood against my door, fidgeting and hesitating, as though he would have proposed something or other, but that he wanted courage.

After a long pause he suddenly and with abruptness, said, 'Who makes your shoes?'

I fixed my eyes upon His Grace in unaffected astonishment at this irrelevant question.

'We will say nothing of the feet and the ankles,' continued His Grace.

This compliment was so very unlooked for from such a quarter, and struck me so very odd, that I felt myself actually blushing up to the very eyes, and I immediately changed the conversation from my feet and ankles to the young Marquis and the Peninsular War.

His Grace, when he took his leave of me, had made no single proposal, nor said one single word, which could in any way assist my guess as to why he did me the honour to call on me.

After this visit, Harriette decided to claim the allowance.

But while these negotiations were in progress, and Harriette was in despair at losing her lover, a rich, good-looking young man called Meyler, one of the dandies though not in the highest flight, began to make advances to her. His affections were at the moment divided between Mrs. Bang, Mrs. Patten, and Mrs. Pancrass, all of Covent Garden—of whom their names are sufficient explanation—but he was more than willing to add to his reputation by an affair with Harriette Wilson. He was also in the good graces of the Duchess of Beaufort, who would have been by no means displeased to see Meyler carry off her son's mistress. It was easy for him to obtain an introduction to Harriette at the opera. She found him 'unaffected and gentlemanlike with a bright glowing countenance for expressing love,' and when he attempted to kiss her on the stairs she refused 'in a coquettish way that gave him every encouragement to repeat his effort.' Worcester, delayed for some days by contrary winds at Falmouth, was by now on his way to Spain, so Harriette wrote to Meyler, asking him to call on her at Julia Johnstone's house, because she knew it would make Lord Worcester miserable if she received him in her own.

When Meyler arrived a slight attack of conscience made her refuse to see him, but he laid siege to her so violently that she began to feel alarmed. It was a choice between keeping or losing two lovers, both highly eligible, and the best way out of it at the moment seemed to be to keep her word to Worcester and go to the country.

'Where is there a village?' said she to Luttrell, the 'father confessor.'

Inquiries elicited the fact that a village could be

found at a place called Charmouth, whither Harriette set off in the Exeter mail, with no company but her maid and a gold toothpick with his hair in it, a parting gift from Meyler. Julia's account was that the village was called Moorcom-Bissett, and that she accompanied Harriette, who could only get the Duke of Beaufort's allowance from an attorney at Bridport if Julia signed for it; which, if true, would point to the fact that the industrious Julia was earning money again as a go-between or female Ponder.

As usual, when both these ladies speak at once, their accounts are hopelessly at variance. Harriette described a rustic, idyllic life, mingling with local society, giving the curate's father aged ninety-five her arm, playing Lady Bountiful to the poor. Julia on the contrary said that Harriette at once made friends among the officers in the neighbourhood—militia, presumably, in default of anything better—and had an illegitimate child by a Lieutenant Devall, which was put out to nurse and its existence hushed up.

'Once she nearly betrayed her *calling* in the country, as we were going to church, by holding up her leg on passing a stile and desiring the clergyman to fasten her bootlace. He had been once a dasher on the London streets and very gallantly complied with her request, saying with a smile :

'Don't your garter want tightening, my love?'

As the promised allowance from the Duke of Beaufort was not forthcoming, and no notice was taken of her letters, Harriette resolved to take fresh legal advice. On inquiry she was told that an attorney of Lyme Regis, one Fisher, of lady-killing reputation, would be able to help her. She wrote to him to ask for an appointment, but the unlucky lawyer, thinking she was suggesting an assignation, answered accordingly; for which mistake he may surely be forgiven. Harriette wrote him a snubbing letter and did not visit him; but she did not forget the affair.

Letters from her lovers cheered her solitude. Worcester wrote from Spain letters of three sheets, crossed and recrossed, full of dearest darlings! angel-wives! loveliest, sweetest, adorable, own own, everlastingly to be worshipped, etc. 'As for your picture,' continued the unhappy young man, 'I could not press my lips near enough to your sweet delicious eyes without taking off the glass; and now, alas! I have kissed the left eye out, altogether, with your under lip.'

Meyler sent her news of his election to Parliament as member for Winchester, and begged her repeatedly to put herself under his protection, sometimes promising to wait for her till Worcester's year of probation was over, sometimes threatening to marry someone else at once if she would not have him.

The question of Harriette was still agitating the Beaufort family. Lady Bessborough, writing on Sept. 24th, 1812, to Worcester's uncle, Lord Granville Leveson-Gower, he who had been so unmercifully walked about Marylebone and Hampstead on a hot summer day, said:

Apropos of throwing away happiness, I must tell
you another part of Ly. Melbourne's letter, which
concerns you more nearly. She was told that Harriette Wilson is living at Ryde in great retirement,
passing for the most Virtuous Woman in the Island;
and that she is waiting for Ld. W.'s coming of age,
when he is to return and marry her. She shows some
of his letters, all ending with yr. affec^{ate} *Husband*.
Probably you know what credit is to be given to
this, but I thought it well to tell you.

This was the first intimation that Harriette had not
given up all her letters to the Duke, as she said she
had done.

The affair now became excessively embroiled.
Harriette returned to London, where Meyler continued his solicitations. She wrote to the Duke to say
that she was willing to transfer her affections to Meyler, if the Duke would guarantee her five hundred a
year. The Duke refused to go a penny higher than
three hundred, to which Miss Wilson agreed; but subsequently the Duke, believing that Worcester had
transferred his attentions to a lady in Spain, the sister
of the second wife of a paymaster in the 10th, with-
drew the offer altogether. Harriette replied that she
still had many letters from Lord Worcester with
promises of marriage in her possession, and that if
he did not at once settle the annuity upon her, she
would publish the letters and put an execution into
his house for the amount due to her.

Upon this the Duke consented to an annuity of two

hundred a year, and an agreement was drawn up by which Harriette, in consideration of receiving the money, swore never to write to Lord Worcester or to hold any sort of communication with him. Having signed this, she immediately wrote to Worcester, saying that she trusted to God and to his good heart, for she still believed him to be fond of her. She then wrote to Meyler, who hired an excellent house for her in the New Road, close to Gloucester Place and became her acknowledged protector. It was not an ideal companionship. Though Meyler had 'an expression in his countenance of such voluptuous beauty, that it was impossible for any woman to converse with him, after he had dined, in cold blood,' he was extremely fickle and had a very bad temper. However, Harriette would kick him out of bed and send him back to his own house if he annoyed her, so things were fairly even. She visited Paris with Meyler and there became very friendly with Brougham (though there is no mention of her in his own memoirs, nor in any subsequent life of him) and consulted him about her allowance from the Duke of Beaufort, which was in considerable danger since she broke her word and wrote to Worcester. Brougham said 'boldly, and at a public dinner table, that it was a mean paltry transaction,' and advised her to bring an action for the recovery of her annuity. Legal proceedings were begun, the Duke offered to compromise for twelve hundred pounds down; Lord Worcester, now considering marriage and heartily glad to be rid of the whole affair, produced the compromising letter; the twelve hundred pounds were paid, and the matter was at an end. Of Brougham's help Harriette could not speak highly enough. A paragraph in which she mentions his kindness is worth quoting, as an example of her other successful attempts to get money from her friends.

As to Frederick Lamb's rage at my publishing these facts, he was fully acquainted with my intention; and had he, now that he is in better circumstances, only opened his heart, or even purse, to have given me but a few hundreds, there would have been no book, to the infinite loss of all persons of good taste and genuine morality, and who are judges of real merit. But I hate harping on people's unkindness, and *vice versa*, I cannot omit to acknowledge the generous condescension of Earl Spencer, who, though I have not the honour to be in the least acquainted with him, has very repeatedly assisted me. In short, his lordship has promptly complied with every request for money I ever made to him, merely as a matter of benevolence.

Lord Rivers, with whom I have but a bowing acquaintance, has not only often permitted me to apply to him for money; but once, when I named a certain sum to him, he liberally doubled it; because, as he kindly stated in his letter, he was so truly sorry to think that one who possessed such a generous heart as mine should not be in affluent circumstances. Lord Palmerston, also, one fine day did me a pecuniary service without my having applied to him for it. Neither can I express half the gratitude I feel, and shall entertain to the end of my life for the steady, active friendship Mr. Brougham has invariably evinced towards me, actuated, as he is, solely by a spirit of philanthropy. When I see a man of such brilliant talents pleading the cause of almost all those persons whose characters I have sketched in these pages with such honest warmth and benevolence of feeling as Brougham did yesterday, to say I look up to him and love him is but a cold description of the sentiments he inspires in my heart.

It is known that Mr. Brougham's spirit of philanthropy was of a generous kind, not confining itself to the narrower meaning of the word.

Julia, on the other hand, who appears to have been jealous of Brougham's partiality to Harriette, remarks in her own restrained style:

A more complete antidote to the tender passion never walked upon legs (broom sticks, I mean) than Henry Brougham, his features apparently stamped on a toadstool, and his eyes like marbles floating in mortar; his chin and nose like the toes of Grimaldi's slipper when dressed for Whang-fong, and the *tout ensemble* of his person so much like that of Sir Murray Maxwell's orang-outang, are sufficient to drive love to the devil.

As for Lord Worcester, after distinguishing himself by his gallantry in Spain, he left the army and made a suitable marriage in 1814. He settled down as a country landowner, went into Parliament, hunted and preserved, and may be found as Duke of Beaufort in *Nimrod's Sporting Sketches*. But where the heart was concerned, he remained as foolish as ever. After the death of his first wife in 1821 he involved himself with two women at once and wrote passionate letters to Lady Jane Paget, signing himself her affectionate husband, while he was contemplating marriage with his late wife's half-sister, a union of doubtful legality which took place in 1822.

Chapter VIII

FAMILY AFFAIRS

*

MEYLER WAS by no means a satisfactory protector, nor was Lord Ebrington with whom Harriette was living at the same time. She had affairs with a number of other men, but sadly missed what she had called in old days, 'a steady friend.' Always extravagant, her debts were mounting fast. In 1814, when peace was declared between England and France, and the Allied Sovereigns visited London, the season was exceptionally brilliant. A gala performance was given at the opera, attended by crowned heads. Harriette described the evening in glowing colours, but Julia said that in that very year she and Harriette had been obliged to give up their opera box for want of funds. 'Besides,' added Julia, 'to her great mortification be it told, she was close confined to her chamber all the time they were in London, with St. Anthony's fire in her face, or rather the fire of champaigne, which about this time she began to tipple very freely.'

In spite of all these embarrassments, Harriette was

able to go to the masquerade at Wattier's Club, given
in honour of the peace. This club, famous for its excellent cooking and its high play, was founded in
1807 and was for a few years extremely fashionable.
After 1819 it fell into disrepute and became a haunt
of blacklegs, but in 1814 it was at the height of its
reputation, and tickets for the fête were eagerly
sought after. Harriette, Amy, and Fanny had invitations, but Julia, less popular, could only get a man's
ticket, through the kindness of Lord Hertford, and
went as a French peasant boy. Harriette went as a
peasant girl 'with a bright red silk petticoat, and a
black satin jacket, the form of which was very peculiar
and most advantageous to the shape.' Fanny was a
country housemaid with muslin cap and apron,
tucked-up gown and pink petticoat, while Amy chose
to go as a nun.

The masquerade, given at Burlington House, was
the most brilliant event of an exceptionally brilliant
season, far eclipsing the masked ball given by the
members of White's Club. The reception rooms were
decorated with orange trees, rose trees, and all kinds
of shrubs, 'tastefully illuminated.' Every lady on ar-
riving was presented with a ticket entitling her to
a prize in a raffle. This 'Lottery of Bijoux' was drawn
after midnight, and the prizes, which varied in value
from a guinea to twenty-five guineas, consisted of
bracelets, watches, lockets, boxes, all decorated with
some image of the Duke of Wellington. Supper was
magnificently served at half-past one for over sixteen
hundred people and the dancing did not cease till seven

in the morning. To animate the spirits of the guests while new arrivals were still pouring in and before the dancing had begun, rope dancers, jugglers and groups of professional singers were performing in the various apartments, a whole ballet was danced, and Grimaldi, the famous clown, gave an entertainment. The various characters described by Harriette can all be found in contemporary accounts, but she reported them far more amusingly than the professional writers.

One of the immense suite of rooms formed a delicious, refreshing contrast to the dazzling brilliancy of all the others. This room contained, in a profusion almost incredible, every rare exotic root and flower. It was lighted by large ground glass, French globe-lamps, suspended from the ceiling at equal distances. The rich draperies were of pale green satin and white silver muslin. The ottomans, which were uniformly placed, were covered with satin to correspond with the drapery, and fringed with silver.

Harriette, wandering into this empty room, was addressed by a masked stranger in a rich white satin Spanish dress and a very magnificent plume of white ostrich feathers in his hat, who seizing her, kissed her to suffocation, said he had always watched over and adored her, and sent her the anonymous bank-notes that she had received from time to time. Harriette, confused, though not unwilling to give and receive more kisses, could only hazard a guess that he was Ponsonby, but before she could discover more he left her. This romantic encounter was not the only adventure of the night. Returning hopefully to the same empty room, she found there another unknown. He was dressed in a long brown robe and unmasked. His complexion was clear and olive, his forehead high, his mouth beautifully formed, his eyes bright and expressive. After some desultory conversation the truth dawned upon them both.

'You must be Lord Byron, whom I have never met.'
'And you are Harriette Wilson.'
We shook hands cordially.

An animated conversation then took place about Lady Caroline Lamb and her novel *Glenarvon*,—which, unfortunately for Harriette's veracity, was not published till two years later,—after which they separated.

I saw no more of him for that evening; but I offered up a fervent, short, ejaculatory prayer to heaven for this interesting young man's better health, and then joined the noisy, merry throng in the adjoining rooms.

For a very unpleasant, malicious account of Lady Caroline Lamb which Harriette afterwards gave, Julia had a highly coloured explanation. She said that Har-

riette did have a servant who had been in the Lamb
family, but that, far from having been Lady Caroline's
maid, she had been assistant kitchen maid at Brocket,
and dismissed for stealing. She came to Harriette
before William Lamb's marriage, and had never seen
Lady Caroline. The rest of Julia's story is improbable
enough to repeat: that after leaving Harriette the servant was with Lady Rosebery, when she became Lady
(Harry) Mildmay after divorce, then with the
Duchess of Devonshire, then with Madame de Stael,
from which situation she was escorted out of France by
gendarmes for theft; that she again met Harriette,
this time in a bagnio in Brussels, and so returned to
her employ.

The graces and the fury were sensibly slackening
in their career. Amy and Harriette were living between London and Paris, in a rather squalid way.
Poor Fanny Parker had received a mortal blow when
her beloved Colonel Parker had broken to her the
news of his approaching marriage. Delicate and con-
sumptive from girlhood, she had little strength left and
could not rally from the shock. The three sisters, Amy,
Harriette, and Sophia were for once united in nurs-
ing her. Lord Hertford's kindness in her last days was
untiring. He had her moved to lodgings in Brompton,
where the air was supposed to be good for invalids, and
ordered straw to be put down before the house.

He was the only man admitted into her room to
take leave of her before she died, although hundreds, and those of the first rank and character,

were sincerely desirous of doing so. I remember Lord Yarmouth's last visit to Brompton, where my poor sister died after an illness of three weeks.

'Can I or my cook do anything in the world to be useful to you?' said he. I repeated that it was too late—that she would never desire anything more, and all I wanted for her was plenty of Eau-de-Cologne to wash her temples with, that being all she asked for. He did not send his groom for it; but galloped to town himself and was back immediately. This was something for Lord Yarmouth.

Queen's Buildings, where Fanny died in the summer of Waterloo, stood on the south side of Brompton Road, near Sloane Street. She was buried in Kensington churchyard, and her name, as Frances Parker, aged thirty-three, can be seen in the register. When the old church of St. Mary Abbot was pulled down in the middle of last century, many of the graves and headstones were displaced to make room for the larger new church, and the stone which marked her grave is not to be found.

And now Julia, deserted by Mildmay, and dependent on the stingy and selfish Napier, had also died, not long after Fanny: at least, Harriette described her death-bed so movingly, that she must have convinced herself, rather to her relief, that a friend who knew too much was now beyond harming her. There was a curious sequel to this.

Three months later Mrs. Dubochet died. Julia said that she was a shocking vulgar woman, very forward and coarse in her language, who used to pervade the Boulevards clad in a riding habit, with a narrow-rimmed beaver hanging gently over her bloodshot eyes, and that her death was due to two pints of brandy per diem. Nugent, on the contrary, as reported by Harriette, said on meeting Mrs. Dubochet in Paris, 'I have often wondered how it happened that so very large a family as yours should not only all be very handsome, but likewise so perfectly ladylike and well-bred. Now it is accounted for: the secret I discovered in your mother. I have not for many years felt such perfect respect and admiration for a woman who at least must be bordering upon fifty. Not only is she still very handsome and delicate; but there is a certain air of modest dignity in her manner which, I believe, the greatest libertine in France could not fail to be struck with.'

These are the two epitaphs of Amelia Dubochet, aged about fifty-five, mother of fifteen children, of whom at least four were notorious.

As for Amy, her subsequent career was involved with that of a very remarkable scoundrel, and almost deserves a chapter to itself. She lived for some years in Paris, where her mother, two of her brothers, and three of her younger sisters also took up their abode; Lord Berwick, always anxious to dissociate himself from his wife's family, having contributed a hundred pounds to that end. In Paris Amy was still under the protection of such old friends as Nugent and Luttrell, made what new friends she could, and still had extremely stingy supper parties, forcing her French admirers to accept her favourite black puddings as a rare English delicacy. Among her acquaintance she had at one time great hopes of the comte de Greffulhe, a very wealthy banker of Dutch origin, who had been naturalised in France and created a peer after the Restoration. As Greffulhe was obdurate, she called in Harriette to her help, but neither Harriette's letters nor Amy's rolling eyes could melt the banker's heart. Harriette, piqued at her failure, came to the conclusion that he was an absurd, affected, mean, contemptible little blockhead, a short, thick man, almost a mulatto, with little purblind eyes and straight, coarse black hair. Further to show her annoyance she insisted upon speaking of him as a Swiss, and adopted the very English fashion of expressing dislike by constantly misspelling his name.

Having failed with Greffulhe, Amy now met her ultimate fate in the person of Nicholas Robert Charles Bochsa, as rascally a musician as ever lived. Son of a composer, Bochsa was brought up to music, became Court Harpist first to Napoleon and later to Louis XVIII, and married a daughter of the marquis Ducrest, Madame de Genlis's brother. His extravagance ran him into debt and he embarked upon what was for a time a very successful career of forgery. Among the charges brought against him were the forgery of bonds with the signatures of Méhul, Boieldieu and other musicians; of a bill for 16,000 francs signed Lafitte and Co.; of a bond for 14,000 francs signed Pozzo di Borgo; of bonds upon the English legation with the name of Sir Charles Stuart, and of documents in the name of the Duke of Wellington. Before he could be brought to justice, he fled to England in 1817. A notice of the Cour d'Assises was published in the *Moniteur* of February 19, 1818, condemning him in contumacy and sentencing him, if he returned to France, to twelve years of forced labour, branding with the letters T.F., and a fine of 4,000 francs. The charms of the '*trop célèbre Bochsa*' so won Amy's heart that she married him at St. George's, Hanover Square, in 1818, ignoring Madame de Genlis's niece, an oversight which was afterwards to cost Bochsa dear.

Bochsa was for some time musical manager to the King's Theatre, and after the founding of the Royal Academy of Music in 1822, he was appointed principal Professor of the Harp and general superintendent of the practice of the pupils. In 1826 an anonymous correspondent, possibly a musician who considered that his claims had been slighted, wrote to a musical paper, the *Harmonicon*, bringing charges against him of being a robber, forger, runaway galley-slave and bigamist. These articles were reprinted by the *Sunday Moniteur* and the *Examiner*, against whose editors Bochsa was foolish enough to bring libel actions. The verdict on both cases was in his favour, but the publicity was dangerous. Part of one of the alleged libels ran:

'ROYAL ACADEMY OF MUSIC

'This silly institution with its cant about morality and religion seems likely to be brought into general contempt by the discussions now taking place about it. Already the Archbishop of York must feel himself in very awkward company when transacting business with his worthy friend, Mr. Bochsa, and the Academy Chaplain has no sinecure in protecting the boys and girls from bad precepts and examples. . . . If the Archbishop and his deputy have power to cast out devils, they will serve their academy best by turning out Beelzebub, the prince of devils.'

Upon this the judge's comment was that he really did not see what Mr. Bochsa could deny except that he was the d–l.

Such a public exposure, followed by a reprint of the article from the *Moniteur*, made Bochsa's position untenable, and the directors of the Academy had to ask for his resignation, which was given in 1827. His musical career does not seem to have suffered greatly.

In 1839 Bochsa, whose concerts were fashionable and well attended, even after Queen Victoria's accession, ran away with the singer, Madame Anna Bishop, wife of Sir Henry Bishop, the composer. Amy may have been dead; if not, she was ignored, even as her predecessor had been. Together Bochsa and Madame Anna Bishop toured Europe (except France, which he never dared to enter), America and Australia. Here, at Sydney, he died in 1856, after an illness brought on by 'the privation of comforts during a tedious voyage from San Francisco to Sydney.' The guileless Australians accepted him at his face value.

He had a magnificent funeral, at which a requiem of his own composition was performed, with words hurriedly supplied by local talent.

> Rest! Great Musician, rest!
> Thine earthly term is o'er,
> And may thy tuneful soul
> To choirs seraphic soar!
> Tho' hushed thy mortal tones,
> Their echoes still remain—
> For in thine own sad chords
> We chaunt thy funeral strain.

Madame Anna Bishop survived him for twenty-eight years.

One other sister is curiously and inexplicably accounted for. In a letter among the Creevey papers for 1819, queried as being from Lord Kinnaird, an old friend of the sisters, the statement is made, 'Lord Lascelles' son has married Harriette Wilson's sister.'

Mary married respectably, a Mr. Borough, 'nephew of Sir Richard Borough, a great Irish contractor.'

Harriette said such very unkind things about the way her sister Lady Berwick treated the youngest girl, Charlotte, that it is a pleasure to find 'An Old Subscriber' writing to a newspaper in 1825 with an account of her ladyship's benevolence. 'One sister Charlotte, who is very beautiful, but has the misfortune to be lame, lives in retirement with an elder sister in a small and obscure lodging in Church Street, Paddington, where Lady B. visits them and supplies their wants.'

On one of her journeys between London and Paris,

Harriette went to see Brummell at Calais, whither he had retired in 1816 to avoid his creditors. She had known him well in London, though never intimately, and confessed that it was curiosity rather than friendship that led her to call on him. His cold and calculating disposition was the last thing in the world to please such a creature of impulse as Harriette, and the stories she had to tell of him, such as his brutal rebuff to Mrs. Armstrong at Amy's party, put him in no attractive light.

I found the beau *en robe de chambre de Florence*, and, if one might judge from his increased *embonpoint* and freshness, his disgrace had not seriously affected him. He touched lightly on this subject in the course of our conversation, *faisant toujours la barbe, avec une grace toute particulière, et le moindre petit rasoir que je n'eus jamais vu.*

'Play,' he said, 'had been the ruin of them all.'

'Whom do you include in your all?'

He told me there had been a riot in White's club.

'I have heard all about your late tricks in London,' said I.

Brummell laughed, and told me that in Calais he sought only French society; because it was his decided opinion that nothing could be more ridiculous than the idea of a man going to the Continent, whether from necessity or choice, merely to associate with Englishmen.

I asked him if he did not find Calais a very melancholy residence.

'No,' answered Brummell, 'not at all. I draw, read, study French, and—'

'Play with that dirty French dog,' interrupted I.

'*Finissez donc, Louis*,' said he, laughing, and encouraging the animal to play tricks, leap on his *robe de chambre de Florence*, and make a noise. Then, turning to me, 'There are some pretty French actresses at Paris. I had such a sweet green shoe here just now. In short,' added Brummell, 'I have never been in any place in my life where I could not amuse myself.'

Brummell's table was covered with seals, chains, snuff-boxes and watches: presents, as he said, from Lady Jersey and various other ladies of high rank.

The only talent I could ever discover in this beau was that of having well-fashioned the character of a gentleman, and proved himself a tolerably good actor; yet, to a nice observer, a certain impenetrable unnatural stiffness of manner proved him but nature's journeyman after all; but then his wig— his new French wig was nature itself.

There cannot have been much illusion between the ruined gambler and the ruined demirep, but Brummell boasting of his French conquests, of the presents Lady Jersey and his other titled friends had sent him, cuts a poor figure beside his philosophical little visitor. Harriette may, as d'Aurevilly says, have envied Brummell his power over the world, but in losing his world he lost the mainspring of his life, while Harriette, battered and raffish, managed to keep some heart of a kind and a good deal of courage till the end of her days.

With her flight to France Harriette's *Memoirs* cease. But by way of *dédommagement*, as she would have put it, for her labours with her pen, she let herself go in an epilogue. This astounding production is entirely irrelevant to the preceding narrative, but it is written with tremendous gusto and must have given its author the greatest pleasure and satisfaction.

> As balmy sleep had charmed my cares to rest,
> And love itself was banished from my breast,
> A train of phantoms, in wild order, rose,
> And, joined, this intellectual scene, compose.

Methought a spirit beckoned me, from the height of a steep mountain: its drapery appeared to be now of earthly texture, and anon but the bright rays of the sun, glittering on a cloud, which enveloped the form of an angel. Her beautiful features were benignly placid. The shadowy paleness of her countenance seemed as though touched by the moon's softest beam; yet it was the bright sun, in the meridian of its splendour, and oppressed me with its heat. To ascend the vast acclivity of the mountain presented a work of such danger and fatigue that I hesitated. The spirit turned from me with an expression of tender sorrow. Its profile, which now became visible, was familiar to me! I threw myself on my knees and raised my clasped hands to heaven! 'I will endure thy sun's scorching rays, O God of Mercy!' said I, 'with the toils and

perils of this thorny road in meek resignation to thy
Divine will. Grant me but life to accomplish the
task!'

A smile now irradiated the features of the beautiful vision. Hope, doubt, and anxiety were blended
in its expression, while the calm of angels' happiness prevailed, as though the spirit had passed the
ordeal of human sufferings. She pointed with her
right hand to the heavens; and as she raised her
eyes in the same direction, I saw a seraphic, radiant
smile illumine her countenance for an instant, and
then the figure was indistinctly veiled by the clouds,
into which, gradually blending, it receded from
my sight into thin air. My tears now fell in despondency at the dangers and labour of the task I
had undertaken; yet I toiled on with indefatigable
industry. 'Oh! for the light of thy benign countenance to cheer me on my dreary road,' said I, sighing heavily. 'Yet no! rest thou in pure eternal
happiness, unclouded by the sight of early sufferings.'

The sharp, burning stones and flints wounded
my feet and caused me extreme anguish. At length
exhausted in body though unsubdued in mind,
I sank down on the earth, hoping by a short interval
of rest, to recover my strength. Suddenly, the air
was fanned with soft refreshing breezes; the
feathered choir chanted their enlivening strains; the
trees about me were covered with ripe, delicious
fruit; luxurious repasts were profusely spread in
groves, where nymphs enjoyed the fragrant shades

or danced and gambolled in wild and careless gaiety. A lovely female, fantastically though tastefully habited, smilingly entreated me to turn from my thorny road and follow her; but gay luxury possessed no charms for one who ambitioned higher joys. Hunger, thirst, and labour, with the goal of happiness in view, were more suited to my character, nor dreamed I of merit in declining mere senseless ease. Again I prostrated myself on the earth and, pressing my hands to my burning temples, prayed for strength sufficient to keep out despondency.

The gates of pleasure now were closed upon me. My head became giddy. My lungs were oppressed, and I was sinking to the earth when I felt myself withheld by the firm grasp of someone behind me, who placed me gently on the ground and presented to my lips some fruit, which instantly revived me.

On opening my eyes I beheld at my side an aged man, whose white beard descended to his middle. 'I am called Fortitude,' said he. 'My hand alone can lead you to the summit of your wishes. We will perform our task together. Nor will I forsake you till you forsake yourself.'

Invigorated by the fruits which were presented to me by Fortitude, and comforted with the prospect of a friend to guide my trembling steps, we now continued our way along the pathless, barren track of the mountain, which seemed to mock my eagerness and retire as I advanced.

Suddenly the atmosphere was impregnated with

the odour of the Indian berry, which grew in immense quantities around me. My senses were affected by it, and a voluptuous indolence began to steal over me. My hand shrunk from the grasp of Fortitude, who continued his firm and undeviating road, frequently beckoning me to follow him. My eagerness now relaxed. My senses were overpowered, and I scarcely regretted my stern guide, when the windings of the mountain concealed him from my sight. At this time I beheld coming towards me a being of extraordinary beauty. His age might be near thirty, judging by the strong growth of a beard, which curled in rich abundance over his chin; but his dark blue eye of fire told him younger.

'I am called Passion,' said he. 'There lies your road to Peace and Happiness,' and he pointed to the height of the mountain. 'Misery is here and, though left of all when you forsake me, I scorn to complain. I deceive none but the weak and the wilful. If this bursting heart, this writhing lip speak not, leave me to the fate I deserve, and which I shall meet undismayed. Misery lies this way,' repeated Passion, tearing his luxurious hair in all the frenzy of maddened sensation, while his teeth gnawed his nether lip till the red current disfigured a mouth of unequalled loveliness. He was turning from me with rapidity.

'Stay,' said I faintly. He snatched me to his heart in all the wildness of frenzy. His heaving bosom seemed to threaten suffocation. His ardent gaze, and the liquid fire flashing from his eyes, dazzled and bewildered me. They spoke of feelings but guessed at by our softer nature; yet coloured by our sanguine minds even beyond reality. The pulsations of his heart were seen, nay, almost heard; and still he curbed the passion which was consuming him; and still he had not pressed the lip, which quivered with delicious expectation. Now with an effort almost supernatural, he threw me from him. His cheeks, late vermilion glow, were changed to the ashy paleness of death; his Herculean strength to the feebleness of infancy.

'Pursue thy happier path,' said he, in accents scarcely audible, 'nor seek thy destruction.'

I threw myself on his bosom— The delirium was succeeded by total insensibility, from which I slowly recovered, and opening my languid eyes, I beheld myself in the arms of a hideous satyr!

The fright and horror which I experienced awoke me.

Chapter IX

AUTHOR AND PUBLISHER

＊

HARRIETTE HAD to face the fact that her days as a successful courtesan were over. She had played her cards badly in the affair of Worcester. She had no longer her sisters or Julia to help her (for whatever quarrels might be raging among them, these ladies were always ready to pass on to a friend any lover not actually in use). The years of the Peninsular War and Waterloo had changed the society in which she lived. The young men about town, who had taken their duties, regimental or otherwise, very lightly, had for the most part served, and many of them with distinction, in Spain and Belgium. They were now marrying and settling down, and Harriette's part in their lives was over. It is a sinister moment in the life of a woman of pleasure when she is first obliged to accept the attentions of second-rate men, such as Meyler, and Harriette was not insensible of this, though with her usual philosophy she accepted the situation. She still had a certain glamour for a few of the younger men who had heard of her past successes, but none of them really cared for her, nor she for them. She lived sometimes in Paris, sometimes in London, writing begging letters from time to time to her old acquaintance, some of whom were generous enough to respond with bank-notes. Among these was Byron, now living in Italy. Her letters to him, some of which have luckily been preserved, are a mixture of bare-faced begging and affectionate admiration. She had already written to him, at the time when he was living in Albany, begging for his friendship and nothing more. The nature of his reply can be guessed from her next letter, in which she rated him soundly for his 'affected, prosing, stupid scrawl', adding, 'You won't recover it' (his good sense), 'till you have said to me, "I was a great beast to remind you of your humble station and of my own rank and talents".'

In spite of this rebuff she had no scruple in writing to him, in or about 1818, to ask for money, though she recognised that she had no claim on him. Byron answered her kindly, promised fifty pounds if he could spare it, and did send her a bill for a thousand francs. After this she had the grace not to persecute him for money again, but indulged herself from time to time by letting her pen have its way in long, adulatory, gossiping letters. She reminded him of their one meeting at Wattier's Masquerade, asking him, 'Are you as dark as at the Masquerade, or were you painted?' and telling him an anecdote which she herself stigmatised as 'beastly', but did not trouble to suppress. A few years later, when living at 60 rue Neuve des

Petits Champs, she drew an imaginary picture of her
old age.

Nothing, I suppose, will ever bring you to Paris,
not even your friend T. Moore—yet I *will* hope
that we shall one day (some twenty years hence)
take a pinch of snuff together before we die—and
as you watch me in my little pointed cap, *spectacles*,
bony ankles and thread stockings, stirring up and
tasting my *pot au feu*, you'll imagine Ponsonby's
Worcester's and Argyle's *Angelick Harriette*.

One of the reasons that Harriette was more than
usually in need of money was that a new and expen-
sive friend had come into her life. Her old friend,
Mr. Smith, the haberdasher, still retained his affection
for her, and she was in the habit of visiting him when
in London. One evening, on leaving his house in Oxford Street, she was walking westwards to her lodgings
when, not far from the corner of Orchard Street, she
was conscious of a gentleman dogging her footsteps.
The situation had no novelty, and Harriette quickly
fell into conversation with the unknown. Their acquaintance made rapid progress, but he would not at
first disclose his name. Harriette had never been so
struck by any man since Ponsonby. He was tall and
extremely handsome, with a large black moustache,
a sure sign at that time of the military profession.
'His bust was so high and so strikingly beautiful that
one could hardly avoid noticing it, even at the slightest glance.' Harriette had always been partial to the

military, not disdaining the militia, or even non-
commissioned ranks when regular officers were not
available. So far indeed had her partiality once carried
her that it gave serious offence to one of her protectors,
who saw her out walking with two privates.

'Zounds,' said the baronet [Sir Charles Bamp-
fylde], rearing up his spiral form, 'If the girl has
no virtue she ought to have some decent pride about
her; and so all this time I have been keeping two
huge guardsmen instead of a mistress.'

These guardsmen were possibly the 'cousins' for
whose refreshment she ran up a bill at the Southamp-
ton Arms, Camden Town. Having omitted to discharge
the bill, she was arrested on Westminster Bridge and
taken to a sponging house in St. Martin's Lane, from
which Mr. Freeling, of the Post Office, bailed her out,
receiving scant gratitude in the *Memoirs* in return.

The story, it need hardly be said, came from Julia.

For some time this glorious creature was known to
Harriette as 'Moustache' for want of a better name,
but gradually he let her know his story, or what he
chose to pass as such. His name was William Henry
Rochfort, and he claimed to be the heir to the Earldom of Belvidere, an Irish peerage. The truth was
that an Irish M.P., Robert Rochfort, married in 1736,
as his second wife, a daughter of the third Viscount
Molesworth. He was subsequently raised to the peerage as Viscount Belfield, and later as Earl of Belvidere.
In 1743 he discovered that his wife, a very hand-

some and accomplished woman was carrying on an intrigue with an unknown lover. The matter was hushed up, and her legitimate son succeeded to the title, which became extinct at his death in 1814. Rochfort founded his claim to the earldom on Lady Belvidere's adventure in 1743, but when pressed was unwilling to go into details. He held the rank of cornet, though vague as to the country in which he was commissioned, and had tried to raise troops for the South American service. A trifling matter of peculation about accoutrements had brought him within the reach of the law, and he was at present a prisoner in the Rules of the Fleet Prison. As the Rules, or the neighbourhood in which prisoners were allowed out on payment of various fees or bonds, were confined to a small area round the prison, it may be thought unusual that the cornet should be roaming Oxford Street late at night. But the discipline was lax in the extreme. At an earlier period Lord Ellenborough, as Chief Justice of the King's Bench, when appealed to for an extension of the Rules, gravely replied that he really could perceive no grounds for the application since, to his certain knowledge, the Rules already extended to the East Indies.

Rochfort preferred, with proper military pride, to call himself colonel, though Julia, with a reminiscence of Monk Lewis, spoke of him as the Rugantino of the Brothel. Be that as it may, Harriette had for the first time met her match. In spite of her detestation of the black moustaches, which Rochfort refused to remove, she became desperately enamoured of this swindling bully. He went so far as to write verses to her (one suspects him of having borrowed them) a stanza of which is subjoined.

> Say, Harriette, why has bounteous Heaven,
> To every end divinely wise,
> That finish to thy features given—
> That lustre to thy lucid eyes. . . .

The course of Harriette's love was not smooth. Rochfort treated her as she had treated her lovers, sometimes encouraging her, sometimes treating her with coldness and brutality. After a more than usually long period of desertion, Harriette went the round of the coffee-houses in the neighbourhood of the Fleet to inquire his whereabouts, but had to be satisfied with the news that he was living in company with a young woman. She then wrote to him, enclosing a lock of her hair and begging him to return to her. Day after day she waited at the window for him to come, but never did that strikingly beautiful bust turn the corner of the street. At last, late one night, a loud knock was heard at the door. Harriette rushed downstairs to her lover's arms, but found only a dirty little boy who gave her a letter and ran away. The letter contained her own lock of hair and a very uncivil communication from Rochfort's 'kept miss', to say that before return-ing the hair, which the colonel did not want, she had rolled it in the dirt and stamped on it.

In spite of these rebuffs, or perhaps because she was experiencing such treatment for the first time in her life, Harriette's devotion to Rochfort remained

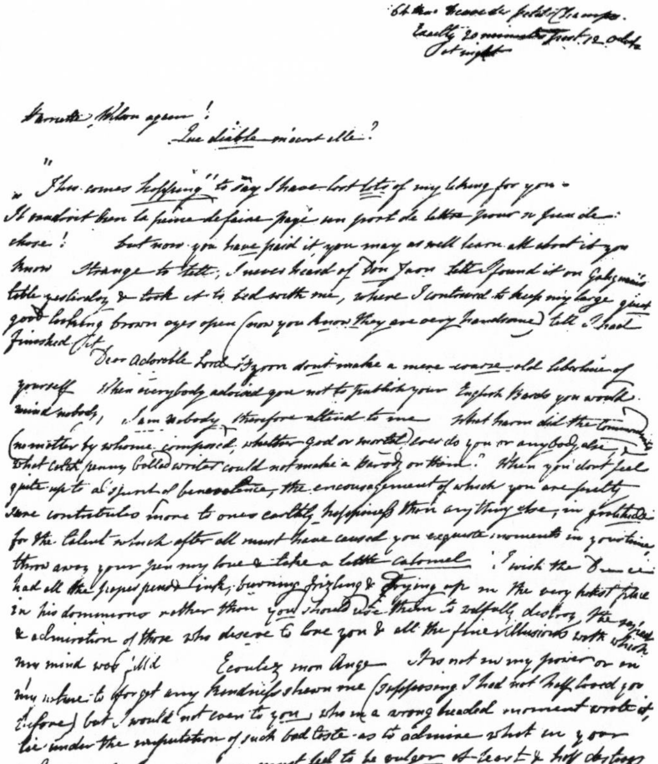

64 Rue Neuve de Petits Champs.
Exactly 20 minutes past 12 o'clock at night

Harriette Wilson again!
Que diable m'écrit elle?

"This comes hopping" to say I have lost lots of my liking for you – Il vaudrait bien la peine de faire payé un port de lettre pour si fine de chose! but now you have paid it you may as well learn all about it you know. Strange to tell, I never heard of Don Juan till I found it on Galignani's table yesterday & took it to bed with me, where I contrived to keep my large & good looking brown eyes open (now you know they are very handsome) till I had finished it.

Dear Adorable Lord Byron dont make a mere coarse old libertine of yourself. When everybody advised you not to publish your English Bards you would mind nobody; I am nobody, therefore attend to me. What harm did the Commandments (no matter by whome composed, whether god or mortal) ever do you or anybody else? & what catch penny ballad writer could not make a parody on them. When you dont feel quite up to a spirit of benevolence, the encouragement of which you are pretty sure contributes more to ones earthly happiness than anything else, in gratitude for the talent which after all must have caused you exquisite moments in your time throw away your pen my love & take a little calomel; I wish the Deuce had all the paper pens & ink, burning frizling & frying up in the very hotest place in his dominions rather than you should use them to wilfully destroy the regard & admiration of those who desire to love you & all the fine illusions with which my mind was filled. Ecoutez mon Ange. It is not in my power or in my nature to forget any kindness shewn me (supposing I had not half loved you before) but I would not even to you, who in a wrong headed moment wrote it, lie under the imputation of such bad taste as to admire what in your cool moments I am sure you must feel to be vulgar at least & half destroys the effect of the most delicious beautiful poetry you ever wrote in your life in the tit-bit.

Harriette on "Don Juan."

unchanged. His ascendancy over her was complete. She managed to pay his debts, made a Fleet marriage —a ceremony involving no binding consequences on the contracting parties—and thenceforward they lived together, chiefly in Paris, which the colonel, for reasons not unconnected with money affairs, found safer than London.

Harriette still had friends in Paris, and kept in touch with some of the officials of the English Embassy there, who obligingly let her letters go to England in the Bag. The Ambassador, Sir Charles Stuart (later Lord Stuart de Rothesay) appears to have been aware of this and raised no particular objection. The regulations as to the use of the Bags to and from the Foreign Office were very slack, and depended largely on the particular Ambassador or Minister in charge.

Harriette now had two to support, for the colonel's dignity would not allow him to take up any trade or profession, so she began to cast about for fresh ways of getting money. In 1823 she discovered Lord Byron's 'Don Juan', and in all seriousness took up her pen to rebuke him for being immoral and spoilt.

64 Rue Neuve des petits Champs
Exactly 20 minutes past 12 o'clock at night.

Harriette Wilson again!

Que diable m'ecrit elle?

'This comes hopping' *to say I have lost* lots *of my liking for you—Il vaudroit bien la peine de faire*

*payé un port de lettre pour si peu de chose! but now
you* have *paid it, you may as well learn all about it,
you know. Strange to tell, I never heard of* Don Juan
*till I found it on Galignani's table yesterday and took
it to bed with me, where I contrived to keep my large*
quiet *good-looking brown eyes open (now you* know
they are very handsome) till I had finished it. Dear
adorable *Lord Byron,* don't *make a mere* coarse *old
libertine of yourself. . . . I wish the Deuce had all the
paper pens and ink burning frizling and drying up in
the very hotest place in his dominions rather than* you
*should use them to wilfully destroy the respect &
admiration of those who deserve to love you & all the
fine illusions with which my mind was fill'd.*

In spite of her disapproval the idea of making some
money out of 'Don Juan' occurred to her, and she
wrote to Lord Byron that she proposed to make a
translation of the poem 'in a sort of new *stile* of French
blank versification.' But though she went so far as
to say that the translation was 'comming out with
great solemnity,' no more was heard of it. She had
hit upon a plan which would bring her in all the
money she needed—almost enough for the colonel's
wants—money which could be earned simply by 'sitting in an easy-chair at No. 111, in the rue du Faubourg St. Honoré, à Paris, writing not for the benefit
of my readers, but for my own amusement and profit
to boot.'

There was in Piccadilly a publishing house founded
by one John Stockdale in or about 1780. His son,

John Joseph Stockdale, was a man of amazing industry. He edited and largely wrote newspapers, published books and prints, wrote and spoke on every kind of question and every possible occasion, associated himself with the London Protestant Club and the Society for the Suppression of Vice, and was entirely unscrupulous. His reputation was at first a good one. He set up as a bookseller on his own account, at 41 Pall Mall, leaving the business in Piccadilly to his brother and sister. He was associated with a patriotic newspaper called the *True Briton and Porcupine*, whose motto was '*Nolumus Leges Angliae Mutari*'. He published a number of such respectable compilations as a *History of Gustavus Adolphus*, *Sketches of all the French Invasions of Britain*, *History of the Campaign preceding the Convention of Cintra*, and an *Abridgement of All the Sciences*.

This perfectly sound and respectable character brought him a strange customer. In 1810 young Mr. Percy Shelley, not yet an undergraduate of Oxford, wished to publish a volume of verse. This he had printed by a small printer at Worthing, whom he found himself unable to pay. He therefore called upon Mr. Stockdale and asked him to take over the stock and do what he could with it. Stockdale, knowing Shelley to be the son of a wealthy man, with expectations, consented—partly, it would appear, won over by the young man's personal charm—and in September, 1810, *Original Poems by Victor and Cazire* was published by J. J. Stockdale, 41 Pall Mall.

The correspondence which ensued may be read in

Hogg's and other lives of Shelley, and in Stockdale's own words. The original poems turned out to be in part borrowed or plagiarised; Stockdale mentioned this fact to Shelley, whom most of his biographers are unable to defend from deliberate lying in this case, and the volume was withdrawn. Undeterred by this, Shelley offered Stockdale a novel called *St. Irvyne; Or, The Rosicrucian.* This was published in the following year at the author's own cost and risk, after having been 'fitted for the press' by Stockdale. It was so unlike Stockdale to undertake any enterprise in which he did not see money, that only two explanations are possible. Either he counted on the poet's father and grandfather to back the speculation, or he was genuinely carried away by Shelley's enthusiasm.

The unpleasant, exalted, Evangelical side of Stockdale's nature, coupled doubtless with a desire to be in the rich Shelleys' good graces, now caused him to take a step extremely irritating to his young client. He took it upon him to write to Mr. Timothy Shelley about his son's works, saying that he was 'rendered extremely uneasy respecting Mr. Shelley's religious, or indeed irreligious sentiments'. Mr. Shelley at once called on Stockdale at his shop. Stockdale accused Hogg of being the corrupter of the young writer, and in his own words 'converted Mr. Timothy Shelley to sanctity', which sanctity caused the father to write one of his more violent and offensive letters to his very trying son. Mrs. Stockdale, always a most industrious scavenger for her husband, collected from some relations who lived near Hogg's family, such details about

his life and modes of thought as might be most useful
to her husband. Further letters were exchanged between Mr. Shelley, young Shelley, Hogg and Stockdale, as the result of which 'all concerned', says Stockdale with great surprise, 'became inimical to me'.

Shelley's bill for his novel was never paid. He
offered a series of moral and metaphysical essays instead, but these were not accepted. 'What degradation,' wrote Stockdale fifteen years later, 'and self-
abasement might have been spared to the widowed
wife and fatherless orphans who perhaps, at last, may
be indebted to my brief memoirs for the only ray of
respect and hope which may illumine their recollections of a father when they have attained an age for
reflection, and shed a gleam of ghastly light athwart
the palpable obscurity of his tomb.' Exactly how
Stockdale might have prevented this degradation is
not made clear, but he was a perfect Rosicrucian in
nobility of language and complete obscurity of sense.

Stockdale, for his misfortune, was of a violent and
quarrelsome disposition and a very poor man of affairs.
Under his direction the business fell into financial
straits and he was bankrupt more than once. To re-
deem his credit he took up the shadier side of publishing, and the business began to bear a dubious
reputation. Nor did he by this step greatly increase
his income, if we are to judge from his description in
the Trade Directory as 'Bookseller and Coal-mer-
chant.' From Pall Mall he moved to 24 Opera Colonnade, one of a row of shops under the arcade on the
north side of the Opera House, in Charles Street, and

from this address he issued various erotic, or to say
the least of it, suggestive works, under the pseudonymous editorship of Thomas Little, a name which he
borrowed unblushingly from Thomas Moore as a
suitable name for amatory writings. The mention of a
few of his publications between 1825 and 1830 will
show the kind of literature in which he dealt.

> *Secret Memoirs and Love Letters of G. H. Ames,*
> *Esq., Banker, and Mrs. Penfold; comprising*
> *Naughty Occurrences in numerous families; Bank-*
> *conveniences and Anecdotes and names of Visitors*
> *to the Minor Key. One Vol. 7s. 6d.*

> *Marlborough Gems* [these were love-letters pur-
> porting to be from the Duke of Marlborough to
> Fanny Davies], *Bristol Gems, New Art of Love,*
> *School for Reverends, Beauty and Marriage Sys-*
> *tems, Robertson's Generative System,* all by Thomas
> Little.

The works by Thomas Little were probably by various hands. One much advertised work, *The Oxonian,*
it is just possible to read. It is a dull mixture of flowery
moral rhetoric, Greek and Latin quotations of an
obvious kind, boring philosophical reflections, and
thoroughly coarse descriptions of the passions of love
and sea-sickness. It seems sufficiently obvious from the
style of 'Thomas Little' that the pseudonymous gentleman was not, as was sometimes stated, the author of
Harriette Wilson's *Memoirs.* He has a heavy manner,

and there is none of what Sir Walter Scott called a 'good retailing of conversation.' That he, or Stockdale in his name, 'edited' Harriette's work in the sense that he improved the spelling and punctuation, and made some additions, is doubtless true; that he actually wrote them, impossible.

Stockdale also published prints of a scandalous nature. In fact, as Lord Glenbervie wrote of him in his journal: 'He unfortunately did not improve in respectability as he advanced in life.'

To this honest tradesman Harriette sent the first part of the MS. of a book she had been writing about her own past life and that of her friends. In it Stockdale at once saw a very lucrative *succés de scandale*. He and Harriette put their heads together and decided on a plan of campaign. Communications were sent to various people whose names figured in the book, telling them that they would find themselves unmercifully quizzed in a forthcoming work by Miss Wilson, and suggesting that a cash payment would prevent unpleasantness. Some took alarm and paid up at once: and to Harriette's credit it must be said that she is not known to have gone back on her word. Whoever paid was safe—and moreover stood a chance of being publicly praised for liberality in the next edition. Some blustered. Fred Lamb, as before mentioned, 'threatened death and destruction,' but would not pay. Wellington—so Harriette said—wrote to threaten a prosecution (a different story from 'Publish and be d–d'), which gave her an opening for some very fine moral sentiments.

I do not mean to say that Wellington threatened to hang me in so many words: but honestly, it was something to say the least, not very unlike it: viz., it assumed the questionable shape of— The prosecution might take a different turn from the circumstance of my having written to him stating that I would certainly publish some anecdotes from real life to try to get paid for them in case my tender lover refused me some small assistance to procure a little bread and cheese or so. Of course it could never enter the brain of anyone save that of stupidity personified to conceive that so great a man as Wellington ever did anything whatever of which he was the least ashamed or minded my publishing. Nevertheless, since he has threatened to bring forward my soft epistles, in which I remember I wrote that old frights like himself who could not be contented with amiable wives but must run about to old procuresses, bribing them to decoy young girls who are living in perfect retirement in Duke's Row, Somers Town, and not dreaming of harm, ought to pay us for the sacrifice they tempt us to make, as well as for our secrecy. However, all I entreat of my late tenderly enamoured wooer is that he forthwith fulfil his threat and produce these said letters in court: and, lest a small trifle of hanging should be the result, but whether of him or me is yet to be seen, I'll e'en make my will, and so good-bye to ye, old Bombastes Furioso. If all the lords and law-givers are like Wellington, in the habit of threatening poor devils of authors and booksellers with prosecution, hanging, and destruction as often as they are about to publish any facts which do not altogether redound to their honour and glory, while they modestly swallow all the *outré* applause which may be bestowed on their luck or their talents for killing men and winning battles, I can no longer be surprised that even Beaufort has maintained his good character up to this present writing, since publishers will quake when heroes bully.

There's no spirit nowadays.

Negotiations with Stockdale were going well, money was beginning to come in, when a change of ambassadors in Paris was responsible for a slight hitch in Harriette's affairs. In the autumn of 1824 Sir Charles Stuart was transferred to another post, and his place taken by Lord Granville Leveson-Gower, now Viscount Granville. Lord Granville, a good if lazy diplomat, spoilt in his youth by the universal adoration of women, was celebrated for his haughty demeanour in public, the result of shyness with inferiors, boredom with most people, and a very good opinion of himself. 'Quite buckram,' was a friend's description of him, and Canning, when Foreign Secretary, found it necessary to write semi-officially to him, warning him against the 'hauteur' which offended his colleagues and other diplomats. When he took over the Paris Embassy he found much to annoy him. His predecessor was huffed at being removed from Paris, to which he felt he had a prescriptive right (and to which he returned before long) and took his revenge rather childishly by leaving the Embassy Hotel in as uncomfortable a state as possible. Indeed a good deal of Lord Granville's official correspondence at this time deals more with the dilapidation at the Embassy and his annoyance with Stuart than with international affairs. With an already irritated temper he began to inquire into the transmission of letters to and from England and found that, through the slackness of his predecessor, the attachés and minor officials were allowing their friends to abuse the privilege of the Bag. Among the entirely unauthorised users of this cheap and useful method of postage was Harriette Wilson, or Madame Rochfort, as she sometimes liked to be called, who by the courtesy of a friend corresponded freely with her publisher at the expense of the Government. Apart from the general impropriety of this misuse of the Bag Lord Granville was naturally annoyed to find that the woman who had once made a fool of him at Somers Town, who had so nearly wrecked the peace and happiness of his sister, the Duchess of Beaufort, by her pursuit of Lord Worcester, was among the chief offenders. Harriette coolly wrote to him to suggest that he should help her to get over the loss of her 'late kind friend' Sir Charles Stuart, by continuing to allow her letters to go by the Bag. Lord Granville, quite buckram at this suggestion, wrote to her, or had written to her, a formal note saying that the regulations of the Foreign Office did not allow it.

To which I replied:

MY LORD,

I was looking about for a fool to fill up my book, and you are just arrived in Paris in time to take the place, for which I am indebted to you.

Yours obliged and obediently,

HARRIETTE WILSON.

It was obviously impossible for Lord Granville to make a public report on this subject, without provoking an unnecessary amount of scandal, so he wrote Canning a private letter, complaining of the annoyance to which he was being subjected. Joseph Planta, the permanent under-secretary of state, replied to him on Canning's behalf as follows:—

FOREIGN OFFICE.

Nov. 30th, 1824.

Private and Confidential.

MY DEAR LORD GRANVILLE,

On the subject of your excellency's Bag, on which I hear from Mr. Canning you have some difficulties, allow me to send you the copy of a Letter which, soon after Mr. Canning came into this office, I wrote to Sir Charles Stuart—for his guidance. On such a subject a good deal must naturally be left to your excellency, but if you are pleased to consider the enclosed as the instruction of the Foreign Office on the question, I think you will be saved much inconvenience and annoyance. We can address a similar letter to your lordship if you like it.

*Soon after this letter was written—we heard that
Sir Chs. Stuart acted so violently upon it as to refuse
even the common letters of many families of such
Rank and Situation as fairly to entitle them to the
Privilege in question. I therefore addressed to him the
Letter No. 2, and that induced him, I suppose, to go
back nearly into the old errors.*

*Your excellency will, no doubt, pursue rather a mid-
dle course—keeping, however, to the* Letter *of our
first Instruction, whenever you think it advisable to
do so. . . .*

Ever your obliged Servant,

JOSEPH PLANTA.

Sir Charles Stuart, with his rather childish show of
temper, does not come well out of this episode, but
Lord Granville had got the instructions that he wanted.
Harriette was not the only offender, though the tres-
passes of others were only dragged in as an excuse for
getting rid of her. There were such complaints of the
size and number of the parcels that Lady Holland was
receiving from Paris by the Bag, that semi-official rep-
resentations were made about her from London to
Paris at about the same time.

Harriette and Stockdale made a determined effort
to keep their lines of communication open at the London end, through Lord Francis Conyngham, whom she
had known in Paris and for whom she professed in
her *Memoirs* to feel 'somewhat of the tenderness of a
mamma.' Writing to Byron about 1818 she said:

I have made a new conquest lately—Lord Francis Conningham; but I hate boys, so I have been setting him to hunt and pull out my grey hairs to destroy his Illusions; *he found ten and I did not know I had* one. *'Better get a* Monkey, *you'll say, than a fine young* blue *eyed man of one and twenty. What a fool he must be!'*

Unfortunately for Harriette, this young admirer had been appointed under-secretary at the Foreign Office, where he worked with Joseph Planta. The two men were friends, and Planta was devoted to Canning. Also Lord Francis had married in the beginning of 1824, and was not in the least anxious to be claimed as a friend of Harriette Wilson's. Lord Granville was determined, Canning's instructions were precise, Lord Francis was only too glad to be out of the whole affair, so, much as Harriette and Stockdale might rage, their letters henceforward had to go by post in the ordinary way, the whole affair being stigmatised by Stockdale as a 'disgusting, un-English—and mean abuse of power.'

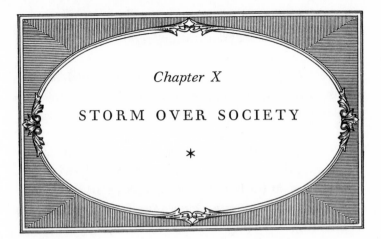

Chapter X

STORM OVER SOCIETY

*

ALL WAS now in train. Stockdale, who had a genius
for publicity, had so well spread abroad the fame
of his wares that on the day, early in January,
1825, when the first weekly part of the *Memoirs* was
issued, a large crowd besieged the little shop in its
eagerness to get copies and he was forced to barricade
his windows. The parts were sold in paper covers, and
at the end of each was an advertisement of the names
of the people to be mentioned in the next number, thus
giving them another chance of buying themselves off.
Stockdale at the same time took occasion to advertise a
new print, of which he had great hopes: 'The Magnificent Painting of the Redemption of Coventry by
the Countess Godiva, taken from the history of that interesting occurrence by Thomas Little, Esq., as detailed in his Beauty, Marriage-Ceremonies and Intercourse of the Sexes in all Nations.' The artist, Joseph,
or Giuseppe Reina, was a Swiss painter of historical

scenes and theatrical decorations, and the picture itself was in Stockdale's possession.

The *Age*, whose leader-writer belonged to the Eatanswill School, took occasion to mention the picture in a disparaging manner:

> This most disgusting and indecent painting has been, and now is, exhibited by the reptile who purchased it, at his bagnio in the Opera Colonnade, and we need not tell our readers that the sole object in effecting this purchase has been to entice young men of fashion to see it, and by tampering their appetites with a lustful style, to induce them to purchase, at an exorbitant price, the engravings taken from it.

Of this interesting print no copies seem to have survived.

Edition followed edition of the *Memoirs* to the number of thirty-five or more in a year; though the word 'edition' must be taken with due caution, as having very little reference to any actual number of copies. To judge by the newspapers of the period, the noise made by the *Memoirs* was prodigious, nor are there wanting references to them in private letters. As early as January 25th, 'Poodle' Byng, so called from his curly hair and his dogs, an old acquaintance of Harriette's, now at the Foreign Office, wrote to Lord Granville in Paris:

'Perhaps you may find time to read this trash ★—

*heard of it you must—it has caused sensation here and
is almost as much talked of as the Mining Shares and
other money Speculations in which the whole town
seem to have embarked with perfect madness. . . .*

*This Publication which I now send you is a sad
black-guard mischievous thing. She says she has forty
to come out. In the next there is to be the D. of
Worcester—and very caustic she intends it to be—tell
me if you chuse me to send it to you? Like most other
people I suppose you like to see what is said of your
relations. . . .*

*They say that there has been a meeting at Brooks's
at which it was determined that nothing in the way of
opposition could be done and that McKintosh proposed
that they should [not?] advertise for a grievance.*

* Not my letter but H. Wilson's Memoirs.'

Again in August he wrote to Granville, not without
some malice :

*I send you some more trash of Harriette Wilson's—
it is too dull to read almost. But as honourable mention
is made of you—it will have more interest in your
eyes.*

Early in February Lord Montagu had written to
Sir Walter Scott mentioning the *Memoirs*. The whole
Cabinet, he said, were reading them, because one member (probably Lord Bathurst, then Secretary for War
and the Colonies, whose name does not, however, appear in any scandalous connection) had been men-

tioned. Canning had said that they were very clever; Lord Melville, on the contrary, had told him that they were very dull.

'I am impatient,' was Scott's answer on February 18th, 'to see Harriot Wilsons biography and have sent an order for it accordingly. I remember (what I trust in Providence she has forgotten) that I had some 25 years ago the honour of supping with the fair authoress, not tête à tête, however, but vis-à-vis, at one of the evening parties of Matt. Lewis where the company was sometimes chosen in that genre. I wont give a hundred guineas, however, to be struck out of the catalogue. I remember she was ugly—remarkably witty—and her society men courted for her mental [rather] than [her] personal accomplishments. At that time she had a sister Lady Berwick who had whitewashed herself and cut Harriot. This was not to be forgiven and as both had boxes at the opera & Harriots was uppermost she had now and then an opportunity of revenging herself by spitting on her sister's head. It is impossible but that the work must be delicious scandal and I will bet on Canning's side without having seen a letter of it.'

There is a further allusion to the *Memoirs* in Sir Walter Scott's journal, towards the end of the year, interesting as showing the truth of her sketches of the dandies of the aristocracy and army, among whom and upon whom she had lived. Several of her former friends were well known to Scott, who was enjoying their discomfiture.

'The gay world has been kept in hot water lately by

the impudent publication of the celebrated Harriot Wilson, who lived with half the gay world at hack and manger, and now obliges such as will not pay hush-money with a history of whatever she knows or can invent about them. She must have been assisted in the style, spelling, and diction, though the attempt at wit is very poor, that at pathos sickening. But there is some good retailing of conversations, in which the style of the speakers, so far as known to me, is exactly imitated, and some things told as said by individuals of each other which will sound unpleasantly in each other's ears. I admire the address of Lord A—y [Alvanley], himself very severely handled from time to time. Someone asked him if H.W. had been pretty correct on the whole. "Why, faith," he replied, "I believe so" —when, raising his eyes, he saw Quentin Dick, whom the little jilt had treated atrociously—"what concerns the present company always excepted, you know," added Lord A—y, with infinite presence of mind. As he was *in pari casu* with Q.D. no more could be said. After all, H.W. beats Con Philips, Anne Bellamy, and all former demireps out and out. I think I supped once in her company, more than twenty years since, at Mat Lewis's in Argyle Street, where the company, as the duke says to Lucio, chanced to be "fairer than honest." She was far from beautiful, if it be the same *chiffonne*, but a smart, saucy girl, with good eyes and dark hair, and the manners of a wild schoolboy. I am glad this accidental memory meeting has escaped her memory —or, perhaps, is not accurately recorded in mine— for, being a sort of French falconer, who hawk at all they see, I might have had a distinction which I am far from desiring.'

What Harriette Wilson would have made of Sir Walter Scott is a thing imagination boggles at.

On February 14th a debate was going on in the House of Commons on the Unlawful Societies (Ireland) Bill—a subject sufficiently far removed from Harriette Wilson, one would think. Dr. Stephen Lushington, a strong reformer and ardent churchman, member for Ilchester and later a distinguished judge, was inspired to say that if the rules which it was proposed to employ against the Irish Clubs and Associations were put into force against some English societies, it would be fatal to many of the highest standing.

He would merely allude to what could be established against a Club of which the Right Hon. the Secretary for the Home Department, (Mr. Peel), was a member. He would name it—it was the University Club (hear, hear). What if it should appear from the recorded proceedings of that very club that two such entries as he should state were inserted: 'The Memoirs of Harriette Wilson, ordered' (continued laughter) —'A plain Bible, rejected' (hear, hear). What were the prominent features in the Memoirs he did not pretend to know, but from what he understood, they very particularly concerned many noble Lords and many Hon. members in that House (hear).

This very disingenuous attack was countered on the

following day by Mr. Bankes, member for Cambridge, and a member of the University Club, who indignantly denied the charge, and said that no such book had been ordered, though he understood that it had been frequently asked for. He also wished to make it clear that he was not a reader of such books.

On the previous Sunday *Bell's Life in London*, a Sunday paper of a sporting and gossiping turn,—the same paper in which Captain Macmurdo was reading about the fight between the Tutbury Pet and the Barking Butcher when Rawdon Crawley called at Knightsbridge Barracks to ask him to carry a challenge to Lord Steyne—printed an instalment of the *Memoirs*. 'First Serial Rights' are nothing new, but it is improbable that either Stockdale or Harriette ever got a penny from *Bell's Life*, which freely used the *Memoirs* as its leading article from February to September.

Bell's Life combined very happily the most scurrilous personal attacks with a fiction that it was acting in the best interests of the public as a *censor morum*.

'A bookseller in the Arcade, Pall Mall—we believe a member of the Society for the Suppression of Vice,' so run its introductory remarks, 'but certainly a great strickler [*sic*] for Church and State—is now publishing a work in numbers which has excited an extraordinary sensation in the beau monde. The lady is, or was, a courtezan, and professes to write, not only the memoirs of herself, but of others, including those of her three sisters who it would seem had chosen a similar frank and professional line of conduct. What renders the work most remarkable is, the circumstance of the open mention of the cavaliers who had the felicity of her ladyship's acquaintance. It is written with sprightliness, and as it affords a peep behind the Curtain of "Life in London", we shall give a few extracts.'

On Sunday, February 27th, after a further instalment of the *Memoirs*, there is a parody of Collins's 'Ode to the Passions'. After several references, coarse and undisguised, to her various admirers, it ends:

> Oh, Harriette, Peer-descended maid,
> Friend of Pleasure, Stockdale's aid,
> Why, oh why, to us denied,
> Wilt thou lay thy pen aside?
> In London's city many a day,
> Thou hadst an all-commanding sway:
> Thy memory keeps thy foes in awe,
> And well recalls what then it saw!
> 'Tis said, and I believe the tale,
> Thy charms with Saints could once prevail,
> And that thy true instinctive page
> Points out the reptiles of the age.
> Now, all at once, together bound,
> They strive to stop the fearful sound,
> And have engag'd, not over nice,
> The fam'd Society for Vice.
> Oh, bid their vain endeavours cease
> And let thy volumes still increase!
> Expose hypocrisy and cant,
> And show the world 'tis all you want!

The 'Saints' is an allusion to the Methodist and anti-slavery connection, especially to Butterworth, the member for Dover, friend of Wilberforce and the elder

Macaulay, who had been unfortunate enough to get his name involved with Harriette's in the gossip of the time. Allusions to him in this connection abound in the less reputable papers.

The 'Society for Vice', or more correctly the Society for the Suppression of Vice, was also an offshoot of the Evangelical Movement. It was founded about 1802 with a very strong committee, including the Bowdlers, Hatchard the bookseller, Zachary Macaulay, and the Rev. Charles Simeon. Its objects were to prevent such vices as the Profanation of the Lord's Day, Blasphemous Publications and Obscene Books and Prints, Illegal Dances, and Cruelty to Animals. In 1825 a further list of members includes Sir T. Dyke Acland, Eton College and the Rev. J. Keate, the headmaster, Mrs. Hannah More and William Wilberforce. By this time snuff-boxes had been added to the list of offences which it caused to be punished, the reason for including these apparently innocent articles being that they often had 'indecent and obscene engravings, highly finished,' inside the lids, and had a 'large and ready market in Boarding Schools for Young Ladies.'

Stockdale is known to have offered himself for membership, but his name is not among the members for 1825. The Society was in existence as late as 1875, when it induced Messrs. Bell and Son to withdraw the Bohn's Library Edition of Rabelais, causing a protest from Swinburne.

If *Bell's Life* felt that it was doing good to the world by publishing Harriette's story, it was a delusion which her publisher fully shared. In a postscript to one of the many editions of the *Memoirs* he expressed himself as follows:

Comparisons are odious, says some saw or adage, therefore, without comparing Harriette Wilson to any of her predecessors, it is due to her from me, her editor, to say that she first introduced order and decorum into the world of fashion, that she reformed and improved the great world, that she established regulations among which was one, that no man should be introduced into her world who had not first been presented to her, and another, that due homage should be paid to her in all public places.

She has drawn within the influence of her dominions great and celebrated characters, whether by the charm of her conversation, the sprightliness of her manners, by the glare of her beauty, by the sweet tone of her voice. . . . It may be attributed to her, as to Orpheus, who as we all recollect, by the power of his music tamed wild beasts and monsters of every kind, that were all obedient to his voice; not that I mean to insinuate that her lovers were wild beasts and monsters, until they were drawn into the vortex of her numerous attractions and then became humanised and polished.

She has just right to rank with the very few impartial and fearless historians of their own times; but she has also the higher claim of having conferred on the moral state of society in Europe, such a benefit as is I believe without parallel.

I shall for the present take my leave, after un-
sparing congratulations on the success of these
Memoirs and on *their moral effects on society and
manners throughout the civilised world*, a consum-
mation which will be assisted in no small degree by
the series of prints, of which the publication has already commenced, and which, I cannot hesitate to
affirm, are entirely unrivalled in this or in any
other country.

Nor was Harriette herself backward in her own
praise.

Now, she exclaims, we are the two greatest people in Europe! Scott in his way, I in mine! Every
thing which comes after us will be but base copies.

Stockdale's fluency, with the tongue or the pen, can
only be described as appalling. On the faintest pretext, or on no pretext at all, he ran into thousands of
words, closely printed pages, or unquenchable oratory.
He combined the less agreeable characteristics of the
demagogue and the tub-thumping dissenter, and was
apt to break out into a high strain of religious and
verbose fervour which sat very ill upon him. Harriette
also had a tendency to these religious outbursts, and
the last recorded publication of hers is a lay sermon
which, if it were not absurd, would be almost blasphemous. It may be this side of her which is responsible
for an otherwise entirely unsupported statement that
she died 'a pious widow.'

The whole law of copyright was in a very loose state, and every publisher had to face a certain amount of pirating against which he was almost helpless. Stockdale was no exception. *Bell's Life* calmly appropriated the earlier part of the *Memoirs*. Some publishers at once rushed out copies of the *Memoirs* and sold them as originals, while others printed small instalments and had them hawked about as broadsheets. Sir Richard Birnie, the magistrate at Bow Street, had given orders to take up hawkers selling the *Adventures of Harriette Wilson*. On March 14th two of his officers brought in a miserable half-starved boy whom they had found in the gateway of New Inn, offering pamphlets for sale and holding a placard saying that they were 'The whole of the Amorous letters from Harriette Wilson to the King, Duke of Wellington and other noblemen.' The boy said he was an apprentice shoemaker, and that business was so bad that his master often sent him out to hawk papers and bring in an honest shilling or two. The report in the *Times* stated that Stockdale had evidently not ventured to institute legal proceedings for the maintenance of his exclusive right to so shocking a publication, and that a number of penny and twopenny numbers of the *Memoirs* were being sold in the streets. After an argument as to the possibility of prosecuting, it was found that the poor boy could be detained only for hawking without a licence, and the magistrates dismissed him. Stockdale at once flew into half a column of small print in the *Times* in his own defence, but succeeded in saying absolutely nothing.

A facetious correspondent wrote to the papers under the heading:

To Heads of Families and Other Suppression People

[This was a hit at the Society for the Suppression of Vice.]

We are delighted to be able to inform our readers on the most undoubted authority, that an edition of the moral and instructive *Memoirs of Harriette Wilson* adapted for families and young persons, by the omission of all objectionable passages, which cannot with propriety be read aloud, by the Rev. Thomas Bowdler, F.R.S., etc., author of the Family Shakespeare, is in the press, and the true friends of undefiled morality and our holy religion may shortly expect this precious addition to their libraries.

This was only the beginning of the trouble that Harriette and her affairs were to bring upon Stockdale and others. In the same year a printer, Pollett, brought an action against him for work done and paper supplied. Pollett stated that at the beginning he contracted to print 1,000 sheets a week, but 'such was the prurient taste of the town' that 17,000 a week were shortly called for. The unfortunate plaintiff was non-suited on account of the objectionable character of the work, the responsibility for which was shared by him and Stockdale.

Early in March Mr. Edward Ellice, M.P. for Coventry, received a letter from Paris which, with some courage, he immediately communicated first to an evening paper, the *Globe and Traveller*, and then to all the daily and Sunday papers of standing.

March 8. No. 111, Rue du Faubourg St. Honoré, à
    Paris.

SIR,

People are buying themselves so fast out of my book, Memoirs of H. Wilson, *that I have no time to attend to them should be sorry not to give each a* chance, *if they* chuse *to be out. Two noble Dukes have lately taken my word, and I have never named them, I am sure—would say you might trust me never to publish, or cause to be published, aught about you, if you like to forward 200 l. directly to me, else it will be too late, as the last volume in which* you *shine, will be the property of the Edetor, and in his hands. Lord — says he will answer for aught I agree to so will my husband. Do* just *as* you *like—consult only yourself. I get as much by a small* book *as you will give me for taking you out, or more. I attack no poor men because they cannot help themselves.*

Adieu. Mind I have no time to write again as what with writing books, and then altering them for those who pay *out, I am done up*—frappé en mort.

What do you think of my French?
                Yours,
            HARRIETTE ROCHFORT LATE WILSON.
Don't trust to bag with your answer.
EDWARD ELLICE ESQ., M.P.
    NEW STREET, LONDON.

What is to be thought of Harriette's English is as much to the point. This is a favourable specimen of her style when her 'Edetor's' eye was not on her.

Harriette, already a 'best-seller'—and entirely on her own merits—beyond the dreams of authors, now found herself also a best-seller on the Continent, though it is improbable that she got any money from her Continental sales. The *Memoirs* were rapidly translated, and appeared in French in Paris and Brussels, in German at Stuttgart. They are very well translated, and include the foreword by 'Thomas Little,' which was also prefixed to the English editions. The French and German editions are not illustrated. The Brussels edition has a lithograph by Burggraf, a fairly well-known Belgian artist, taken from the portrait by Hoffay, which is prefixed to one of the English editions.

A letter written to *Bell's Life* at this time is interesting as bringing up the question of the name Wilson. This name she had adopted early in her professional career, and some people spoke of her sister as Amy Wilson, though Amy always answered to the name of her protector for the time being. It seems an easy enough name to take, but there were other insinuations afoot. The letter in question is worth quoting in part, as giving a slightly different account of Harriette's past life.

If this Lady's Memoirs had been completed she might perhaps have recollected a little dirty girl whose name was Du Bouchet, who was five-and-twenty years ago a regular tramp in St. James's Street, and the courts adjoining, being picked up by a nobleman and converted into a lady; after growing too old for any success in begging from those persons of high rank, whose names she could collect from the Court Guide *(her constant practice), she liberated a prisoner from Fleet, and set him sailing after his pretensions to an Irish peerage; if she should see this, she will know who wrote it, and perhaps I may get a round sum not to say any more. She was never handsome, though she had good eyes, but was hog-backed, narrow chested and had an awkward shuffling gait, and was not at all like the handsome portrait which is published as that of Harriette Wilson; but this can be of no consequence now, as she must be next summer in her 42nd year. But who am I who can recollect these things? Why,*

AN OLD RAKE.

South Molton Street, Grosvenor Square.

It would seem not improbable that Harriette had at one time turned down this agreeable old gentleman, whose suggestion that she should buy him off is decidedly ingenious. In another part of his letter he alludes to the *Memoirs* 'which she wrote, or were written for her, by her Ambrosial friend'.

Now, ambrosial was an epithet much in favour in certain circles as a kind of synonym of erotic; but there may have been something more behind it, for two days later a letter appeared in the *Morning Chronicle* and other papers from a certain S. Bertie Ambrosse, stated by Stockdale to have been steward to Sir

John Douglas, whose wife was involved, not credit-
ably, in Queen Caroline's affairs. This gentleman
wrote to refute indignantly any suggestion that the
word Ambrosial applied to himself. He admitted that
there had been a general report to that effect, but
averred that he had never seen nor communicated
with Miss Wilson, nor had any hand in the *Memoirs*.
He added that a novel of some notoriety called *Six
Weeks at Long's* had also been attributed to him, but
entirely without grounds.

The jokes about Ambrosial continued, however, to
circulate, and four years later, in a copy of verses
about Harriette, dealing with various names she had
borne, the stanza occurs:

> 'Next, Wilson, all know that you took;
>   'Twas given by A—br—e perhaps,
> Who wrote that most exquisite book,
>   Brimful of lies, scandals and scraps.
> The Colonel [Rochfort] denies that you bore
>   That name, and perhaps you did not,
> You certainly bear it no more—
>   The sooner the better forgot.'

This is at present an unsolved puzzle—perhaps
hardly worth insisting on, except that these persistent
rumours, like the rumour of Mr. Dubochet's relationship to Chesterfield,* have sometimes a grain of truth
that makes them worth following up.

In August *Bell's Life*, which had temporarily
dropped Harriette in favour of some even newer scandal, began to serialise the rest of the *Memoirs*. In an

* See Notes.

earlier number the editor had explained that 'many parts of the *Memoirs* are written with a warmth which, however it may suit the morals or manners of the age, does not meet our notions of propriety.' He found himself later able to reconsider this attitude, and in announcing a fresh series of extracts he explained that *Bell's Life* was doing public good, for not only did it make such extracts from the book as were *fit to read*, but by giving its readers these samples, it saved them the expense of having to buy a seven-and-sixpenny book. This was indeed a golden age for the Press.

During this year Harriette seems to have been backwards and forwards between Paris and London to interview Stockdale, though the exact occasion on which a Mrs. Graham Campbell met Harriette at Dover Pier, knocked her down and pulled her hair out, is not ascertainable, nor the reason for this violent action, though it may be suspected. While she was in London she was seen, though not acknowledged, by some of her old friends, one of whom surprised Harriette very much by coming out with a rival book. Julia Johnstone, whom Harriette says she had seen dead and almost buried, had been alive all the time; at least Julia said that she was alive, which would require some contradicting. Annoyed by Harriette's success, and the way in which her own career was described, Julia flew to her pen and wrote the *Confessions of Julia Johnstone, written by Herself in Contradiction to the Fables of Harriette Wilson*. This book, to which reference has often been made, fell perfectly flat, which must have

mortified Julia beyond expression. In truth, it deserved
to. But it has interest as giving what sounds like a
fairly accurate though unkind portrait of Harriette
Wilson at the age of thirty-nine; a portrait not unlike
the description of herself which she gave to Byron,
with her spectacles and bony ankles.

' *'Tis not many weeks since I saw this industrious
piece of capricious biography, and my visual organs
bare testimony to the correctness of my memory.*

*Imagine to yourself a little woman in a black beaver
hat and long grey cloak. No tightening at the waist to
show the figure of the wearer, nor any ornament to be
seen whatever. Her figure, at a short distance, might
not inaptly be compared to a mile-stone with a carter's
hat resting on its summit. Her once little feet are now
covered with list shoes, to defend them from attacks of
a desultory gout, which she has suffered long in both
extremities. Her face, at the time I allude to, was
swollen with this disorder to distortion. She has no colour, le couleur de rose a disparu [sic], and in its place
appears a kind of dingy lilac, which spreads all over
her once light countenance, and appears burnt into
her lips. The* crow's feet *are wide spreading beneath
her eyes; which, though sunken, still gleam with
faded lustre through her long dark eyelashes. She
bears the remains of what was once superlatively
lovely—the wreck of the angel's visage is yet to be
seen; it looks interesting in decay—not the decay
brought on by age and infirmity, but beauty hurried*

away prematurely, from the practices of a licentious and dissolute life; such is the once celebrated Miss De-bouchet, alias Wilson.'

This was Julia Johnstone's last word.

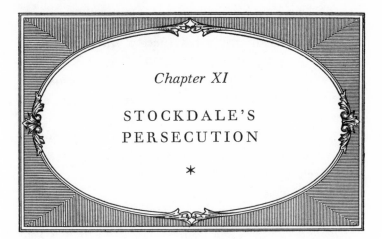

Chapter XI

STOCKDALE'S
PERSECUTION

✳

ALTHOUGH BROOKS'S, according to Poodle Byng,
had decided that Harriette's victims were power-
less against her, and would do better to leave things
alone, there was a strong general feeling that some
kind of stand must be taken. A certain Robert Blore,
a stone-mason in Piccadilly, had been made to look exceedingly foolish in the *Memoirs,* accused of having
offered marriage to Fanny Parker and speaking in the
regular Cockney way. Blore, a respectable married
man, who had known the Dubochets as children,
brought a libel action against Stockdale, tried in the
Court of King's Bench on July 10th, 1825, laying his
damages at £500. It is said that this suit was backed by
many of Harriette's other victims, but whether this is
true or not, it is certain that Stockdale was uneasy
about the matter. He had already managed to
have several bankruptcies—never, curiously enough,
through his own fault—and was not at all anxious to

lose money again after his success with Harriette's book.

The libel was clear enough. Blore had been married for many years and had a family ranging from a son of twenty to young children. A letter had been published in the *Memoirs*, purporting to be written by Fanny Parker from the Isle of Wight, parts of which have already been quoted. The passage of which Blore complained was as follows:

Apropos! Talking of vulgarity, I have had a proposal of marriage since I saw you, from Mr. Blore the stone-mason, who keeps a shop in Piccadilly. Parker says it is all my fault for being so very humble and civil to everybody; but, you must recollect, this man was our near neighbour when we were all children together, and I cannot think I had any right to refuse answering his first civil inquiry after my health, by which he no doubt thought as a man of good property and better expectations, he did me honour. Since then he has often joined me in my little rural walks in the morning. When first his conversation began to wax tender, I scarcely believed my ears. However, these soft speeches were speedily succeeded by a proposal of marriage! You know my foolish way of laughing at everything of this kind, which was what encouraged him to argue the point after I had begged to decline his polite offer.

'Look ye here, my dear lady,' said he, 'these here officers cut a splash! And it's all very well being called Mrs. Parker, and the like of that; but then it's nothing

*compared to a rale husband. Now I means onorable,
remember that.'*

I was interrupting him. *'Come, I don't ax you, my
dear, to make up your mind this morning. Marriage is
a serious kind of a thing, and I wants no woman for to
marry me till she has determined to make an industrious, good wife. Not as I should have any objection
to your taking a bit of pleasure of a Sunday, and wearing the best of everything; but at the same time, we
must stick to the main chance for a few years longer,
if ever we wishes for to keep our willa, and be raley
genteel and respectable. Not but what I've got now as
good a shay and oss as any man need to wish for, and
an ouse over my ead, full of handsome furniture, and
plenty of statters* [statues], *still I looks forward to
better things.'*

Though it is morally and physically impossible for
a woman, be she what or whom she may, to attach
herself to anything so low and vulgar as this poor Mr.
Blore, after she has acquired the taste, by the habit of
good society, still I certainly have a right to feel
obliged to any honest man who yet considers me
worthy to become his partner for life; and I could not
have said anything cross or harsh to him for the world.
You have no idea what difficulty I had in making him
believe that I would not marry him.

'There, my dear,' said he, after I had assured him,
over and over again, that I must really decline his offer.
*'There, my dear, I will leave you now. I don't want
you to decide all at once; but, remember, you must
not let what I a been a-saying about the main chance,*

frighten you; because you'll find me a very reason-
able, good-natured fellow: and as for going to the play,
if you are fond of that, I can get orders for the pit,
whenever I like.'

Harriette made no secret of the fact that she had
herself written Fanny's letter, which was all pure invention. 'As for Mr. Blore,' she wrote later, 'I certainly in my usual thoughtless way made him court
Fanny ten years too late in life. I did not know he was
married when I made him propose to Fanny, and there
is no doubt he was single when he used to court Fanny
as a very young girl.'

The unlucky Blore complained bitterly of the injury done to his domestic life and his professional connection by this statement. Stockdale, who vastly enjoyed conducting his own defence, spoke so fast that
he was at times almost inaudible to the reporters, who
nevertheless managed to give a very good account of
his speech. He said that the whole affair was most un-
expected, had taken him entirely by surprise; that he
had a sore throat, had sat up all night to prepare his
defence, and was the victim of a general conspiracy.
The *Memoirs* of Harriette Wilson had been described
in harsh terms by the learned Council for the Plaintiff; but he ventured to say that it was one of the most
important works, from its tendency to improve the
morals of society (always excepting those of divine
origin) that had ever issued from the press. He was a
poor worm of a publisher, and the object of his enemies was to destroy him.

Stockdale wished to call witnesses, including most of those men whom Harriette had made fun of, but such evidence was ruled out as inadmissible, much to his disappointment. The Lord Chief Justice summing up produced a verdict in Blore's favour, with damages £300, and £78 10s. costs.

As Stockdale had to pay, while Harriette got off scot free, there was for a short time a certain amount of feeling about the law suit; the first real rift in the pleasant and profitable relationship of these two adventurers. But business came first. Harriette had been writing a book about the visit of an English family to Paris, and Stockdale had every hope of recouping himself for his losses by its means. In September of the same year he published *Paris Lions and London Tigers*, with coloured plates, at 7/6. ('Dandies' had become 'tigers' in London and 'lions' in Paris.) It is a poor and tasteless book with none of Harriette's sparkle. In fact Thomas Little's—or Stockdale's—or, more probably, Harriette's preface, is the most amusing thing about it.

Here's a piece of pork and greens, as exclaimed a good-humoured countryman, who got into some dilemma, with his cart-horses, one day. Here's a piece of pork and greens! This comes of notoriety. No sooner had the following little volume got wind, than all the world was on the qui vive, to learn, what characters it was to contain. One got at one, and another at another, and then the last proof-sheet was dropped on its way to the printers. Thus, by degrees, several of the persons which it introduces, acquired publicity, and all the world was agog to give to airy nothings a local habitation and a name.

The London newspapers duly announced the meeting of Harriette with her publisher, at Calais. The latter had scarcely betaken himself once again to his harness, and seising [*sic*] his pen, in manful guise, at his bookselling desk, than he received an anonymous letter, *franc de poste*, from Paris, apprising him that its sagacious writer had developed many of the characters which figure on the following pages.

Harriette, tenderly sympathising with her unhappy publisher, who had not forgotten that most extraordinary verdict which had been given against him in Blore's case, and resolving to be secure against such a recurrence in future, drew on her imagination for her modern romance of *Paris Lions and London Tigers*, but neither may she nor her publisher be at rest!

His anonymous correspondent, assisted as he says by many other persons, no less *comme il faut* than himself, avows that the list hereto subjoined is a true key to the characters of this romance, as far as it goes, and Stockdale, thinking the joke too good to be altogether lost, has handed the elegant epistle to me, to turn to the best possible account.

Ecce signum! Thomas Little.

The key has little interest, as the characters in the book have no real relation to their originals. Such equivalents as Sir Violet Sigh-away for Sir Harry Mildmay, or Lord Chatterbox for the Earl of Clanricarde, can hardly be taken seriously. Harriette and her adviser were being more careful. But at the end of the key there is a delicate hint of blackmail. A number of fictitious names are mentioned as being 'in want of an owner.' In spite of this, the book fell very flat. Harriette was no writer of fiction, though as a reporter she was excellent. One point of interest is the appearance of Rochfort as Mr. Bellfield, the second title (wrongly spelt) of the Earldom of Belvidere, which he claimed. His loving Harriette paints him in glowing colours as a model of beauty and virtue.

But, as 'Thomas Little' said, neither might she nor her publisher be at rest. The persecution by enemies continued unabated. Mr. Fisher, the attorney of Lyme Regis, whom Harriette had pilloried as a black-eyed lady-killer, and accused of misinterpreting her intentions, having taken his time to consider the libel and doubtless encouraged by Blore's success, now brought another action against Stockdale. This was tried in May 1826 in the Court of Common Pleas, before the Chief Justice. Harriette's old friend, *Bell's Life in London*, enchanted at this fresh publicity, gave the case a prominent position on its front page.

Fisher v. Stockdale. This was an action against J. J. Stockdale the publisher of the *Memoirs of Harriette Wilson*, brought by a gentleman named Fisher to recover compensation in damages for the injury he had sustained by the publication of a libel in that work, imputing to him immoral habits, and intercourse with certain loose females, La Belle Harriette's acquaintance. Part of the libel consisted of a supposititious conversation between the plaintiff and certain ladies. The Lord Chief Justice animadverted very strongly on the abominable work and conduct of the defendant, in stabbing the reputation of honest persons for the sake of lucre. The Jury returned a verdict for plaintiff. Damages £700.

As Stockdale was only too ready to explain with tongue and pen, it was not so much the damages that outraged his feelings as the imputation that he had acted on any but the highest moral grounds. He also took the liberty to doubt that Mr. Fisher was himself, declaring that he had in his possession letters from Fisher under the name of Hugh Evans Fisher, of Bath, whereas in the *Memoirs* he was known as C. F. Fisher, of Lyme Regis. But as he did not go beyond vague accusations, the case stood, and the damages and costs were to be paid.

Bell's Life was now in full cry after Stockdale and Harriette. 'The celebrated Harriette Wilson,' it stated, 'arrived yesterday at the White Bear in Piccadilly, from Dover. She has not yet announced whether she will be "At Home." ' On May 8th, the Sunday following Fisher's triumph, *Bell's Life* printed a doggerel poem of some merit entitled,

ST—CKD—LE AND HARRIETTE W—LS—N

A London Eclogue.

'Twas at the hour when most agree
To take a sober cup of tea
(A very economic meal,
As sundry folks in London feel,
Who are not able to afford
Each day to sit at dinner board),
St—ckd—le and Harriette W—ls—n met.
(The Colonel too, a little wet—
His custom of an afternoon),
With recent verdicts out of tune.
To Fisher, Blore, large sums were given:—
To one *three* hundred, to t'other *seven*.
Much St—ckd—le feared lest such a sample
Make others follow the example. . . .

ST—CKD—LE

I like it not: some speedy plan
Must be adopted, or, by Heaven!
Three hundred first, and after *seven*,
Will take away all sort of profit.
You laugh! but I am certain of it,
'Twill take the gold, as has been said,
Entirely off the gingerbread.

HARRIETTE W—LS—N

Baboon! your (sic) talking nonsense. Zounds!
What is a paltry thousand pounds?
Let them proceed, but don't you pay
A single *sous* in any way.
Place on my counsel full reliance,
And set the rascals at defiance.

ST—CKD—LE

But they will send me off to jail,
If I to pay the verdict fail.

HARRIETTE W—LS—N

And let them send you, if they dare;
I'd like to see them send you, there.

ST—CKD—LE

Perhaps you would; but I may wish
You'd suffer also. Mrs. ——

HARRIETTE W—LS—N

Pish!
Why should I suffer, I who wrote,
And for *your gain*, each anecdote?
Your wish I think not only rude,
But savours of ingratitude.
If you get *into jail*, why then,
You've only to get out again;
And nothing is more easy, now,
Surely I need not tell you how.
If you don't know, the Colonel here
Can make the method plain and clear;
(I mean when he's awake) for he
With many a prison has made *free*,
And been made free of many a prison,
Therefore I say so, and with reason.

Harriette then tries to comfort Stockdale by suggesting that his new print of Godiva may recoup him for losses on the book. He says he is losing on both, although he has advertised the print as being done from Harriette herself.

HARRIETTE W—LS—N

Baboon! Impostor! Hubble-bubble!
You know my book has made you rich.

ST—CKD—LE

You lie, you most infernal ——

Kind reader, guess the word intended;
Had he his sentence fully ended.
But lovely Harriette, taking up
Her tea, just pour'd into her cup
Discharg'd it in poor St—ckd—le's face.
.   .   .   .
The Colonel with the noise awoke,
And St—ckd—le, fearful of a scrape,
Thought it more prudent to escape.
Then down *three pair*, into the street
Rushing, it was his chance to meet
A man!—but, reader, don't turn pale if
I mention that it was a bailiff:
Producing a long slip of parchment
He shew'd him what the word *to march* meant;
Then took him—but you do not care,
If to the Devil, or elsewhere.

For these verses Fisher managed to get damages
against Clement the proprietor and editor of *Bell's
Life,* but he would have done better to leave matters
alone.

There now began the period always alluded to by
Stockdale as 'Stockdale's Persecution.' The general
conspiracy to crush the worm was in full swing, but
though it succeeded in ruining him for the time being
in a worldly sense, Stockdale, like other victims of general conspiracies, throve upon it morally and found
himself able to forgive and pray for the adversaries
with unction and freedom. The author of the *London
Eclogue* may have meant the end of his poem in jest,
but it was very near the facts. After Fisher's successful

action in 1826, Stockdale had to pay not only £700 damages, but in addition £105 10s. taxed costs. The righteous man, living in the bosom of his family at Winter House, Acton, and conducting a blameless business at 24 Opera Colonnade, suddenly found himself—as had often, and always inexplicably, happened before—in that unpleasant position where liabilities are greater than assets. He was also deep in a quarrel with his landlord, Mr. Winter, on the subject of trespassing cattle, straying poultry, broken hedges, and worst of all the question of a field of potatoes. His courage and cheerfulness, his energy in writing long offensive letters, were unbounded. If it is permissible to compare a publishing worm with so great and good a man as Mr. Micawber, one might find points of resemblance between them. Stockdale's trust that something would turn up, his invariable surprise at his money difficulties, his indignation with his wife's family who did not see their way to advancing small sums, his lofty language, his inability to keep away from pen and ink, his devotion to an equally devoted wife and children, are all in the best tradition. When he speaks of his family it is in a strain that Wilkins Micawber himself might have envied.

Mrs. Stockdale is the mother of six children, who are living. The oldest of these, a male, is now in his twentieth year; the youngest, a female who has not yet entered her second year. I am better known than represented, and most of those who are loudest in my censure, know that they are liars to their own consciences. Mrs. Stockdale, as a wife and a mother, equally defies their censure, and contemns their praise. My children, according to their ages, would confer dignity and lustre on all that is good, and noble, and amiable in the country, and I will add, however I may be charged by the ignorant, with partiality and presumption, that they would grace the royal court itself. The conduct of my grossly persecuted and oppressed family would have done no dishonour to the proudest annals of Imperial Rome.

Of Stockdale's other side, it is enough to say that Chadband, Stiggins, and Uriah Heep exist to show what religious hypocrisy can be; and Stockdale was equal to all three.

Upon this devoted little family, with four maid-servants, the persecutors were about to descend. Having made no attempt to meet his obligations, Stockdale was not unnaturally shocked and surprised to receive one day when at his shop a warning that Fisher was about to put in an execution. Begging for a little time, he hurried by coach to Acton to break the news to Mrs. Stockdale, 'now for the twenty-second time in the family way' [of the fate of the other fifteen nothing is known], fearing that the shock might endanger her health. Fortified by religious faith and a complete want of understanding, she received the news with such serenity that her husband felt strength given him to return to town. Here he found that his chaise and horse, which he had stabled as was his custom at the

White Bear in Piccadilly, had already been seized in execution. Returning to Acton by coach again as swiftly as possible he found a man in possession of Winter House. The furniture was already being removed; the piano, an instrument to which his daughters were extremely partial, was so roughly handled that its silk front was burst in getting it downstairs; the beer and wine were being driven away in a carriage with the blinds drawn. Three straw mattresses were all that was left for a family including nine females. His son Miah begged for his canary. The ruffians in charge allowed the boy to keep his pet, but his childish plea for a dog, a quantity of poultry, and a pig, was brutally refused. Stockdale at once took up his pen and wrote to a maiden lady with whom he had no acquaintance, asking her to take his two elder daughters in any capacity for a small salary. To the eternal dishonour of maiden ladies at Acton, she refused.

On returning once more to town, a horrid scene met his eye. The sheriff's officers were now in possession of his shop, and a sale by auction was announced to take place. All his books, pictures, and prints were to be put up for sale, including the 'magnificent national picture of the Redemption of Coventry by the Countess Godiva'. Even at the auction the hideous machinations of his enemies pursued him. 'A friend on whom I had relied to bid for the family became so paralysed, perhaps from intensity of feeling, that his voice could not be heard.' Godiva, that national picture, for which Stockdale asserts that he had frequently refused five thousand guineas, was 'doubled in two, injured by the blows of a hammer, the marks of shoes, and other acts of carelessness,' and finally knocked down for 75 guineas. One of his maidservants came from Acton expressly to bid for the picture, and when the bidding went beyond twenty-eight pounds, the whole of her savings, she burst into tears, deeply affecting the bystanders, and went back to Acton, where she performed her duties with even more ardour and cheerfulness than in happier days.

A neighbouring bookseller, Mr. Brooks of the Royal Arcade, bought up a quantity of books, but this was less from philanthropy than from a wish to make a good bargain for himself. The result of the sale, conducted in a spirit of illiberal vindictiveness, was that the stock, worth at a moderate computation many thousands of pounds, even without Godiva, did not fetch enough to pay Fisher's damages and the costs.

Low in spirits, Stockdale returned to Acton, to find that villains had stolen the remaining poultry and the gate bell. The fateful question of the potato field now lifted its hydra head again, and for the short time of freedom that remained to him Stockdale corresponded with his landlord on a hitherto unprecedented level of mutual abuse, complicated by the introduction of Mr. Winter's demand to be compensated for the damage the myrmidons of the law had done; while the Stockdale family suspected Mr. Winter of having instigated the forcing of the coachhouse door with a crowbar.

The blow now fell. On September 5th, 1826, the persecutors, acting through the regular officers of justice, had him arrested and taken to the Fleet.

Anyone who wishes for an account of Stockdale's confinement need not waste time in reading his voluminous and often distasteful letters to his wife. The whole of the correspondence on both sides was published later by Stockdale, and a better matched pair in hypocrisy, malice, and nauseating insinuation could hardly be imagined. But as far as his actual prison experiences go, they can all be read, far better related, in the life of Mr. Samuel Pickwick, who was in the Fleet just two years later. Everything is just as Dickens set it down. The inspection by the turnkeys, the crowded rooms and corridors, the anxious wives with ailing children sharing their husbands' captivity, the 'chummage'—4/6 in Stockdale's case, but Mr. Martin, Mr. Simpson and the drunken chaplain offered Mr. Pickwick 3/6, though the regular chummage was 2/6—the whistling shop where spirits were illegally sold by the turnkeys, the poor side, the racquet courts, all are there.

Stockdale, as might be expected, experienced none of the headache or heartache which Mr. Pickwick was to feel. He settled down at once to the enjoyment of a mixed but delightful society, including several ladies and 'that fine fellow Johnson, the smuggler.' In spite of their total destitution his family appear to have had resources, for not only did Mrs. Stockdale get a fresh set of servants, making several troublesome journeys to take their characters, but she sent, by the boy Miah, quantities of food to her husband, and from time to time some clean linen. Except on the night when the sofa bedstead broke down under him because his bed-

maker had forgotten to put up the middle leg, Stockdale found everything pretty comfortable. Bugs were
his worst enemy. He had his bedstead washed with
copperas to drive them away, but they sought refuge
elsewhere, their presence, traceable directly to the
persecutors, gave Stockdale the opportunity for some
fine amateur preaching, ending with the noble words
'Our enemies are daily cutting their own throats. They
are like pigs which always cut their throats with their
forefeet or claws when they swim.'

There were frequent allusions in his letters to the
geese and chickens his wife sent in to him. Anxious
and affectionate messages passed on the subject of
health. When thanking Mrs. Stockdale for some apples
and cigars, he took occasion to warn her that pork af-
fects the bowels, while she implored him to eat two
roasted apples a day to promote regularity. 'Get a pudding for my birthday on Sunday,' is one of his messages, 'I think I shall be forty-nine or fifty.' He took
every opportunity of reassuring his wife as to his welfare. 'I intend to drink my love to you all, which indeed I never omit, when I take my half pint of ale, one
glass of wine, and nightly wine-glass of gin and water.
These trifling little recollections seem to sanctify my
confinement.'

As rum is not mentioned, it may be taken that, as in
Mr. Pickwick's time, 'that partickler wanity' was not
to be obtained in the establishment.

But all good things come to an end, and on October
24th, Fisher, probably seeing no chance of getting the
rest of his money while Stockdale was in prison, was

glad to compound for fifty pounds down, the rest to
be paid in instalments. Stockdale was released, not a
day too soon for the peace of the British aristocracy.
During his confinement he had collected several very
'maculate' stories, from the best authorities, about people of title, and his industrious wife had been writing
her recollections of the upper classes with a view to a
little blackmail.

'I was going to add,' writes Stockdale to his wife,
'a story of Lord Pomfret, but as it is rather maculate,
it shall be yours in private, as Coriolanus said.'

His wife was not backward in maculate anecdote,
but there were degrees of maculacy beyond her innocent mind, and she had to write to her husband to ask
him what he thought the much advertised 'Goering's
elastic generating bedstead' was likely to be; which
question found Stockdale, for once, completely at a
loss.

However, in the great joy of family reunion, these
threats to public reputations were temporarily laid
aside, and Stockdale applied himself to re-establishing
his business. He had succeeded in letting his shop in
the Opera Colonnade and required a fresh place of
business. Hardly was he out of the Fleet than he took
rooms in St. James's Square, and there began to publish a weekly journal called 'Stockdale's Budget'. Its
dull scurrility makes it impossible to read. It is full of
libels, slanders, police news, reports of crim. con. cases
with all the details, and every kind of 'maculacy'. Its
chief interest lies in the republication of what have
seemed to the best authorities to be the actual letters

which had passed in 1810 and 1811 between Stockdale, Shelley and Hogg, and a series of newsletters
from Paris, written by Harriette Rochfort, as she was
then calling herself. They are entirely valueless, not
even containing any Paris news, but they show us that
Harriette was living with Rochfort at the same address
in the rue du Faubourg St. Honoré. There is a brief
allusion to Amy, whose husband, Bochsa, had just obtained damages against the two editors who had called
him a forger, bigamist, runaway and galley-slave;
though truth must have been, with the exception of
the term galley-slave, the only libel here involved. 'I
cannot think,' writes Stockdale in one of his letters to
Harriette in the *Budget*, 'how your sister Amy, who
does not want sense, came to let her husband meddle
in such an affair.' This is the last that is heard of Amy.

After six months of most disgraceful attacks on
Mrs. Coutts, Sir Francis Burdett, Canning and others,
the Attorney-General, Sir James Scarlett, who had
also been grossly treated, stopped publication. To the
end of his life Stockdale could never understand why
a plain-spoken, reputable journal, which only aimed
at purifying morals, should have incurred the dis-
pleasure of the authorities. But he was born to be persecuted and was able to take it meekly, hoping, though
without much success, to inherit the earth.

Echoes of the Fisher v. Clement case continued to
ring through the law courts. In 1827 *Bell's Life*,
which not unlike some Sunday papers of later years,
enjoyed nothing so much as a good rousing libel action,
retorted upon Fisher by having the suit retried in the

Court of King's Bench on a Writ of Error. The Court reversed the judgment, upon which *Bell's Life* remarked:

Bell's Life in London triumphant and the Lawyer Floored.

In 1828 the game was still afoot. The ill-advised Fisher again appeared to try to get redress for what he considered the libel. To the impartial observer there is nothing injurious to him in the *London Eclogue*, which only laughs at Harriette and Stockdale and their methods. All Fisher had to complain of was being mentioned in the poem at all.

The case, Fisher v. Clement (proprietor and publisher of *Bell's Life in London*) was tried for the third time in the Court of King's Bench. The proprietorship of Mr. Clement was admitted and the publication of the alleged libel in *Bell's Life* of 28th May, 1826. Sir J. Scarlett, for the defence, spoke of the general good character of Clement and his paper. 'As to the publication of Harriette Wilson's *Memoirs*, there could be no one who detested it more than he did; but she, a poor abandoned creature, could not have brought it before the world. It was Stockdale who published the scandalous memoirs of that abandoned strumpet for the sake of the horrid profits. The sheets were perused, corrected and settled by Stockdale himself, and they were published for his benefit. The verses merely held Stockdale and Harriette up to ridicule.'

After the gross attacks which Stockdale had made

upon Scarlett in *Stockdale's Budget*, we may admire
the moderation of the late Attorney-General's language.

The jury, after Lord Tenterden's summing up, up-
held this view and found for the defendant, and *Bell's
Life* came out with a leading article in a high moral
tone, extolling itself again as a *censor morum*.

Chapter XII

CLARA GAZUL

*

BY THE short-lived 'Stockdale's Budget,' by recurring allusions in *Bell's Life*, Harriette's name had been kept in the memory of the public. In the autumn of 1828 she came back to London, bringing with her the Colonel and a French maid called Julia Le Toille. She took a house in Trevor Square, Knightsbridge, then and long afterwards a place of equivocal reputation; No. 16, at the south-east corner. She had some more literary works in view, and while her attention was taken up with them, one of her brothers paid marked attentions to Julia. This unbrotherly action led to strong steps on Harriette's part, and she and Rochfort found themselves in trouble with the police. Her old friend *Bell's Life in London* gave a spirited account of the affair.

SUNDAY, FEBRUARY 15, 1829.
HARRIETTE WILSON ONCE MORE!

The famous Harriette Wilson, alias Madame de

Bouchere, alias Madame Rochfort, was on Thursday brought up to Marlborough Street before Mr. Dyer, the Sitting Magistrate—charged with assaulting a young French female, named Julia Le Toille.

Madame Harriette was accompanied to the office by Mr. Rochfort. She was dressed in a fashionable black silk dress, with a rich cashmere shawl flung negligently over her shoulders, and her head surmounted by a huge French many-coloured bonnet, from the point of which hung a rich white silk veil, but of a texture delicate enough to afford a perfect and distinct view of the features of its owner.

Before the case was gone into Mr. Rochfort begged to address a few words to the magistrate, for the purpose of stating that the name given to the lady, who was the defendant in the case in the warrant upon which she was taken into custody, was not at all her proper name, nor did she ever, at any time of her life, bear the name of Wilson; in fact, he said, his name was given, not with any view to the ends of justice, but to bring about exposure; for the complainant knew full well that the lady's real name was Harriette de Bouchere, because she was well acquainted with Madame de Bouchere's brothers, and others of her family.

Clements, the officer, said that when he went that morning to the house of this lady, No. 16 Trevor Square, Brompton, accompanied by Andrews, another officer, he placed Andrews at the back of the house to prevent the object of his search escaping that way, while he himself knocked at the street door. Mr. Rochfort had tried to keep him out, saying there was no such person as Harriette Wilson, named on the warrant, residing in the house.

Mr. Rochfort here interposed that he did, through ignorance of the English law, resist the officer, but had then given in.

The sum of the complaint was that Julia Le Toille, a girl of about eighteen, had been brought over from Paris by Madame de Bouchere, as a lady's maid, under a written agreement of 300 francs a year; that Madame de Bouchere had accused her of some improprieties, which had no foundation, had ordered her to leave the house at once, and on Julia's refusal had knocked her off a chair where she was sitting flat onto the floor.

Harriette, in defending herself, said she had brought Julia to this country to try to save her from the disgrace that must attach to her by remaining in her own, because there she had been guilty of the impropriety of having a child by a gentleman. Harriette said she discovered recently that there was some very improper understanding between the complainant and Mr. de Bouchere, her brother, the couple having remained out together till four in the morning, which determined her to dismiss the girl. As for the alleged assault, she said Julia had deliberately fallen flat on the floor with a view to this charge. All who knew her (Harriette) through life, knew very well that she was of anything but a violent or turbulent disposition;

indeed she was always remarkable for the mildness and gentleness of her nature.

The magistrate said she must put in bail to appear at the Sessions, one housekeeper (or, in modern usage, householder) of respectability being sufficient.

Harriette said she really did not know to whom to apply for such a purpose. 'We have been upwards of seven years absent from this country, and we are almost, at present, foreigners in it; and besides I do not like troubling my friends upon such a matter: there are plenty of persons of the first consequence who would be happy to come forward, but I don't like to trouble them on so trivial an occasion.'

Rochfort then suggested that his and Harriette's securities together would be sufficient, as she was a housekeeper. Harriette, on being questioned, said she held her house on a lease for fourteen years and the furniture was her own and paid for. Clements, the officer, said the house was a very handsome one and richly furnished. The magistrate agreed to take the joint recognisances of the defendant and Rochfort, as the former was a housekeeper, and the latter swore he had vast estates in Ireland. Accordingly they 'departed in a hackney-coach, as they came.'

When the magistrate was reading the written agreement between the plaintiff and the defendant, he remarked that the lady was described as Madame Rochfort, and asked Mr. Rochfort if he were the husband of the lady, to which Rochfort replied that he was not, though the lady was known by that name for some time in France.

The reporter of this scene unkindly added, 'The present appearance of this unfortunate woman makes it difficult to conceive that she could ever have been attractive either as to person or manner; her features are now ugly and coarse, her person bad, and her manners vulgar, with a harsh discordant voice. She appears now about fifty-five years of age.'

Harriette was little more than forty. Perhaps Julia's description was not exaggerated.

The upshot of this unfortunate scene was a copy of verses in *Bell's Life*, entitled *Ode to Harriette Wilson, alias Made. de Bouchere, alias Made. Rochfort, on her late appearance at the Marlborough Street Police Office*. It deals with the question of the various names she has borne and has a refrain of 'The sooner the better forgot.' One verse was quoted earlier, another deals, not kindly, with her appearance.

> 'No wonder when now fifty-five,
>   You're better than when but fifteen,
> 'Tis a pity you cannot contrive
>   To make yourself fit to be seen.
> To Police Office when you were brought
>   By warrant, refusing to trot,
> There was no one that saw you but thought,
>   "The sooner the better forgot".'

On the same day there is a report of Rochfort's second appearance at Marlborough Street, 'to eat his words as to his possessions in Ireland.' He seems to have been a little confused; at first said the property belonged to his mother, then was not quite sure whether he had a mother, or if so, whether she had any property anywhere; and finally took refuge in asserting that the magistrate must have misunderstood his original statement. He also complained that he and Harriette were being inundated with anonymous letters and abuse, but the magistrate did not offer to help in this matter.

Harriette paid her rates regularly at Trevor Square and continued her literary work, but this time she does not appear to have consulted Stockdale. As usual she was in want of money, and it had occurred to her that she might do all her blackmail for herself instead of sharing with a publisher. The story of the new work with which she proposed to fill her pockets is obscure, but its extreme rarity makes it appear probable that her blackmail was so successful and so many people paid to be left out that it was hardly worth while printing many copies. In 1830 a novel in three volumes called *Clara Gazul* was published anonymously by the author at 16 Trevor Square. The name *Clara Gazul* naturally tempts one to look for some kind of relation between Harriette and Prosper Mérimée, but though Mérimée at one time affected the society of the demi-monde he does not mention Harriette, nor she him.

The opening sentences run:

My mother, Dona Euphrasia, was bred to the stage, so was my grandfather. My mother had made her successful debut at Madrid ten years before I was born.

On ne connoit pas toujours son père c'est un malheur.

Harriette had used that quotation from Pigault Lebrun (?) before.

It would be possible to see a parallel between this opening and the first pages of the preface to Mérimée's *Théâtre de Clara Gazul,* which was making a stir in Paris in 1825, but it would be unwise to insist upon it. Spanish romanticism was in the air in Paris, where Harriette spent most of her time, and one name is as good as another.

Before the actual novel begins, there is a leisurely sequence of prefaces, of which the first is the *Intro-duction,* containing an account of Harriette's early life, with which she had not yet favoured her readers. It is followed by a notice headed *To the Public.* As this bears upon the question of how much Stockdale was responsible for Harriette's *Memoirs,* it may be of interest to quote it in full. It is dated London, January, 1830. Harriette's grammar and construction, to which she always sat easily, give way entirely in her efforts to justify everyone concerned.

It is but fair to state of a man who has been so harshly dealt by, that Mr. Stockdale, as my pub-lisher, conducted himself towards me liberally and honestly.

At the same time, I must, in justice to myself, declare that in the latter part of my *Memoirs,* independent of so much extraneous matter being introduced, under the head of my *Memoirs*, which never belonged to them, and for which *I* have been reproached; many expressions have been put into my mouth which never issued from my pen.

It is, therefore, to prevent a recurrence of the like annoyance, that I am compelled to acquaint the public, that Mr. Stockdale *has* now published nearly the whole part of my *Memoirs* which I wrote and sold to him in MS.

Some few *pages* may yet remain in his hands, but I should imagine, indeed, I am almost positive that of *my composition*, he cannot have sufficient to form a single number or part of a volume, such as was at first sold for half a crown.

The MS. of the remaining *unpurchased* and consequently *unpublished* parts, about half a dozen in number have not been *out of* and are still in my possession, and without intention, at present, on my part, of being given to the public.

I give this information very reluctantly, as I should be truly sorry to injure the father of a family, of whom, with the above exception, I have no cause to complain.

After the *Introduction* and notice *To the Public*, Harriette, still 'sitting in an easy chair, at No. 111, in the rue du Faubourg St. Honoré, à Paris' arrives by gradual degrees at the *Preface*, which deals chiefly with the genesis of *Clara Gazul*. According to Harriette's account, 'an illustrious and in my opinion very amiable nobleman' recommended her to write a sketch-book or light novel. True to her principles of always aiming high, she at once consulted 'a gentleman belonging to the company of Edinburgh Reviewers.' This critic, whom she describes as 'a well-known Whig from principle, a poet by inclination, a dramatist from taste, whose compositions were unfortunately untasted by the public, an atheist *par excellence*, and a very gouty subject *malgré lui*' was enthusiastically in favour of the plan. 'In case of publication,' he wrote, 'the knowledge that it was written by you would ensure a sale so that at least people would be forced to pay you before they could abuse.' This is perhaps the worst light in which the Edinburgh Reviewers have yet been seen.

There follows a brief description of some of her characters, with hints at the identity of the living people from whom they are drawn. The authoress protests that her work is of a highly moral nature, inasmuch as all the bad characters come to bad ends. 'But,' she adds, 'I have traduced no character by such FALSE calumnies as have been practised against myself.' With her usual disarming frankness she continues: 'As to plot, it is what I fear I have no sort of taste or talent for, and the reader may despise my brief attempt in that department, without the possibility of making me think worse of myself than I have always done hitherto.'

Certainly the plot of *Clara Gazul*—if it may be said to exist at all—is, as Harriette herself admitted, as devoid of taste and talent as one might wish. It would be quite useless even to attempt to give any outline of the story. Clara herself takes but little part in the novel, and is merely a peg on which to hang descriptions of people and places. Among the characters are a noble Italian lady seduced by a Cardinal; a venerable father; a brutal brother; a newly born baby thrown into a blazing fire by ruffians of both sexes (in the brutal brother's pay) who subsequently fall into the fire themselves owing to excess in spirituous liquors and share the baby's fate; a brigand called Alberto, who wrote a very successful poem in German called 'Robbers and Soldiers' and had a profusion of jetty ringlets and jewellery; and quantities of monks, soldiers, pages, waiting-women and natural children. Clara's only dramatic contribution to the book is her love for Ligonia, who is apparently Alberto's brother, but in any case had murdered a third brother from the highest motives.

After murdering his brother he entered the Russian service as a private soldier—and in 1814, upon the occupation of Lyons by the Cossacks, he was absolutely billeted in his native town, upon his orphan niece's house. Having however changed his name and being greatly altered by his grief and service, he was not after such a lapse of time recognised by anyone. . . . I have disguised the real name of 'Ivanchoff' which he bore in the Russian service, under that of Ligonia.

Clara had an assignation with Ligonia, in the course of which he 'drew aside his mask, raised me in his

arms, and hid his face in my bosom. IT WAS THE
SWEETEST MOMENT OF MY LIFE.'

Then there is the page Eugenio, who was the
natural son of Napoleon and a lady whose identity
is 'concealed as the Countess de Polignac.' He woos
Clara, but as her affections are already another's, he
goes to London and stays at the Clarendon Hotel.
This hotel, which stood till 1870, was between Old
Bond Street and Albemarle Street, with a frontage to
both. It was kept, during Harriette's palmy days, by
a French cook, Jacquiers, who had been with Louis
XVIII (while in England) and later with Lord Darn-
ley. It contained large suites of apartments where
royal and noble personages used to put up during their
stay in London, and was celebrated as the only hotel
where a genuine French dinner could be obtained,
but the sum charged seldom amounted to less than
three or four pounds; a bottle of champagne or of
claret in 1814 usually cost a guinea.

From the Clarendon Hotel Eugenio writes long
gossiping letters to his mother about London society.
Upon the night of his arrival he had the misfortune
to get mixed up in a brawl at Covent Garden Theatre,
and it would have gone ill with him before the magistrate had not the Earl of Ricketty obligingly offered
himself as bail, and carried Eugenio off to breakfast
in his rooms. Here Eugenio had the pleasure of meeting Lord Dolittle (Lord Dudley), whom he had
known at Naples as Mr. Delford, the Marquis of
Boobeedon (Lord Boringdon?), and Lord Pickle. Lord
Pickle expressed himself with much freedom about

French actresses, declaring that 'he hated them all.'

'Why the deuce do you visit them then?' said Lord Dolittle, his mouth full of roast partridge.

'Visit! Hem! Why, what is a man to do in such a blackguardly place as Paris? I go to half a dozen of these nasty things sometimes of a morning, for the vice and viciousness of it. I am naturally vicious.'

Eugenio had been forced by her relations into an engagement with the Lady Anna Maria D. In despair, he hit upon an effectual remedy or antidote for love.

A dentist who resided in the metropolis, was entrusted with his secret. This artist permitted him to hire two complete rows of false teeth exactly like his own, which being very neatly packed in a small, pink card-box, the dentist was induced to make out an elegant bill, on the top of which his name, address and profession was elegantly printed.

The bill ran thus—and was addressed to Eugenio. 'To a complete set of composition teeth and gum set in pure gold £15 15s.'

This parcel Eugenio contrived to drop on her lady-ship's carpet—and the marriage was broken off by her friends.

Eugenio then visits 'Harriette Memoirs,' whom we may take to be Harriette described by herself. The portrait appears to be on the whole an impartial one. She is attractive, though not beautiful, and takes her colour from her surroundings.

A stupid companion (Eugenio writes to his mother) appeared to paralyse her and change every feature in her face. Vainly did she labour to go through the forms of politeness, in order to avoid wounding him by her neglect, she was so absent as to have appeared almost insane, and her face seemed to lengthen with the torturing annoyance she evidently experienced in her efforts to collect her ideas and listen to a dull every-day character.

Observe Harriette Memoirs in the society of a man she respects and desires to attach; you will then see one of the most pleasant and unlearned women in England; playful in her wit, which is the more piquant from the almost imperceptible dash of libertinage which serves but to excite curiosity; respectful in her address she has the knack of inspiring those whom she would please with esteem as well as love.

During her whole career she has honourably discharged every debt she ever contracted, and when in the hurry of leaving a foreign country anything was forgotten, she never failed to forward the sum due to her creditor after her arrival in England.

Her misfortune is ill-health. Her qualities are her love of truth and singleness of heart. At this period, when her youth has passed away, she is infinitely more refined in her taste and more difficult in her choice of society than she was formerly. If her face has lost some of its youthful beauty, perhaps it has gained something in character and expression; and with regard to her talents for conversa-

tion, these are unquestionably improved by time
and reflection, aided by her good sense. Her person
is pretty, but her clothes are hung about it so loosely
that it is difficult to guess what they conceal or
disfigure.

Harriette very seldom reads, but retains what
she does read for ever. She is as difficult in her
choice of books, as acquaintances; the weakness of
her nerves disqualifies her for deep study.

I take Harriette to be a very high-couraged person whose strength of mind would be found equal
to any sudden emergency. Though the world call
her profligate, she is strict and severe in her principles of candour and honesty. . . . Her temper
and disposition are happy, for she can amuse herself harmlessly in solitude and never find the day
long enough for her occupations.

To conclude the subject, I, who have well studied
her character, and I believe impartially, do positively acquit Harriette Memoirs of the least particle
of selfishness, while I give her credit for a very
affectionate heart.

As there was no key published to this romance, one
can but guess at the characters. If it was entirely a
roman à clef it would certainly have been worth while
for certain people to pay for the suppression of their
names. Some of those who remain are easy to place;
the Duke of Inverary for the Duke of Argyle, Canwin
for Canning, Cocker for Croker, O'Rioter for O'Con-
nell, Mr. Birch for Brougham (who is unctuously

praised), de Beaumont for de Gramont, and Lord Dudley for Lord Dolittle—this last being openly given away by Harriette. But for the engaging Lord Pickle and all the foreign and English nobles who pass through the pages, originals are still to seek; or, as Harriette wrote in her *Paris Lions and London Tigers,* 'are in want of an owner.'

Here, for the last time, Harriette drops into poetry, the occasion being her hatred for a member of the Paris Embassy. To vent her spite upon the unnamed offender, she imagined that he had died upon the day when the Embassy Bag was to be made up for London, thus greatly inconveniencing 'the Chevalier,' Sir Charles Stuart.

> Under this stone reposes beau Minacious,
> Whose sudden death was really quite vexatious,
> And mourned by his good master the Chevalier
> Because he died most luckless on a bag-day.
> As Mouchard too! he brilléd as a spy,
> Never so well shall we his place supply. . . .
>
> A snail's a nasty little slimy reptile
> That we recoil from—it rouses not our bile;
> And if on impulse we should cast it from us,
> We blush to think an insect should have ruffled us.

These are not good verses, but Harriette seems to have been in very good spirits when she composed them.

It is, on the whole, surprising that *Clara Gazul* dropped dead from the Press, except on the supposition, already mentioned, that Harriette had earned her money before publication and only had a few copies printed. The edition was in three volumes, and there is an example extant bearing the label of the Lyme circulating library, where Mr. Fisher's painfully acquired notoriety doubtless made it much in demand.

Stockdale, who disappeared from trade directories between the years 1826—the year of his 'Persecution' —and 1835, was so little offended by Harriette's acting as her own publisher that he lifted bodily some of the portions of the Introduction to *Clara Gazul*, which deal with her early life, and incorporated them in a new edition of the *Memoirs* and the *Paris Lions and London Tigers* which he brought out in 1831. This edition, in nine volumes, contains Stockdale's own account of the Persecution and his confinement in the Fleet. It is also interesting for another long instalment of Harriette's *Memoirs*, which would appear to be those alluded to in her notice *To the Public* at the beginning of *Clara Gazul*. Either she or Stockdale, probably both, pressed for money, decided to use the hitherto unpublished parts, hoping for another easy harvest, but the chapters which remained were so poor and dull that they fell to the ground by their own weight and could not make anyone go to the trouble and noise of a libel action. One would say that Stockdale had bought the other parts from Harriette and hashed them up to his own liking, for it is only in a very few places that her authentic fire and impudence are found.

This edition is also remarkable for an index which

spreads over a volume and a half and leaves nothing to the imagination. A few extracts will show its range.

ADULTERY. Insufferable, by anyone not of royal blood, except in private, like Lords Cowper and Maryborough.

Our Saviour's remarks on.

MUTTON. A hot leg of, thrown by Lord Berwick at the footman.

STOCKDALE, J. B. (*this is Master Stockdale Junior, the 'Miah' of the persecution*).

Notices the appropriateness of the psalms.

Considerateness of.

Remiss.

To get another pig.

Not thanked, for his chicken and pork.

STOCKDALE, MARY (*J. J. Stockdale's sister who carried on the bookselling business in Piccadilly*).

Sisterly feelings of.

Has lost a glorious opportunity.

Contrasted with jews.

The whole ends with a 'sermon written but never preached by Harriette Wilson'; an unpleasant by-product of the Evangelical movement.

In the following year Harriette published another edition of *Clara Gazul*, this time adding her name, 'Harriet [sic] Wilson', to the title page. It was identical with the first edition and seems to have roused no interest. Although it was published as from Trevor Square, she had left that address at the end of 1830, and vanished with her colonel.

Once more only she is heard of. In November,

1832, her brother-in-law, the second Lord Berwick, died at Naples. He was succeeded by his brother, William Noel Hill, envoy for many years to the court of Sardinia. A natural feeling moved Harriette to write and condole with the new Lord Berwick on his loss; an even more natural feeling moved her to ask him for money. Her letter, dated from Paris, is in the possession of the present Lord Berwick, but there is no record of any answer.

From this date Harriette and Rochfort, '*homme très inconnu*', as the *Biographie des Contemporains* justly calls him, pass into obscurity. Harriette is said to have died in England in 1846; the colonel's fate is not known.

Harriette had long outlived her notoriety as courtesan and blackmailer, but her literary work kept her alive in a way that would have surprised her very much.

If, in reading her Boswell, she noticed Dr. Johnson's remark that no man but a blockhead ever wrote except for money, she would have agreed heartily, and so long as her old friends were anxious to buy themselves out of her *Memoirs*, she cared very little for immortality. But she must have got a good deal of pleasure out of her writing, for she was a born writer in the pleasant slip-shod style, with occasional flashes of wit, an excellent eye for character, and a turn for an apt phrase. 'A talking at each other conversation'; 'Mademoiselle Sophia *vouloit faire paroitre les beaux restes de sa vertu chancelante*'; Miss Ketridge's 'uninteresting little Dutch cheese.' The truth

of her characters to nature was praised by Sir Walter
Scott, her dialogue was brilliant. Her defects were extreme prolixity—the *Memoirs* run to something near
250,000 words—a fine disregard for chronology, and
a tendency to believe that everything she said was true.
From her long, rambling story of her own career between fifteen and thirty, one gets a very definite
impression of the woman herself, very like the self-
portrait which she drew in *Clara Gazul*, and agreeing,
on the whole, with allusions to her which exist in
contemporary memoirs and letters; an impression of
an agreeable rattle, a frank, high-spirited creature,
caring almost as much for a handsome face as for a
long purse, entirely without morals, but with a code
of her own, to which—to the great discomfiture of
various would-be admirers—she almost invariably
conformed. Her career reminds one in some ways of
that of Becky Sharp; the rapid rise of a girl living by
her wits and charm, the few years of brilliant success
and adulation among the best of London society, the
squalid bedraggled conclusion with religion used for
social purposes, but there is this difference: Becky
desired respectability with all the strength of her
narrow little heart, to Harriette the very word was
what she would have called a dead bore. Her preju-
dice against the middle classes remained as strong as
ever, and if she could not live with the aristocracy,
she was content to hob-nob with small tradesmen.
It was a very long time since she had put Fanny's
love-letter into the meat pie. Between her and Queen
Street, with Craven and Sheridan passing the house,

there lay a strange journey. The days when she and Julia and Fanny held the dandies; the opera boxes, the champagne, the talk, the love-making; her passion for Ponsonby, Worcester's fond and foolish adoration. Other days to be remembered less willingly; Meyler's contemptuous pursuit, the raffish life in Paris, the colonel to be fed and clothed, all her shifts to beg and borrow money. Then the success of her *Memoirs*, old lovers offering a hundred guineas to be cut out, the pleasure of seeing Stockdale paying substantial damages for her indiscretions; Trevor Square and the French maid, a little more blackmail with *Clara Gazul;* the old sense of fun flashing out. Then nothing. The little woman in the black beaver hat and long grey cloak whom Julia had seen. The woman whom Harriette had foretold to Byron, in her little pointed cap, spectacles, bony ankles and thread stockings, stirring up and tasting her *pot-au-feu*: Ponsonby's, Worcester's and Argyle's Angelick Harriette.

Harriette's signature.

NOTES ON THE CAREER OF
HARRIETTE WILSON

THE *Memoirs of Harriette Wilson,* which have been
from time to time reprinted, but never very widely
known, have till now been the principal source of
information about their writer. Her own contemporaries are not communicative about her. Her fashionable friends, all of course men, were not for the most
part inclined to letters, and she probably played a
much smaller part in their lives than she believed herself, or would like to have us believe. Also, a politician,
a general, or a man of fashion turned respectable
country gentleman, does not vaunt in print an acquaintance with a woman no lady in his circle visited.
Of her early years, and her life after she left England
in or about 1815, little or nothing was known.

A few years ago my attention was drawn to an
advertisement in a second-hand catalogue of a novel
by Harriette Wilson, dated 1830, and described as
very rare. The title, *Clara Gazul,* with its reminiscence of Mérimée, was intriguing, and I began to
make desultory inquiries into the matter. The book
contains not only what must be one of the worst
novels ever written, even judging by the standards of

to-day, but also Harriette's own account of her child-hood and youth, up to the point at which the *Memoirs* begin. Further search in contemporary newspapers brought to light a great deal of material, all very unflattering to my heroine, but of interest to anyone who had read the *Memoirs*. As many of these news-papers made their circulation by publishing lies and their income by suppressing them, their evidence is about as valueless as Harriette's. There are, never-theless, certain facts, including a good many libel actions, which cannot be disputed.

There is another source, possibly even more un-reliable than the *Memoirs* or the Press, the *Confessions of Julia Johnstone, written by herself in Contradiction to the Fables of Harriette Wilson*, 1825. Mrs. Johnstone, for nearly all these ladies cling to the respectability of Mrs., was a professional friend of Harriette's and would like to have been thought a rival. She had a ready and at times an amusing pen, and the success of Harriette's *Memoirs*, which inci-dentally told Julia's own story in a far from flattering way, seems to have driven her into print within a few weeks. Both ladies are as inaccurate as it is possible to be, and would indeed probably have scorned accu-racy as low, but while Harriette's lies appear to be largely the result of laziness, indifference, and a muddled way of thinking (when not actually inspired by a wish to blackmail), Julia's are so inspired by jealousy and rage that she becomes almost inarticulate in her virtuous passion to expose her former friend.

What adds to the difficulty of trusting Julia is that

it appears quite probable that she was dead at the time when her *Confessions* appeared. Stockdale states that the *Confessions* were written by a John Mitford, or a Captain Richardson, who were paid by his enemies to discredit his publications: but Stockdale is as unreliable as any of them. Be that as it may, the *Confessions* furnish one or two facts that can be verified, such as the date of Fanny Parker's death and the place of her burial.

There is also the edition of the *Memoirs* in 1831 which contains a long and rambling account of Harriette's early and later life, supposed to be written by herself, but not very much in her style. This edition contains information about Rochfort; information that can be verified to some extent by the Peerage, Mrs. Delany's letters, and Julia Johnstone's *Confessions*. Most of the nine volumes are entirely worthless, but there are gleanings here and there, and a good deal of curious information about that remarkable character, J. J. Stockdale, whose career still waits a biographer.

Among the unpublished Granville papers at the Record Office, there are allusions to Lord Granville's difficulties with the abuse of the Ambassador's Bag. While the letters are very guarded and Harriette's name is not specifically mentioned, the facts and dates leave little doubt that she is the person referred to. It is possible that among the mass of letters yet further allusions might be found.

Harriette's own letters, and the letters that she printed as from her admirers, must be read with

caution. Julia Johnstone says that she herself helped
Harriette to write a great many of her letters, and
being a good business woman where affairs of the
heart were concerned, Julia kept copies of all her correspondence. In this way, she says, she was able to
prove that Harriette had printed letters both to and
from herself in a form quite different from the original. What might be merely a malicious accusation is
given considerable substance by the letters extant from
Harriette to Lord Byron. These—mostly begging
letters—were written at any time between the years
1812 and 1823; only one is dated, but the others can
be placed approximately. They had been kept by the
recipient, and are among the Byron correspondence
in the possession of Sir John Murray, who has kindly
allowed me to see them. They were published in the
Cornhill Magazine for April, 1935, with some omis-
sions and changes in punctuation and spelling.

These letters are written in the same delightful,
free and easy, talkative style as the best part of her
Memoirs, but when she reprinted them in the
Memoirs, from memory or from copies she had taken
at the time, she altered them almost beyond recogni-
tion, and did not improve them. Her second thoughts
on literary matters were always a mistake and her
whole charm as a writer lay in her spontaneity and
gift for reporting conversations.

One curious, if improbable, story of Harriette's
ancestry must be touched on. In April, 1825, while
Harriette's *Memoirs* were still appearing in parts, a
correspondent wrote to the *English Spy* to give his

account of Harriette's paternal grandmother. In a few words the tale he had to relate was that Harriette's father, John Dubochet, was a natural son of the Elizabeth Debouchette who was Lord Chesterfield's mistress and mother of his son Philip Stanhope. No one seems to have taken any further notice of this contribution to history, though it has a faint air of probability which is extremely alluring. Lord Chesterfield's liaison with Elizabeth du Bochet (as she is called in the will by which he left her £500 'as a small reparation for the injury I did her') is a matter of history. Her son Philip was born in 1733. If she had had another son, not necessarily by Chesterfield, within a few years, he would have been between forty and fifty at the time of Harriette's birth; this would fit every circumstance of John Dubochet's age. It is an enchanting vista to explore if one lets fancy roam. How amusing it would be to persuade oneself that some of Harriette's facility in writing had come to her indirectly through her grandmother's liaison with Lord Chesterfield; a kind of heredity not unknown to biologists. But this way madness lies. Harriette had evidently never heard any rumour of such a connection from her father, who indeed appears to have been inordinately proud of his Swiss birth.

As for Harriette's statement that her father was at one time secretary to General Burgoyne, but was lucky enough to be away (or, as she states in another place, 'safely quaffing his bottle of Burgundy') at the time of Burgoyne's surrender, we may think what we please. Burgoyne's surrender to Gates took place in

October, 1777. John Dubochet's first child was born
in March of that year, but whether he was in London
or not in the autumn, remains to be discovered. He
certainly held no military rank. But doubtless the
statement was the offspring of Mr. Dubochet's fertile
mind and his daughter's inaccurate remembrance and
spirited rendering of the same.

From among this welter of rumours, lies, contra-
dictions, allusions; from Army Lists, from Ratepayers'
Lists, I have attempted to reconstruct that part of
Harriette's life which she does not tell us in the
Memoirs. She never mentions dates, and it is hardly
worth searching too closely into her chronology. Such
dates as the death of Lord Ponsonby's father, the
gazetting of Lord Worcester, the Wattier Masquerade, are indisputable: the rest can be left alone without any serious loss.

In the spelling of the name Dubochet I have used
throughout the form found in the majority of entries
in the register of St. George's, Hanover Square, where
all the children were baptised, and in most of the
Ratepayers' Lists Dubochet, Dubotchet, Dubouchet,
Debochet, de Bouchere, are all found. In writing to
Byron she wrote the name as Du Bochet, but Dubochet
is the most common official form.

Of her death I can at present find no particular
evidence, beyond the date given in the *Dictionary of
National Biography*. There is at Somerset House the
record of a will made on September 8th, 1846, by
Harriette Wilson, of the parish of St. Peter's,
Knightsbridge, but no address is given, and the few

bequests, all of small sums of money, are to people with unknown names. Neither is it known whether she used the name Wilson in her last years. In the register of deaths I find nothing under the names Wilson or Dubochet for that year. It is not of very great matter.

INDEX

INDEX

(The dates, where given, are for identification, or to indicate that there is matter of interest in the D.N.B.)